Praise for *PLAY MONEY*

"Julian Dibbell has long been one the best foreign correspondents in cyberspace. But *Play Money* is investigative reporting from the future, taking readers to hidden levels of reality never dreamed of. Somewhere, William Gibson is wishing he had written this book." —ANDREW LEONARD, *Salon*

"There are whole new societies and economies blooming in the digital desert of online game world. Not many people can claim to understand them as well as Julian Dibbell, and nobody can claim to write about them with as much intelligence, wit, and storytelling verve."

—MCKENZIE WARK, author of *A Hacker Manifesto*

"*Play Money* is a treat. Dibbell's sharp analysis of the nature of play, and the point at which it becomes part of work, is some of the best around."

—T.L. TAYLOR, author of *Play Between Worlds*

"Dibbell gives us a witty and incisive tour of a subculture well on its way to becoming *the* culture. His attempts to wring a real living from a consensual hallucination seem quixotic, at first. But *Play Money*'s electric meditation on play and work challenges comfortable notions about other consensual hallucinations—money, value, reality—and leaves you casting sideways glances at your "real" twenty-dollar bill."

—D.B. WEISS, author of *Lucky Wander Boy*

"This may very well be the best narrative non-fiction yet written about virtual worlds. Through both his experiences and his journalism about them, Dibbell has upgraded the level of conversation about the liminal space between work and play, reality and fantasy, and value and money. *Play Money* is an entrancing book told with rare ease and immediacy."

—DOUGLAS RUSHKOFF, author, *Cyberia*,
Get Back in the Box, and *Testament*

"There's a billion-dollar market in virtual item sales, and it's making lots of people ask, 'Why would anyone pay real money for play objects inside games?'. Find the answer in the pages of *Play Money*, because Dibbell's first-hand experience as a trader in virtual economies is the best window we have into this exploding market."

—EDWARD CASTRONOVA, Associate Professor and
Director of Graduate Studies Department
of Telecommunications, Indiana University

"Dibbell's accounts of virtual economies practically convulse with sinister wit, and find action and intrigue hiding almost everywhere: in empty buildings and in abandoned rooms where screens glow all night."

—JOHN DARNIELLE, founder and lead-singer
of The Mountain Goats

PLAY MONEY

Or, How I Quit My Day Job
and Made Millions Trading
Virtual Loot

JULIAN DIBBELL

Basic Books
A Member of the Perseus Books Group
New York

Hardcover published in 2006 by Basic Books,
A Member of the Perseus Books Group
Paperback published in 2007 by Basic Books

Basic Books are available at special discounts for bulk purchases in
the U.S. by corporations, institutions, and other organizations. For
more information, please contact the Special Markets Department
at the Perseus Books Group, 2300 Chestnut Street, Suite 200,
Philadelphia, PA 19103, or call (800) 255-1514, or e-mail
special.markets@perseusbooks.com.

Cataloging-In-Publication data is available at the Library of Congress.
Hardcover ISBN–13: 978-0-465-01535-1
Hardcover ISBN–10: 0-465-01535-2
Paperback ISBN–13: 978-0-465-01536-8
Paperback ISBN–10: 0-465-01536-0

10 9 8 7 6 5 4 3 2

For Lola, for real.

"Play cannot be denied. You can deny, if you like, nearly all abstractions: justice, beauty, truth, goodness, mind, God. You can deny seriousness, but not play."

JOHAN HUIZINGA

"People have told me I need to get a life."

JOHN DUGGER

"i do this for a fucking living, rich. this is my entire fucking job."

DESTINY

CONTENTS

< vii >

CONTENTS

< viii >

CONTENTS

< ix >

ACKNOWLEDGMENTS

This is a book about make-believe value in make-believe worlds, and it makes the case, I like to think, that there really is no other kind.

That said, there are no made-up characters in this story. It depends for its substance on what real people have really done and really said, and I would be a lout if I didn't begin by thanking, broadly, all those really real people for their contributions to the narrative. In particular, my thanks go out to every game designer who's had a hand in shaping the remarkable massively multi-player online game genre, and especially to Richard Garriott, Raph Koster, and all who helped construct the great, enduring Ultima Online. To them and to their customers, whose virtual labors constitute the economies I came to experience and to write about, I owe a debt of gratitude that probably will bankrupt me before I can pay it off.

Slightly more manageable is the thanks I owe former *Wired* magazine features editor Adam Fisher, who long ago encouraged my fascination with virtual economies of every sort, and whose genius for fanning a writer's smoldering curiosity into the bright flame of a story gave this book its first shove forward. Next in line: Stanford Law School's Center for Internet and Society and

< xi >

its director, Lawrence Lessig, who gave me the gift of a yearlong CIS fellowship and, with it, the chance to even contemplate embarking on a project as preposterous as the one this book chronicles. Early encouragement came also, and crucially, from Lydia Wills, as humane and ass-kicking an agent as any writer could hope for (pH34r her), and from Megan Hustad, who acquired the book for Basic.

Once underway, the authoring process proved, to my surprise, much less the chore it tends to be and much more the intellectual party one longs for it to be, and for that I'm thankful to many. My fellow virtual-world explorers at the collaborative blog Terra Nova (terranova.blogs.com) kept me lively and occasionally brilliant company throughout: Edward Castronova, Dan Hunter, and Greg Lastowka, especially, provided both material and moral support, and conversations with anthropologist Thomas Malaby, both online and off, provided insights I would not trade for all the gold in Azeroth. Thomas Keenan of Bard College, T. L. Taylor of IT University of Copenhagen, and Michael Connor of Liverpool's Foundation for Art and Creative Technology all helped out with valuable opportunities to share my story and my ideas with students and scholars from around the northern hemisphere, and a well-timed assignment from Nicholas Thompson, former editor at *Legal Affairs* magazine, gave me the chance to share them, most informatively, with the Internal Revenue Service.

In the final shaping of the book I had excellent editorial guidance from William Frucht, my end-game editor at Basic, from the eternally recurrent Adam Fisher (who wasn't getting paid for it this time), and from the exceptionally generous Tim Kirk, a great storyteller and a greater friend. And in the final stages of a hair-raising production schedule, copy editor Lori Hobkirk helped me through with sound advice and heroic patience.

< xii >

Of course, the true heroes (and/or casualties) of any book's gestation are the people who had to spend it living under the same roof as the author, so let me praise them now. Jessica Chalmers, bless her soul, was far more supportive of my efforts to get this book off the ground than the circumstances required. Jacob and Amelia Mazzarella, ages eight and ten, bore up generously under the deprivations my obsessive revision work entailed. Lola Chalmers-Dibbell, age five, asked only that I tell her a story nearly every time we got into the car for a drive of longer than fifteen minutes, and though I doubt she realized how liberating an effect these forced improvisations had on my writing habits, it's largely out of gratitude for this that I've dedicated the book to her. As for Jennifer Cole, what can I say? She was, and is, an angel.

One special mention remains. Thirty-three years ago, as I sat on the carpet of a fourth-grade classroom weeping bitter tears over the cruel difficulty of long division, the teacher, Elene Kallimanis, sat beside me, held my hand, and calmly talked me through the assignment at hand. This year she did it again, volunteering to check in briefly with me on a weekly and, finally, daily basis as I raced to finish the manuscript, and her levelheaded tactical and strategic advice made all the difference. I hardly cried at all this time.

< xiii >

PART ONE

The Noob

On Tuesday, March 11, 2003, I announced to my family, my friends, and anyone else who happened to look at my website that I was embarking on a new profession: I was going to start a business selling make-believe commodities, and I was going to get rich doing it.

That was the extent of what I could have told you about the plan. I didn't know then just how routinely surreal the year ahead would prove to be, or just how deep my fascination with the Internet's vast, densely populated virtual worlds would pull me into the half-illusory economy those worlds sustain. I could have sketched the general backdrop for you: a global exchange of fictional goods for very real currencies amounting, in total, to what is surely the most improbable half-billion-dollar-a-year industry on the planet. But the cast of characters remained uncertain, the pivotal scenes unwritten. The powerful industry player I would come to think of as my professional mentor, Mr. Big; the elite Markee Dragon team of virtual gold brokers I would soon look up to and eventually ascend into the ranks of; and the murky underworld of gray-market gold farmers I would eventually know better than I was entirely comfortable with—my acquaintance with them all was still remote, a hint, no more, of things to come.

< 2 >

Nor had I caught much more than passing glimpses of the insights that lay ahead. A dogged intuition told me something world-historic was afoot in the territory I was moving into. But I would have been embarrassed to admit I thought so. The profound economic and cultural changes I see inscribed so clearly now in the project I embarked on—the radical confusion of production and pretend, the emergence of play, and of computer games specifically, as key to any understanding of what the world economy has become and where it's headed—still lay beyond my power to articulate.

As for when, exactly, it first occurred to me to get into this line of work, I honestly don't remember. But if I had to guess, I'd say it was not long after I got my sorry ass pwned outside the dungeon Despise in the midst of yet another run to harvest lizard men.

I'd been doing lizards for a month or so. Like all new visitors to the world the lizard men inhabited, I lacked skills and money, and killing these not very likeable creatures had proven a good way to acquire both. Night after night, I would hop on my horse, load my backpack up with blood moss, black pearl, sulfur, and other magical reagents essential to the casting of spells, and head out to Despise, the lizards' lair, for an hour or two of solid slaying. It was easy work, and satisfying. The lizard men were iguana-green, ridge-backed, and stupid; over and over, they kept hissing the unfathomable phrase "Vess-stim-sah!," which no doubt meant something darkly menacing in lizard-man language but sounded, after the four- or five-hundredth time you'd heard it, more like a bad case of Tourette's. I knew the lizard men were only computer programs, but they had killed me often enough when I was just starting out that I still felt a tiny thrill of revenge watching them die.

Tonight I was killing them in waves. The dungeon was infested with them, and I would ride through it drawing their dim, robotic

< 3 >

attention to me until I had a band of seven or eight pursuing me through the torch-lit tunnels. Then I would lead them to a narrow, desolate passageway, speed ahead to the end of it, and lay down Flame Field spells behind me. A half dozen walls of flame would fill the corridor, and the lizard men would march into the midst of the inferno trying to get at me, hemorrhaging hit points as they did. I'd let them get almost to my end of the passage, then ride back to the other end, leading them through the fire fields again. Two or three rides back and forth and the lizard men were corpses, heaped up amid the dwindling flames. The rest was two minutes' worth of cleanup: one by one, I clicked on the dead bodies, carving off hides and then cutting the hides into sheets of spined leather, which I stowed away in my horse's pack. I had a regular customer for the leather, a guy who seemed to live in Eastern Europe somewhere and paid 30,000 gold pieces for every thousand sheets. What he did with all that leather I had no idea, but as long as he kept paying for it, I didn't really care.

Eventually, my horse's pack was full, and it was time for me to make a quick run to the bank. A random lizard man was approaching me, bent on murder. "Vess-stim-sah!" it growled. I hit it with a lightning bolt, just for laughs, then teleported magically to the busy capital city of Britain, where amid the usual crowd of fellow adventurers gathered outside the bank to hawk their loot, I deposited my own in a private bank box, clicking the horse's backpack open and dragging its burden onto the pile of leather already accumulated in the box. Then I teleported back to the entrance to Despise, and prepared to ride in for another session of lizard whacking.

Wassup? said the lone horseman loitering on the small meadow just outside the dungeon portal.

The stranger stood some thirty paces from where I'd materialized, and his greeting was written in light-blue letters that hov-

< 4 >

ered just above his little cartoon image on my screen, like a thought balloon.

Heya, I typed back.

Vas Ort Flam, he replied, casting a spell, obviously, though I couldn't have said exactly which one.

Corp Por, he added, whereupon my computer speakers rumbled with the sound of an explosion and my own little cartoon image was surrounded with a cartoon cloud of fire and smoke. There immediately followed the sound of an electric crackle and the sight of a blue bolt of energy emanating from the stranger toward me, and it was only as the bolt hit home that I realized, at last, that for the first time since I'd started playing this game, I was under attack by a fellow player.

By then it was more or less too late. Standing to fight was out of the question—the attacker's magery skill clearly outclassed mine by a good twenty points—so I turned to flee. Sheer cliffs blocked my escape on one side, however, and deep water blocked it on the other, so in the end all I could do was run in circles, hoping to make a difficult target for the enemy's cursor. This didn't last long. The first two spells had sapped my strength to within a few hit points of death, and the next energy bolt that hit me finished the job. My screen dimmed for a moment, and in the next moment a dead body—mine—lay on the ground at my horse's feet. I was now a gray, shrouded ghost standing impotently over the corpse as my slayer came to loot it.

fucking noob, he said, after a quick examination of my backpack's contents. *next time bring something worth taking*

maybe then I won't do this, he added, loosing an energy bolt at my horse, which immediately dropped dead.

ah you bastard, I typed. But I knew there wasn't much point. Ghosts couldn't talk, and all the killer would see on his screen when I typed was a pathetic, moaning *OooOOoooOooo* . . . Be-

< 5 >

sides, he was already halfway gone, disappearing in a haze of sparkly pixels as he teleported off. There was nothing left for me to do but run through my usual post-death routine: set out walking, find a healer who could resurrect me, walk back to my corpse, gather up my clothes and reagents, teleport back to Britain, buy a new horse, stable it, and call it a night.

I logged out and switched off the monitor.

It was 3 a.m. and a good moment, all things considered, to take stock of the pursuit that had been occupying most of my leisure time for the last three months. The bolt-casting stranger had just rudely reminded me of my place in the hierarchy that bound the hundreds of thousands of players who shared this gamespace with me. He was right: I was a noob. A newbie. Bottom-most rung on the ladder of accomplishment and fated, therefore, to endure from time to time the sort of humiliation that had just befallen me. *Vanquished*, I suppose, would have been the properly swashbuckling word for the condition he'd reduced me to, but players generally preferred variations on a phrase that sounded somewhat more like prison slang and somehow felt more appropriate:

I'd been *owned*.

0wnz0red.

Pwned.

This was educational. The experience hadn't felt good, exactly, yet there'd been a visceral sort of thrill to it. My pulse had pounded from the adrenaline rush of the chase, and when the assailant had killed my horse, I'd felt my face flush with something that approached genuine indignation. The encounter had engaged my limbic system as much as my intellect, triggering reflexes wired deep into the biology of human motivation. A window had opened into the magnetic core of the game, and I could see more clearly than ever what kept me and all the other players

< 6 >

coming back: It was the same thing, more or less, that kept most of us going to our jobs each day, or going to school. It was a desire not to fall to the bottom of the social food chain, a desire to rise through the ranks, to achieve and acquire as a way of marking our status within the massive monkey troop that is human civilization. To own and not be owned.

I knew then that I was in trouble, and just what kind of trouble it was. Like most players, I had joked about being addicted to the game. And sometimes—after I'd lost half my workday to a four- or five-hour "lunch break" of game play, or as I lay in bed actually *hoping* for insomnia so that I could get up and slay lizard men for a couple hours—I wondered whether it was more than a joke. But now I saw plainly that, at least as far as certain quarters of my brain were concerned, this was more than an addiction. It was a parallel life. A career, in fact, and in some ways a career more straightforwardly rewarding than the writing career I had chosen to follow in my real life. And as long as there was room to rise in this career—as long as there were bigger monsters to slay, bigger piles of gold to amass, and a distantly attainable day when I might have some sort of revenge on the prick who'd killed my horse—then I would go on feeling compelled to pursue it right up to the limits of the sensible.

Something had to give. The twenty hours a week I was devoting to the game were no big deal compared to the sixty, seventy, and even eighty hours some players put in. But a kind of nausea welled up in me when I considered what I was getting in return for that investment of time. Fun was the chief result, to be sure, but what was that? "An occasion of pure waste," according to one famous sociologist's definition of play: "waste of time, energy, ingenuity, skill, and often of money." Pointlessness, in this widely held view, is precisely the point of play. It gives it whatever meaning it has. Yet somehow, now that I was stopping to give it some

< 7 >

thought, the pointlessness of playing this particular game, given its uncanny similarities to the pursuit of an actual profession, filled me with a mild existential horror. I knew then that I would either have to quit the game cold turkey or find some way to do what was in principle impossible: Give the game a point. Make it productive. Turn the imaginary career into a real one.

I thought about quitting for a few days. I really did. But in the end I opted for the impossible, having reason to believe it might be the easier of my options.

< 8 >

PART TWO
Tijuana

"Sorry about the mess," said Lee Caldwell as he led me into the living room of his Orange County, California, home. "The maid hasn't been by today yet."

He was right about the mess, but I doubted there was much the housekeeper could do about it. Caldwell was thirty-one years old, his three housemates were all in their early to late twenties, and bits of bachelor-pad detritus (an empty pizza box, a half-finished can of soda) could predictably be seen here and there. It wasn't mere litter, however, that cluttered the living room beyond all hope of tidiness. It was wall-to-wall hardware. A half dozen computers, along with their attendant peripherals, wiring, and workstations, filled the room in no particular order. Programming manuals and computer-game cheat books spilled from wire-rack shelves. Something serious was going on here, though you would have been hard pressed to say at a guess exactly what. You got the impression, at any rate, that despite the vague party-house vibe pervading the place, the people who lived here were no slackers.

In fact, they were businessmen. Caldwell and his housemates were partners in an enterprise they called Blacksnow Interactive, and this was its headquarters. Blacksnow made money selling

< 10 >

things on eBay and other online sales sites, and in this, of course, it was no different from the masses of other small-scale businesses that had discovered the advantages of doing commerce over the Internet. In at least one aspect of its business model, however, Blacksnow was distinctive: It sold things that didn't, strictly speaking, exist.

More precisely, the goods Blacksnow dealt in existed only within the bounds of make-believe digital worlds called massively multiplayer online role-playing games—MMORPGs for short, MMOs for shorter. There are dozens of these worlds in operation around the globe, with millions of players inhabiting them, each a complex virtual geography of sprawling land masses, busy towns, dangerous wildernesses, and semi-magical physics. Each too is a complex virtual economy, in which players—masquerading as elves, dwarves, wizards, spaceship captains, comic-book heroes, or whatever other fantastical entities the setting demands—compete for scarce resources that in one way or another help them get ahead in the imaginary world of their choosing. The resources vary widely—they may be high-powered weapons, invincible armor, choice real estate, rare collectibles, or basic commodities like lumber, leather, metal ore, and, of course, money. Nor is it entirely clear what makes these things as desirable as they are, since the games themselves never really come to an end, never produce an ultimate winner or loser, never, indeed, quite define what the point of playing is. But in this, of course, the games resemble nothing so much as real life, and just as often happens in real life, players tend to reduce the hazy, intractable question of what it's all about to a simpler, unspoken rule of thumb: He who logs out with the most toys wins.

All of which helps, somewhat, to explain this curious fact: There are many, many MMO players who, lacking the time, the patience, or the ability to acquire fantasy goods through fantasy

< 11 >

means, will instead purchase them from other players with cold, hard, real-life cash. In game-industry jargon it's called real-money trading, or RMT, and the trades involved can move astonishing amounts of cash. The record sum for a single item is the $100,000 paid in October 2005 for an "Asteroid Space Resort" in the Swedish-based, science-fiction-themed game Project Entropia. But it's hardly unheard of for players to spend tens of thousands of dollars over the lifetime of a game character, equipping their virtual selves with all the trappings of power and prestige that separate average players from those distinguished, in the gamer vernacular, as *uber*. In the mythical realm of Azeroth, for instance—home to the six million players of the current MMO market leader World of Warcraft—merely getting yourself off to a respectable start might entail buying a level 60 Alliance warrior account from a departing player ($1,999 on eBay), a Dwarven Hand Cannon ($20 worth of gold coins at the in-game auction house), a pair of Abyssal Plate Legplates of Striking ($10 at the auction house), an extremely rare Baby Murloc Pet just for kicks ($500 on eBay), and maybe five thousand extra gold coins for living expenses ($250 from an online virtual-currency broker). And that's just one night's expenditures, for one player, in one of the many games that sustain this etheral market. Worldwide, annual sales of virtual goods run to an estimated $880 million and growing.

Which in turn is just a fraction of the total wealth created annually by inhabitants of the world's MMOs. For every item or character sold on eBay and other Web sites, many more are traded within the games themselves—some for barter, most for fanciful in-game currencies (with, of course, not-so-fanciful out-of-game exchange rates: at twenty to the U.S. dollar, the Azerothian gold coin of World of Warcraft trades at a rate comparable to the Russian ruble's; on the lower end of current virtual-money markets, Lineage II's Adenian adena trades at

< 12 >

around a million to the dollar, slightly better than the Turkish lira did before its revaluation in 2005). The goods thus exchanged number in the high millions, if not the billions, nearly every one of them brought into being by the sweat of some player's virtual brow. Magic weapons won in arduous quests, furniture built with tediously acquired carpentry skills, characters made powerful through years of obsessive play—taken as a whole, they are the gross domestic product of fantasy land.

And not just in a manner of speaking. In December 2001, Edward Castronova, then a professor of economics at California State University–Fullerton, had published a paper analyzing the circulation of goods in Sony Online's 400,000-player EverQuest, then the largest of the U.S.-based MMOs. Taking the prices fetched in the $5 million EverQuest auctions market as a roughly reliable reflection of in-game property values, Castronova calculated a full set of macro- and microeconomic statistics for EverQuest's fictional world, the realm of Norrath. He measured its money supply and its export market. He examined the tenacious roots of Norrathian inflation and the market-shaping effects of in-game transaction costs. And most strikingly, he totaled up a Norrathian GDP—the sum value of all the goods looted and crafted and otherwise brought into existence by EverQuest players in a given year—of $2,280 per capita. This implied an average hourly income of $3.42 and placed Norrath in the upper third of world economies, just below the island nation of St. Vincent, a notch or two above Russia, and well above such countries as China and India.

Now, take Castronova's numbers and his methods and a bit of guesswork and apply them to the collective output of all existing MMOs, worldwide, and you arrive at this conclusion: The workforce toiling away in these imaginary worlds is generating a quantity of real wealth on the order of $20 billion each year.

< 13 >

Blacksnow's piece of that pie was the merest sliver, but it was enough to earn the principals a more-than-respectable living. "We'll probably bring in thirty or forty grand this month," Caldwell told me. Mentally totaling up their holdings in the various games they dealt in—the sci-fi-ish Anarchy Online, the medieval Dark Age of Camelot, and the MMO genre's founding title, Ultima Online—and glancing around at the computers with which they accessed those assets, he added, "We've got about $800,000 in inventory sitting around in there at the moment."

Caldwell was short, paunchy, and pug-faced, with close-cropped hair and a frat boy's sense of style. Not exactly the Future of American Enterprise personified, I suppose, yet he seemed in some way larger than life to me—and not just because he was the first person I'd ever met face to face who made his living in an imaginary economy. I would in time meet others, some more intelligent than Caldwell, some more successful, but none with quite his flair for locating the most unsettling implications of his line of work and then somehow turning up the weirdness dial to eleven.

Take, for instance, the reason I had gotten in touch with him in the first place: the as-yet unsettled but already legendary court battle known officially as *Blacksnow Interactive v. Mythic Entertainment, Inc.*

Mythic Entertainment ran Dark Age of Camelot, the game in which Blacksnow had had its greatest economic success, and like most game companies, Mythic took a disapproving view of the shadow market in items it considered to be its exclusive property. "I hate it with every bone of my body," Mythic president Mark Jacobson was known to say, and in this, he reflected the opinions of a great many MMO players as well.

It was easy to see why players might hate RMT: Their every learned instinct about games told them it was cheating, as brazen an injustice as pulling out a real twenty-dollar bill in the middle

< 14 >

of a Monopoly game and giving it to another player in exchange for Boardwalk and Park Place. But it was rare to find a game-industry executive as passionately opposed to the practice as Jacobson, because in fact the players—their customers—had always been deeply ambivalent about it. MMOs may be games, after all, but they are hardly Monopoly, and their vast complexity and open-ended format leave considerable room for debate about the ethics of buying virtual prowess. ("It's like showing up to a knife fight with a gun," argued one side of a message-board discussion I saw once; "No," the other side calmly replied, "it's like showing up to a knife fight with a knife you bought from somebody else instead of handcrafting it yourself.")

The end-user license agreement all Dark Age of Camelot players were required to click on, however, was not at all ambiguous: "[P]laying the Game is intended for the entertainment, enjoyment and recreation of individual natural persons, and not as corporate, business, commercial, or income-seeking activities . . . [P]laying the Game for commercial, business, or income-seeking purposes is strictly prohibited." What part of *strictly prohibited* the boys of Blacksnow did or didn't understand was, as far as Mythic was concerned, beside the point. What they were doing, and in particular the scale on which they were doing it, couldn't go unanswered. And so Mythic took action: It contacted eBay and informed the company that Blacksnow's auctions were in violation of Mythic's intellectual property rights, which in turn was all it took to get the auctions shut down.

The standard response, had Blacksnow opted for it, would have been to roll with the punch: Go find other auction sites to sell on, maybe beef up sales on Blacksnow's own retail site, and carry on making money as if nothing much had happened. But though Caldwell's partners seemed inclined to go that route, in the end he prevailed on them to take a road less traveled: In late

< 15 >

February 2002, in the U.S. district court of Southern California, Blacksnow filed suit against Virginia-based Mythic for "unfair business practices" and "interference with prospective economic advantage." The suit asked for unspecified compensatory and punitive damages, and it sought as well a clear and final ruling that the sort of trade Blacksnow and thousands of other Dark Age of Camelot players were engaged in did not in any way infringe on Mythic's copyrights.

Who knows why Caldwell chose to stand and fight. Maybe he just wanted to be as big a pain in Mythic's ass as he possibly could be. Even if that's all he was after, though, the only way for him to do it was to force the American legal system to come to grips with the strange and knotty question at the heart of Blacksnow's business model: Exactly who owns the wealth of virtual worlds? The companies that create those worlds? Or the players who fuel their economies?

"What it comes down to," wrote Caldwell himself in a press release issued soon after the suit was filed, "is, does a MMORPG player have rights to his time, or does Mythic own that player's time?" I saw the press release online a little later, and while some might have felt that the American legal system had more important matters to grapple with, I sensed in Caldwell's question a faint, tectonic rumble of profound socioeconomic disruption—the sound, perhaps, of a three-century-old intellectual-property regime colliding with the limits of its ability to make sense of twenty-first-century reality. This was not the only place that sound could be heard, of course. The battles that rage around networked file-sharing, digital piracy, free software, international pharmaceutical patents, and other hotspots in today's explosive economy of intangibles were already well underway. But in Blacksnow's challenge to Mythic's copyright claims, it seemed to me, lay something of another order: Here

< 16 >

were the traditional economics of the intangible being stretched to the point of surreality.

I wanted a closer look. So I got an assignment from *Wired* magazine to write about MMO economies, and I got going. I pored over specialized websites educating myself in the intricacies of the virtual market. I interviewed players who had bought and sold in that market. I opened accounts on a game or two and got a first-hand taste of the obsessive play that keeps the market alive. And then, finally, I called up Lee Caldwell and talked to him for a while.

And when I did, I learned something interesting about the way Blacksnow did business. So interesting, in fact, that by the time I showed up at Caldwell's door, in late April of 2002, there wasn't a lot else about the business that I very much wanted to hear about. Not the lawsuit. Not the wall-to-wall hardware. Not, certainly, the half-digested tech-biz hype that Caldwell spouted, as if Blacksnow were just another plucky Internet startup riding the technological wave of the future.

"This is another world," Caldwell was saying. "The Internet has really affected the world like nobody has understood yet. There's gonna be greater impact, people are gonna be spending more time on their computers. TV is gonna go the way of the dinosaurs eventually. There's more and more people doing stuff online than ever before. There's more women coming online. There's more older people coming online. There's more poor people coming online."

I took notes dutifully and asked all the questions Caldwell seemed to want me to ask. Then finally, at a lull in the conversation, I asked the one question I'd been wanting an answer to since the moment I'd arrived:

"How soon can we go down to Mexico?"

< 17 >

CHAPTER 3

The view from the upper floors of the Grand Hotel Tijuana is something to behold, and I should know. Shortly after my visit with Lee Caldwell, I spent three days beholding it, there being not much else for me to do under the circumstances. I had come to Tijuana in search of a clue to a sort of puzzle, and outside my window the puzzle was all I saw: a wretched jumble of shops, shacks, and modest high-rises spreading all the way from my hotel to the U.S. border in the near distance, where suddenly the landscape changed to a brown-grass nothingness of pristine, empty hills. It was an allegory—a picture in geography of what feels more and more like the central fact of life on this globalized planet: the steady migration of material wealth into realms of the immaterial, of virtuality and emptiness.

This much I knew. But I knew, too, that somewhere amid the Tijuana streets below me lurked a picture even more vivid, an image that not only embodied the uneasy abstractions of contemporary economic existence but, perhaps, illuminated them. A clue, in short. And the clue was eluding me.

More to the point, Lee Caldwell was eluding me. When I'd left his house in Orange a week before, he had promised to meet me here. He was going to lead me, at last, to the clue I sought. It was

< 18 >

the secret, he claimed, of Blacksnow's success: a rented Tijuana office equipped with a high-speed Internet connection, eight PC workstations, and three shifts of unskilled Mexican workers paid to do what most employers would have fired them for—play computer games nonstop from punch-in to quitting time. The Mexicans were young men, mostly, and a few young women, but they were not, by disposition, gamers. They played according to tightly scripted guidelines given to them daily by their on-site supervisors, and they earned piecework wages, paid by the amount of make-believe loot they piled up. They were farmers for hire, harvesting the resources of imaginary worlds, and they made about $19 a day doing it.

It was a brilliant idea, in its way, though its brilliance lay more in its brazenness, perhaps, than in its insight. The economic arithmetic that made it viable, after all, was easy enough to grasp. Edward Castronova had essentially laid the numbers bare already when he'd pegged the average hourly income of EverQuest players at $3.42—a rate most Third World workers would feel privileged to earn. From Castronova's analysis to Blacksnow's Tijuana loot farm, then, was just a matter of filling in the blanks.

And fill them Caldwell and his partners most assiduously did. They kept a close eye on the shifting opportunities for wealth production in the games they farmed, and wherever an opportunity emerged that promised revenues sufficiently in excess of the going Mexican wage, they swooped.

For a while the big money-maker was an activity in Dark Age of Camelot called consignment crafting. This was a tedious method of improving a character's trade skills (armor crafting, say, or weapon smithing) that paid tidy sums of gold coins to players patient enough to sit through it. Blacksnow's Tijuana staff, of course, were paid to be patient, so it was no big deal for

< 19 >

one of them to take a character from level 1 in a trade skill to the maximum level 500 in a week's time, acquiring in the process not only gold, but a highly skilled character account that could itself be sold on the open market. "At the time," Caldwell had told me, "the price of gold was high enough that we could pay the Mexicans $112 a week, and they would make about 150 gold [approximately $300 worth] in about thirty-eight hours, plus the account, which we were selling for a hundred bucks."

Four hundred dollars' return on $112 in labor costs was a sweet margin, but generally Blacksnow had to hustle to stay close to profit levels like that. When the profitability of consignment crafting dropped with the price of DAoC gold, Caldwell and the gang shifted Tijuana's focus back to the older and more dependable Ultima Online, where the workers could still farm productively for them in a variety of ways: slaying high-level monsters for loot, harvesting hidden treasure, mining the hills for metal ore to smelt down into ingots. For the most part, the commodities thus gathered were sold in-game, for gold pieces, with the resulting stockpiles of currency selling in small lots on eBay or at wholesale volume to other retailers. "Currency is a quick turnaround," Caldwell had said. "The guys in Mexico, with UO gold, they can still do 800,000 a day each, 900,000 to a million if they work together. That's $25 a day."

I tried to imagine it: Eight working-class Mexicans sitting in a small office staring at computer screens, typing and clicking away like telegraphers tapping Morse code, some of them playing mage characters, some playing warriors, all of them joining forces now and then not so much for the camaraderie as because it was the only way to defeat the highest-level dragons and orcs and thereby maximize their productivity. "Not everybody likes the job," Caldwell had allowed. "Not everybody's a factory

< 20 >

worker. Not everybody can sit there at the computer and do it for hours and hours and hours, day after day after day." Still, he'd insisted, those who kept at it had no complaints. "Conditions aren't like what I'm used to, but apparently they love 'em. We buy food and everything; we order pizzas or Chinese food and everybody loves that. And they're playing video games instead of working in a field somewhere. They love it."

Well, maybe they did. But somehow, as thoroughly as Caldwell had detailed the workings of the gold farm, I still had a hard time picturing it. It was just a little too surreal, for one thing; but more than that, it was just a little too perfectly emblematic. When I tried to envision the particulars of the operation, I could barely penetrate the haze of world-historical significance that seemed to envelop it. If I closed my eyes and thought about what Blacksnow was up to, I was less likely to see the mouse-clicking hand of a Mexican gold farmer than the face of Karl Marx, captioned "All that is solid melts into air."

That phrase is from the *Communist Manifesto*, and it has long been cited as evidence that Marx, however questionable his own prescriptions for change, had a keen eye for the changes that the modern industrial regime was already working on the world of his day. Capitalism is a permanent revolution, Marx observed— a constant revision of the tools of production and the social relations they entail. In its hunger for new methods and new markets, it leaves untouched no realm of the economy, no region of the world. Globalization has been one consequence of this hunger, obvious even in the middle of the nineteenth century. But here, in the passage anchored by those memorable seven words, Marx hints at an even broader consequence: a relentless drift toward abstraction at every stage of the productive process. A melting away of the solid—the tangible, the material—in the face

< 21 >

of a system forever impatient to discard what exists and create what doesn't.

A century and a half later, Marx's hint has become a global fact, omnipresent and ineluctable. Look at any quarter of the world's economic landscape, and you'll see the forces of dematerialization either on the rise or in full swing. Money, arguably a virtual reality to begin with, cut its last ties to tangible value three decades ago, when the world's currencies went off the gold standard for good. Other financial instruments—commodity futures, mortgages—have billowed up into complex derivatives many layers of abstraction removed from the material goods they represent. Meanwhile, back in the marketplace, material goods themselves cede pride of place to brands, copyrights, patents, and other intangibles more and more central to the creation of wealth. And production, finally, increasingly outsourceable to any jurisdiction on Earth, takes its last step away from the agrarian setting that once defined it and becomes an activity unattached to any particular piece of land, local or national.

In Blacksnow's gold farm I saw all these tendencies reduced to a sort of economic parody: offshore peons harvesting the bounty of a "land" that exists nowhere and anywhere. Copyrighted bitmaps masquerading as iron ingots. Gold coins more ephemeral than any paper dollar.

But the crowning jest, not so much economic as technological, was the digital frame in which the whole scene was set. Blacksnow's story seemed to capture, as no broad historical narrative ever could, the peculiarly mythic role computers have come to play in capitalism's flight from the material. Lubricating the global flow of capital, privileging mental over manual labor, expanding the value of intellectual property, computers, and their allied technologies (robotics, telecommunications) have been

< 22 >

consummate enablers of the postmodern economic condition. But more than that, the computer has been an icon of that condition—a concrete engine of abstract production and, as such, a tantalizing promise of economies finally set free of matter and its many inefficiencies.

People once believed more fervently in that promise than they now admit to. The late, lamented Internet boom inspired visions of an ethereal global marketplace lying just beyond the horizon. Capitalism's dematerializing trajectory, if you believed the boldest predictions, was to culminate at last, and soon, in a commercial utopia sometimes referred to as the virtual economy—a realm of atomless digital products traded in frictionless digital environments for paperless digital cash. And so it had, I realized now. Only, who would have guessed that this culmination would so literally consist of the buying and selling of castles in the air?

Such were the ironies that presented themselves to me as I sat in my hotel room, contemplating Caldwell's description of his Tijuana operations. They were juicy ironies, to be sure. But I had the nagging sensation, as well, that they only partially captured the meaning of Blacksnow and the virtual economy that sustained it. As easy as it was to frame Blacksnow's story as a portrait in miniature of the late-capitalist order of things, I couldn't help feeling that the relationship between the two went deeper than that. I sensed that the Tijuana loot farm wasn't just a metaphor but, as I've said, a clue. More than simply reflecting a truth about the twenty-first-century world, I suspected it might very well reveal one.

Not that I could have said, at the time, exactly what that truth might be. But now, I think I can. What Blacksnow's story was trying to tell me about contemporary economic life was this: It is becoming play. A game.

< 23 >

This is not an entirely unprecedented observation. "Casino capitalism" is political-economist Susan Strange's label for an international economic system in which speculative financial dealings—wagers in all but name—have come to dwarf in monetary value the global trade in goods and services. More broadly, cultural theorists such as Jean Baudrillard and Guy Debord have argued, in various ways, that life under advanced capitalism immerses us all in a largely imaginary reality, a media-saturated Disneyland-writ-large, drained of the heft and consequence that have historically distinguished real life from play. Or, if you like a little more kung fu in your critical theory, you can find the same argument roughed out in *The Matrix*, where, in an unsettlingly familiar future, the daily grind of economic production turns out to be no more than the rules of what is essentially a vast multiplayer computer game (and where Baudrillard's critique of postmodernity as "the desert of the real" is quoted twenty minutes into the narrative, just so you don't miss the point).

My point, however, is both narrower and more sweeping. I'm not talking about games as a metaphor. I'm talking about games as a symptom; about Pac-Man, Asteroids, Mortal Kombat, Counter-Strike, Halo, World of Warcraft, and the fast-growing, multibillion-dollar computer-game industry in general as the side effect of a far profounder development in the history of play: its decisive infiltration of that most serious of human pursuits, the creation of wealth. I'm suggesting that when the economic system of the world has come to such a pass that the labor of online gamers can contribute more to the global GDP than two out of three sovereign nations, then no proper account of that system can neglect to account for its relationship to play. And I'm arguing, finally, that that relationship is one of convergence; that in

< 24 >

the strange new world of immateriality toward which the engines of production have long been driving us, we can now at last make out the contours of a more familiar realm of the insubstantial—the realm of games and make-believe. In short, I'm saying that Marx had it almost right: Solidity is not melting into air. Production is melting into play.

< 25 >

CHAPTER 4

The sun began to set on my third day in Tijuana. I looked out the window of my hotel some more, wondering which of the buildings in the tumbling cityscape below might house the Blacksnow loot plantation. I waited for Lee Caldwell to call. He was still up in Orange County, as far as I knew. When I'd called his cell phone the day I arrived in Tijuana, he seemed oddly surprised that I had actually followed up on our plans to meet there. On the second day he started making vague suggestions that now might not in fact be the best time for me to visit the factory. And by the end of the day he was putting it bluntly:

"I'm sorry, man, I really am. It's not me. It's the partners. I guess I hadn't really cleared this with them, and they just don't think the publicity is a good idea right now. If the game companies found out what we're doing, you know... And we're not even sure we're in line with the Mexican business laws, honestly."

I pleaded. I wheedled. I dangled visions of the glowing light in which I would paint Blacksnow Interactive if he granted me access. "You guys are entrepreneurial pioneers," I said. "You're fucking heroes!"

< 26 >

Caldwell laughed weakly. "Right. I don't think we'll be looking like heroes. We'll be looking like Kathie Lee, running some sweatshop down in another country."

He stopped answering my calls after that. And now, as the day went dark, a small, unsettling notion began to nag at me: Maybe the gold farm didn't exist. Maybe it was just the fictional creation of a small-time hustler hungry for publicity. I found it hard to believe Caldwell could have made up all the operational details he'd given me, but how did I know, ultimately, just what level of con job the man was capable of? And how delightfully ironic, of course, to think that Blacksnow's elaborate scheme for harvesting imaginary resources may itself have been nothing more than the product of someone's imagination.

Not that I was savoring the irony. I picked up the phone and dialed a number I'd been scrupulously avoiding for the last week or so: that of Blacksnow's lawyer, Steve Krongold. I knew he'd told his clients not to talk to the press while their suit was pending, and I figured there was a good chance he'd flip when he learned they were talking to me. But at this point, I reasoned, only Krongold could convince them to open up the factory to me, and only a hard sell could convince him it was in his clients' best interests to do so. It was my last shot and a long one.

"Steve, I'm down in Tijuana waiting for a chance to have a look at Blacksnow's factory operations here," I said when Krongold answered. "And I just wanted to check in with you and see if I could get your help with the situation." I began to make my case. I told him what a handsome profile of his clients I was planning to write, and I was working up other desperate angles, such as, for instance, the favorable view a judge might take of these nice young men's contribution to the Mexican economy, when Krongold interrupted me.

< 27 >

"Wait a minute. Back up," he said. "Tijuana? Factory? What exactly are you talking about?"

It was then I knew I was not going to see the gold farm. If they hadn't told their own lawyer about it, then whether or not it actually existed was now beside the point: Krongold, presumably, was about to give his clients a scorching lecture on the dire consequences of ever talking to me again.

I got in my rental car the next day and headed north. I never heard another word from any of the Blacksnow principals, and whatever slim hopes I entertained of regaining their confidence dissolved entirely two months later, when the Federal Trade Commission announced a summary judgment against Caldwell and Blacksnow partner Richard Phim, fining them $10,000 for a previous online business venture selling computers they'd neglected, by and large, to actually deliver. Poor Steve Krongold: Apparently his clients had forgotten to tell him about that little operational detail too, and not long after the news of it got out, they disappeared on him, defaulting on their legal bill and obliging him to withdraw their suit. Thus ended *Blacksnow v. Mythic*, which had scarcely gotten underway, leaving its questions hanging over the world's burgeoning virtual economies.

Thus, too, the Blacksnow gold farm disappeared for good into the realm of myth. Months later *Wired* would publish my brief report on the factory, running it alongside my larger feature on the virtual economy, and the news would thenceforth circulate among gamers as something neither quite urban legend nor matter of record. There would be plenty of time for me to stew over the collapse of what could have been a spectacular scoop, but for now it didn't really matter to me anymore which of Lee Caldwell's various assertions were true or not. Clue or no clue, those three days in Tijuana had shown me enough to know that the story was no longer

< 28 >

about his curious intellectual-property claims or his even curiouser business practices. It was definitely headed someplace else.

As it turned out, I still had a few more road trips ahead of me before I got there, and many, many lizard men to immolate. But crossing the border into San Ysidro that morning, I was already on my way.

< 29 >

PART THREE
Stolle's Tower

CHAPTER 5

Not long after I got home from Tijuana, a 43-year-old Wonder Bread delivery man in Stillwater, Oklahoma, logged on to eBay and, as people sometimes do these days, bought himself a house there. Not a shabby one, either. Nine rooms, three stories, rooftop patio, walls of solid stonework—it wasn't quite a castle, but in most respects it put to shame the modest red-brick ranch house the man came home to every weeknight after a long day stocking the supermarket shelves of Stillwater. Excellent location, too; a long, long way from Oklahoma and nestled at the foot of a quiet coastal hillside, the house was just a hike away from a quaint seaside village and a quick commute from two bustling cosmopolitan cities. In short, the house could only have been better if it had actually existed, and even that might have been no great improvement in the buyer's eyes. He wasn't in the market for a real house, after all. He wanted his own small piece of the vast computer database that was Britannia, the mythical world in which the venerable MMO Ultima Online unfolds. And for $750, he got it.

The buyer's name was John Dugger, and I spoke to him by telephone a few weeks after his purchase. By then, it no longer surprised me that people spent real money on this sort of thing.

< 32 >

But that's not to say I understood why they did. Dugger had given up a week's wages to own what was at best a digital doll-house, and I grasped only dimly what had inspired him to do that. I suppose I could have simply asked him, and eventually, I would. But the real question, I sensed, was at once more specifically economic and more broadly social: How exactly does a seven-kilobyte piece of digital make-believe turn into a $750 piece of upmarket real estate? And the real answer, I suspected, was a bigger one than Dugger alone could have given me.

So I got into my car and set out to find it.

At a construction site in Indianapolis, Indiana, Troy Stolle sat in the passenger seat of my car, hard hat in his lap and a Big Mac in his hands. "Whoa, A/C at lunchtime," he observed, "that's a rarity." Outside, the temperature was ninety-one degrees; the air was thick with humidity, dust, and the rumble of bulldozers. A hundred yards away, the outline of a future Costco megastore shimmered in the heat, slowly taking shape as workers set rebar and poured concrete. Stolle's job, as a form carpenter, was to build the wooden molds the concrete got poured into and then rip them down after it dried. It was not a cushy gig even in the nicest weather, and in heat like this it could kill you if you didn't drink water constantly. Stolle's arms and hands were flecked with cuts and bruises, and at the moment he had a pounding headache from the early stages of dehydration. Or maybe from the two-by-four that had smacked him in the head earlier that morning. He wasn't certain which.

He was sure of this much, though: This job was a cakewalk compared to the work he'd put into raising a virtual tower in Britannia two years before. "That was a lot more stressful."

A lanky, bespectacled 29-year-old, Stolle looked less like the third-generation construction worker he was than like the second-

< 33 >

generation sword-and-sorcery geek he had become. When Stolle was 10, his father, a union electrician, died of a heart attack, leaving behind a cherished 1967 paperback edition of *The Lord of the Rings* and a copy of the Dungeons & Dragons rule set. All through high school, on through his four-year union apprenticeship, and well into his first years as a journeyman carpenter, Stolle spent vast stretches of his free time immersed in the intricacies of D&D, Warhammer, Battletech, and other tabletop role-playing and strategy games.

Then came Ultima Online. The first successful MMO, UO went live in September 1997, and by December Stolle had a character, a blacksmith he called Nils Hansen. The business of bettering Nils's lot in life quickly came to absorb him more intensely than any game ever had. In short order, he added two other characters: an archer, who went out hunting when Nils needed hides, and a mage, who cooked up potions to make the archer a better hunter. "I had everybody interlocked so that they totally supported one another," Stolle said. And to give this little team a base of operations—a place to store equipment, basically—he paid about 40,000 gold pieces for a deed permitting him to build a small house. He found a nice, secluded spot in northern Britannia, placed his cursor there, and double-clicked the building into existence.

The house worked out fine for a while, but in a game whose essence is accumulation, no house stays big enough for long. Stolle's trio needed new digs, and soon. The hitch at this point in Britannia's history, however, was that real estate was acutely hard to come by. Deeds were still available, but there was nowhere left to build. The number of homeless was rising, the prices of existing houses were rising even faster, and the natives were getting restless. At last, the game designers announced a solution—a whole new continent was being added to the map.

< 34 >

Stolle started preparing for the inevitable land rush months before it happened. He scrimped and saved, sold his house for 180,000 gold pieces, and finally had enough to buy a deed for the third-largest class of house in the game, the so-called large tower.

On the night the new continent's housing market was set to open, Stolle showed up early at a spot he had scouted out previously, and found twelve players already there. No one knew exactly when the zero hour was, so Stolle and the others just kept clicking on the site, each hoping to be the first to hit it when the time came.

"It was so stressful," Stolle recalled. "You're sitting there, you double-click the deed once and then click on the spot. And so I did this for four hours, standing in one place." Finally, at about one in the morning, the housing option switched on, and as a couple thousand build commands went through at once, the machine that was processing it all swooned under the load. "The server message pops up, and everything just freezes. And I'm still clicking. Even though nothing's happening, I'm still clicking—boom, boom, boom. For like ten minutes, everything's frozen. You see people kind of disappearing here and there. And then it starts to let up. And a tower appears! Nobody knows for sure whose it is. Guys are like, 'Whose is it? Did I get it?' I double-clicked on it, and I couldn't tell. And so then I double-clicked again—and there was my key to the tower."

Just like that. In a single clock cycle and a double mouse-click, Stolle had built himself a real nice spread.

But of course there was more to it than that. In addition to the four hours of premature clicking, Stolle had had to come up with the money for the deed. To get the money, he had had to sell his old house. To get that house in the first place, he'd had to spend hours crafting virtual broadswords and plate mail and the like to

< 35 >

sell to a steady clientele of about three dozen fellow players. To attract and keep that clientele, he'd had to bring Nils Hansen's blacksmithing skills up to the highest level possible. To reach that level, Stolle had spent six solid months doing nothing but smithing: He had clicked on hillsides to mine metal ore, he had headed to a forge to click the ore into ingots, he had clicked again to turn the ingots into weapons and armor, and then he had headed back to the hills to start the process all over again, each time raising Nils's skill level some tiny fraction of a percentage point, inching him just slightly closer to the distant goal of one hundred points and the illustrious title of Grandmaster Blacksmith.

Take a moment now to pause, step back, and consider just what was going on here: Every day, month after month, a man was coming home from a full day of bone-jarringly repetitive work with hammer and nails to put in a full night of finger-numbingly repetitive work with "hammer" and "anvil"—and paying for the privilege. When I asked Stolle to make sense of this, he had a ready answer: "Well, it's not work if you enjoy it."

Which of course begs the question: Why would anyone enjoy it?

The psychologist Mihaly Csikszentmihalyi has done thousands of interviews over several decades in an effort to understand how people achieve and maintain what is sometimes called happiness. One of the people he interviewed is an assembly-line worker whose job requires him to repeat one simple task all day long, taking no longer than forty-three seconds each time he performs it, for a total of almost six hundred times a day. "Most people would grow tired of such work very soon," Csikszentmihalyi writes, with some understatement. "But [this man] has been at this job for over five years, and he still enjoys it." Why? Because

< 36 >

when he is on the job, he thinks of only one thing: how to get better at it. He watches his performance times like a sprinter training for an Olympic match, analyzing his moves, his tools, shaving a few seconds off his record whenever he can. After five years on the job, his best day's average is down to twenty-eight seconds per operation, and whenever he performs close to that, his work becomes, in Csikszentmihalyi's description, "so enthralling it is almost painful for him to slow down."

"It's better than anything else," the worker himself reports. "It's a whole lot better than watching TV."

In Csikszentmihalyi's analysis, what this man regularly experiences at work is a condition called "flow"—an exhilarating and uniquely fulfilling convergence of attention and purpose. "An activity that produces such experiences is so gratifying that people are willing to do it for its own sake," he writes, "with little concern for what they will get out of it, even when it is difficult, or dangerous." And no wonder. Flow, as described by Csikszentmihalyi and his informants, is a trip: "Concentration is so intense that there is no attention left over to think about anything irrelevant, or to worry about problems. Self-consciousness disappears, and the sense of time becomes distorted." There's a touch of mysticism in the concept—Csikszentmihalyi himself suggests that Zen monks were onto it before he was—but in fact, he insists, nearly everyone experiences it to greater or lesser degrees at various points in life, and it's not too hard to isolate the conditions that give rise to it. Above all, flow depends on "a sense that one's skills are adequate to the challenges at hand"—assuring we are neither overwhelmed nor understimulated by the tasks we face—and on the context of "a goal-directed, rule-bound action system that provides clear clues as to how well one is performing."

Given how closely these conditions match the description of a well-designed game, it's no surprise Csikszentmihalyi focused

< 37 >

initially on players of one sort or another—chess masters, mountain climbers, music makers—as the paradigm of human consciousness in flow. The surprise came later, when he discovered that *workers,* too, in almost every sort of occupation, are just as often in flow's grip. In fact, one study, in which he asked more than one hundred people to record the quality and circumstances of their everyday experience at randomly scheduled intervals, found that the respondents were "in flow" *more* frequently at work than at leisure. Three times more frequently, to be precise. "So much for the dichotomy of play and work," Csikszentmihalyi remarked.

And yet, there is another, equally curious aspect of his findings that points in a somewhat different direction. For though the research finds flow happening more often on the job than anywhere else, it turns out also to be true that workers, even in the very moment of reporting themselves immersed in every known condition and symptom of flow, will also typically say that they would rather—in that same moment—be away from work than at it. Flow alone, in other words, does not suffice to turn work into play. And while it may be true, as Csikszentmihalyi seems to suggest, that flow's indifference to the border between what we call work and play confirms that the border is in fact a fiction, that hardly renders the fiction meaningless. Nor does it cancel the seductive, motivating power that the category of play derives from that fiction—a power work somehow can't duplicate and flow, all by itself, can't quite account for.

And finally, if we really want to understand what made Troy Stolle do it—what drove him through the long, mouse-clicking nights of his career as a Britannian blacksmith—then we will definitely have to look beyond the Zen placidities of flow. As sociologist T. L. Taylor argues in *Play Between Worlds,* her illuminating ethnographic study of EverQuest players, "flow" only partially

< 38 >

captures the range of mindstates typical of MMO play, not all of them especially pretty. Even "play" itself comes in for a nearly fatal stretching of its definition here, particularly among that class of MMO aficionados known as power players, the geeks among the geeks, whose obsessions with game statistics and maximally efficient skill gains lead fellow players to deride them as humorless drones who couldn't possibly be enjoying themselves.

Not that anyone in MMO-land gets away clean from the embrace of joyless "fun." Even the most purely social players, for whom the game is all about camaraderie and chitchat, will at some point or another feel themselves more obliged than eager to show up and put in an appearance. The hardcore role-players will wake up one day feeling, like a dead weight on their chest, the strain of endless texting in stilted Renaissance Faire English— yet dutifully go on theeing and thouing all the same. And everyone, of course, must make a separate peace with the profound ambivalence of the "grind": the tantalizing, enervating treadmill of monster bashing, which promises a never-ending daily burst of experience points, gold, loot, and other tokens of self improvement but all too often leaves you feeling sick, unhinged, and inexplicably compelled, at the end of a long, late night, to try for just one more mongbat or ogre lord or lizardman when every rational fiber in your body is cringing at the sound of dawn's first songbirds tweeting outside the window.

"Well, it's not work if you enjoy it."

True enough. The part that Stolle apparently forgot to mention, though, is that somehow, through some obscure mutation of postindustrial human consciousness, it's still play even when you sort of hate it.

And if that sounds plain nuts to you, don't worry: When even a sophisticated conceptual framework like flow theory can't entirely make sense of it, how should you?

< 39 >

Perhaps a slight adjustment of the framework, though, might help. The perspective of psychology, after all—flow theory's disciplinary home base—is not the only angle we could approach the question from. And while it's true no other human science is as centrally preoccupied with the questions of personal desire, motivation, and evaluation that concern us here, there is one that comes close: economics.

Modern economics, according to its textbook definition, studies the allocation of resources under conditions of scarcity. More colloquially, you could say it's about the ways people try to get what they need in a world where they can't always get what they want. Either way, it's not called the dismal science for nothing: Deprivation, solidly embedded in the discipline's founding assumptions, literally defines it.

In this, contemporary economics echoes a founding assumption of Western culture itself, as ancient and as rooted as the book of Genesis, which defines the human condition as a fall from leisure and plenty into scarcity and work. We've been dreaming of the garden ever since. Throughout the rich Western tradition of utopian thought, the most desirable of all possible worlds has typically been imagined as a realm devoid of scarcity. Pie in the sky, manna from heaven, the land of milk and honey: All are shorthand for places or moments of limitless abundance and ease. And though the occasional long-haired visionary has insisted that these utopias might be found or built on planet Earth, the rest of us have by and large accepted that their only place is in our wishful thoughts.

Recently, however, a loose conspiracy of visionaries (mostly long-haired, as it happens, albeit unusually well-funded) created an earthly environment that fits the bill more closely than most. With its effortlessly reproducible wealth of data and light-speed transcendence of geography and time, the Internet, from the

< 40 >

start, was rumored to be a place where scarcity had no place. And as anybody in the record business or otherwise dependent on certain scarcities of information for a living can tell you, this rumor has proved in a bewildering variety of ways to be true.

But in certain realms of the emerging online universe—and in some ways just as bewilderingly—scarcity has thrived. In particular, when people have used the Internet not just to document and reflect on the world we live in, but to re-create and redesign it, they've discovered that worlds of limitless abundance and ease aren't necessarily as attractive in fact as they are in dreams. Given the endless malleability of the digital medium, a virtual world can in principle simulate any improvement on the real one imaginable, and not surprisingly, many of the Internet's earliest virtual worlds tried hard to do just that. In commercial, graphics-intensive spaces like World Inc.'s Worlds Away and Time Warner's The Palace, designers erased constraints long considered to be among the real world's most regrettable flaws: Users could fly, could duplicate objects at will, could generally get whatever they needed from the world without having to do much more than hang out socializing. And sure, people liked these places—who wouldn't? But in the end, the worlds they actually wanted to be in—badly enough to pay an entrance fee—were the ones that made the digital necessities almost maddeningly difficult to come by. All else being equal, in other words, the addictive, highly profitable appeal of MMOs suggests that people will choose the world that constrains them over the one that sets them free.

And economically speaking, that too is plain nuts. It was Edward Castronova, the Adam Smith of EverQuest, who first arrived at this conclusion. As the first economist to look seriously at virtual worlds, he was naturally puzzled by their mute refusal to take his discipline's most cherished truth very seriously at all. Scarcity, in traditional economics, is a necessary evil, but it is

< 41 >

above all an evil. Whatever stands between people and the things they want, whatever constrains them, is a bad thing. Conversely, whatever minimizes that constraint is a good thing—and typically worth paying good money for. So why were so many people now doing exactly the opposite, paying fifteen bucks a month to plow through the infinite constraints of MMOs?

Castronova identified this question as a special case—a peculiarly suggestive one, it turns out—of a broader problem he called the "puzzle of puzzles." The puzzle of puzzles, he wrote, is the first challenge facing any economic theory of games, which arises "primarily because economics is constructed from a model of human behaviour that asserts a universal conflict between our ends and our means." Consider, on the one hand, a jigsaw puzzle with 900 billion pieces, which proposes an end beyond any person's means, and on the other, a puzzle with only two pieces, which annihilates any distance whatsoever from means to end. In the world according to economic theory, the two-piece puzzle always gives better bang for buck—beating any other kind of puzzle, in fact, since none can claim more thoroughly to resolve the conflict between ends and means. Yet in the real world, as it shouldn't take a Milton Bradley executive to explain, both the two-piece and the 900-billion-piece are equally unmarketable.

As a technical matter, this riddle isn't hard to solve. Conventional economics can be tweaked to recognize the entertainment value in a certain degree of constraint; equations can even be written to compute that value (let $S = aR - b[C - W]^2$, Castronova helpfully suggests). But on a more philosophical level, the puzzle of puzzles can't really be unraveled without also tugging hard, finally, on the thread that holds mainstream economic thought together. As long as games remain closed and relatively simple systems, as they have throughout most of history, it's easy to dismiss their curious embrace of constraint as a mere exception to the economic

< 42 >

rule. But once games start to take on the complex shape of worlds and yet maintain their power to amuse and obsess us, you have to wonder: Could it be that scarcity is not so much a necessary evil as an economic good? Could it be that the real world's never-ending abundance of scarcity has prevented us from recognizing, until now, that we've actually developed a taste for the stuff?

Well, why not? In an atmosphere of oxygen, our bodies learned to breathe; in a world of scarcity, the soul might just as likely learn to need the universal obstacle to its desires—just maybe not, you know, so damn much of it. This, at any rate, is the lesson Castronova derives from the puzzle of puzzles, and more specifically, from the puzzle of virtual scarcity. "What we're learning is that scarcity itself is an essential variable," he writes. "We just haven't needed to worry about it before. Thanks to God, the Man, or whoever's running this show, we're used to taking scarcity for granted. The emergence of virtual communities means that we have to make it explicit."

And whether or not this lesson ultimately makes Troy Stolle's nightly reenactments of his daily grind seem any less perverse, it should at least make the fact that I can log on to eBay this minute and buy 100,000 imaginary iron ingots for $7.99 seem not only a little less improbable but just about inevitable. Economic theory tells us, after all, that scarcity breeds markets. And markets will seep like gas through any boundary that gives them the slightest opening—never mind a line as porous as the one between real and make-believe.

Or as Castronova had explained to me the day I met him, months before I'd even heard of Stolle's tower: "The minute you hardwire constraints into a virtual world, the economy emerges. One-trillionth of a second later is when that economy starts interacting with ours."

< 43 >

CHAPTER 6

From Stolle's house in Indianapolis, I drove to the quiet, former coal-mining town of Beckley, West Virginia, and there, in the downstairs den of a pleasant split-level house, I got to know a 31-year-old man named Bob Kiblinger. This was a good place to get to know him, for it was in that den that Kiblinger's most comfortable sofa was located, and it was on that sofa that Kiblinger himself could be found roughly fourteen hours a day, just about every day of the week, conducting business. As sole proprietor of UOTreasures.com—the largest retailer, by far, of second-hand Britannian items—Kiblinger spent much of his days scanning eBay listings on his laptop in search of assets undervalued and overlooked.

He was the second UO professional I'd met in person, and a very different sort of person from the first. Physically larger than Lee Caldwell—a head taller and probably half again his weight—Kiblinger didn't seem to take up nearly so much space. His face, shaved clean and framed by close-cropped dark hair, was gently boyish rather than rowdily so: round and open and typically on its slow way to a grin. Even his girth seemed less imposing than accommodating, more like an extension of the sofa cushions than a product of all the hours he spent sitting on them ("I need to get a T-shirt that says 'Body by Ultima,'" he joked). He lived

< 44 >

in tidy bourgeois respectability with his fiancée, an animal-rescue worker; their African grey parrot, three cats, and two dogs; and a shiny black Ford Explorer. And very much unlike Caldwell, he seemed perfectly happy to leave it at this—content with where the business had led so far, and not at all obsessed with how much farther it might take him.

I guess it's obvious, in retrospect, that this encounter was a pivotal one for me. If all the professionals I met along the way had been as outlandishly driven as Caldwell, it might never have crossed my mind that there could be a place for me in this profession, too.

But that's not why I'd come to see Kiblinger. I was there because on one particularly lucky day a few weeks earlier, as he had sat on his couch eyeballing the eBay offerings, he'd caught sight of a diamond in the rough: UO account, fifty-two months old, Grandmaster Smith, large tower. And not a single bid, he'd noticed.

Troy Stolle's account was definitely an opportunity. Kiblinger sized it up at about $1,500 worth of stuff, possibly $2,000. He fired off an email asking Stolle how much money he wanted to close the deal and hand over the account. Stolle emailed back: $500. Minutes later, Kiblinger was on the phone to Indiana, making arrangements to finalize the transaction. Before he hung up, the two men chitchatted a bit: Stolle got to talking about the unfortunate reasons he'd sold the account—about how he'd been out of work since 9/11, and how the bills were piling up. Kiblinger could hear an infant crying in the background, and part of him hoped the carpenter would never find out just how much he stood to make on the deal.

But business was business. Kiblinger knew that to keep his income up to speed he needed at least three or four fat, high-margin trades like this each week, and they weren't getting any easier to come by. Once upon a time, back when UO was young and most

< 45 >

players still hadn't gotten wind of the auction markets, his percentage on a deal often as not hit quadruple digits. Players sold him thousand-dollar accounts for a hundred, and Kiblinger just took the money and kept his mouth shut, knowing full well that in their eyes he was the crazy one. Not long before, he might even have agreed with them. "I would have done the same thing," he said. "If I had an account I was giving up, and you said you were going to give me a hundred dollars for it—for something that's not real—I would have said, 'Here, take it.'"

That was three years earlier, when Kiblinger was twenty-eight years old, married, working for Procter & Gamble in Cincinnati as a chemist (he shares two patents on the odor-busting fabric spray Febreze), and feeding his UO jones at night and on weekends. Within a year, his marriage was over ("Yes, it's true, an Ultima widow"), he had moved back home to Beckley, and he was brokering virtual worlds full-time. When I asked him how much he was earning by then, Kiblinger smiled affably and declined to answer, except to say that it was—and remained—a lot more than he had made at Procter & Gamble.

Kiblinger's caginess, I knew by then, was par for the course. There were dozens of people out there making a real living selling virtual goods, and none that I had spoken to was particularly eager to disclose their profits. A few would talk off the record, and none of those claimed to be netting less than six-figure incomes or fifteen-percent margins. But those were fragile numbers, threatened on all sides.

Hackers were among the biggest threats. To stay ahead of the latest tricks for stealing players' hard-won property—and to safeguard an inventory that routinely swelled to tens of thousands of dollars worth of goods—Kiblinger checked the UO cheat sites several times a week. Even worse were the dupers—counterfeiters who looked for software bugs, known as dupes,

< 46 >

that let them double and redouble their gold on command, turning a single piece into billions with just a few dozen mouse clicks. Not a bad deal for the dupers, but for the Britannian economy it was deadly: some of UO's earliest dupes had inflated the currency to the brink of worthlessness. Even now, the resulting monetary surplus kept the game designers busy thinking up "gold sinks"—typically expensive luxury items that could only be bought from NPCs (automated "non-player characters," often vendors of supplies and other goods), thus taking large sums of money out of circulation. Pricey housing deeds, neon-bright hair dye, and rare blue armor were among the many gold sinks that had been deployed to drain player wealth from the dupe-addled money supply.

Ultimately, though, the scariest threat to the dealers was the game companies themselves. Well aware that his income existed at the sufferance of UO's corporate overseer, Electronic Arts, Kiblinger tried to make sure his inventory never got much higher than $15,000. "It's scary to have that much cash tied up in the business at any given moment," he said, "when anytime they wanted to Ultima could just say, 'We deem this outside the rules of the game. You're done.'" That they hadn't done so yet was in some ways mystifying. Sony had come down hard on the EverQuest RMT market the year before, getting eBay to wipe its listings clean of EQ auctions, and by now Ultima Online was the only major MMO left that officially tolerated real-money trading.

But even seemingly market-friendly moves could play havoc with the traders' livelihoods. Recently EA had announced that Ultima players could now, for a mere $29.95, order their own custom-built, high-level characters straight from the company. At the far end of this line of thinking lay concepts like MindArk's Project Entropia, home of the $100,000 virtual space resort, in which every item in the game was available for sale direct from

< 47 >

the company—a move that could, if widely adopted, finally make corporate peace with the independent auction markets by rendering them completely superfluous.

In the meantime, though, Kiblinger remained relatively safe from competition. To watch him in action once he finally got his hands on an account like Stolle's was to understand, a little, the uncommon expertise it took to make this business pay. As he logged on for the first time and started taking inventory, the casual once-over of his initial appraisal sharpened to a laser focus. Wandering through the newly auctioned house in the cartoon body Stolle previously inhabited, Kiblinger became a value-sifting machine. He was equipped with a massive mental database and could cross-reference the most obscure imaginary item with its latest market price.

Houses were invariably the most valuable items, and the easiest to judge. But almost as much money could lie hidden in a far subtler class of objects known as "rares"—curiosities whose value consisted entirely, as the name suggests, in their scarcity. The original rares had been accidents, pieces of the graphical scenery—rocks, piles of horse dung, patches of waterfall, even error messages—that were supposed to be fixed in place but had somehow been left untethered, so that players could pick them up and carry them home. By the time Kiblinger got into the market, these freaks of virtual nature were hundred-dollar collectibles, and for a long time they were his bread and butter. Eventually, the designers caught on to their popularity and started peppering the landscape with "semi-rares": decorative fruit baskets and other knickknacks that popped into existence every month or so in some remote backwater of the land. In this way much of the economic steam was taken out of the rares scene, and Kiblinger was compelled to shift his focus to the perennially tight housing market.

< 48 >

But the true rares remained big-ticket items, and so he was obliged to keep in mind, as he sorted through a new account, that an innocuous-looking piece of horse crap still might sell for as much as $75. Such arcana made the job of sweeping out a typical account a two- or three-hour affair.

In the case of Stolle's, with nearly two thousand items locked up in the tower, the job took even longer. But by the end of the night, the account was stripped: Ownership of the house was transferred to one of Kiblinger's characters, assorted rares were relocated to storage and cataloged, and the rest was warehoused for future sorting. The messy complex of characters and possessions that had been Troy Stolle's virtual identity was broken down into parts far more valuable than the whole. The most valuable items were listed on eBay within a day or two, and one by one they went off to the highest bidder.

But the most valuable of all was the last to go. Not that Kiblinger lacked for house buyers in the month that Stolle's tower stood at auction. He sold one property to a single mom in Aspen, Colorado. He sold another to a manager for a database company in California. Yet another went to a woman in Norfolk, Virginia, who bought the house for her mother, an Alzheimer's sufferer whose last link to reality was her regular UO sessions with her daughter. If not for the vagaries of luck and circumstance, any of these bidders might have wound up with the tower that Troy Stolle built.

In the end, of course, it went to John Dugger, a Wonder Bread deliveryman in Stillwater, Oklahoma.

< 49 >

CHAPTER 7

"A wage of $3.42 an hour is sufficient to sustain Earth existence for many people," writes Castronova, again referring to the average wage in EverQuest's mythical Norrath. "Many users spend upwards of eighty hours per week in Norrath, hours of time input that are not unheard of in Earth professions. In eighty hours, at the average wage, the typical user generates Norrathian cash and goods worth $273.60. In a month, that would be over $1,000, in a year over $12,000. The poverty line for a single person in the United States is $8,794." Do the math, Castronova suggests, and the bottom line is this: "Economically speaking, there is little reason to question, on feasibility grounds at least, that those who claim to be living and working in Norrath, and not Earth, may actually be doing just that."

Troy Stolle stopped living in Britannia months before he sold his account. And Bob Kiblinger rarely logged in anymore except to inventory the remains of somebody else's existence there. But John Dugger was another story.

Separated from his wife for the previous four years, Dugger lived alone. When he got off work in the afternoon, his three young daughters were usually at his house till their mom picked them up, and sometimes they spent the night or a weekend. The

< 50 >

rest of the time, Dugger could be found in what he called his dungeon, a section of the garage walled off to make a small, barely ventilated room, where he sat five hours a night, eyes fixed on his computer screen and on the tiny, make-believe self he maneuvered through Britannia's cartoon landscape.

"People have told me I need to get a life," Dugger said. And picturing him there in his dungeon, I was inclined to think those people were right.

But then I followed him into Britannia one day, and I found myself thinking again. It was a few months after our first conversation, and in the interim I had tracked the story of his tower from its origins in Troy Stolle's mouse-clicking ambitions to the day Bob Kiblinger sold it, and I wanted to see it for myself, finally. So I opened a UO account of my own, rolled a blacksmith character I called Alhinud, and got myself acquainted with the basics of Britannian geography and how to get around in it. And then I called up Dugger and asked for a tour, and as we went on talking on the phone, we both logged in and teleported to his house. He showed me around then, and as we walked our characters from room to room, I could see just how busy he'd been transforming the place in the months since he bought it.

The first floor, once the austere workshop of a hardcore craftsman, had become a bright, busy, public gallery for Dugger's collection of rares and semi-rares. "That bucket of water you see on the floor there is a true rare," he said proudly, narrating the tour in a sharp Okie twang that didn't quite fit the armor-plated knight paladin onscreen. "It cost me 600,000 gold." The second floor had metamorphosed from a blank, all-purpose storage area, basically, into a verdant indoor forest of lime-green cactuses and other potted plants. Likewise the roof, which had come furnished as a sort of game room, complete with playable chess and backgammon sets, was now buried beneath the lush foliage and waterworks of a

< 51 >

rooftop garden designed by Dugger's in-game girlfriend, the Lady Lickeretta.

"I did pretty much leave the master bedroom alone, though. I liked the way they did it," said Dugger. As it happened, he had no idea who "they" were. At first he thought the previous owner was the person who met him at the house to transfer the deed, a young woman named Blossom. But that turned out to be one of Kiblinger's characters—and not even Kiblinger at the keyboard but his cousin Eugene, who he sometimes paid $10 an hour to run around Britannia doing the deliveries that otherwise took up most of Kiblinger's work day.

So now Dugger could only guess. "There's some stuff in the house that the label says was made by a Lord Nils something or other, so that might have been one of the characters on that account," he surmised. "And to be a lord, that means he hasn't died in a very long time, so that means he was pretty good at what he did."

Dugger excused himself to run his character upstairs to the bedroom and in a minute said over the phone: "Yeah, here it is. 'Nils Hansen.' N-I-L-S H-A-N-S-E-N."

There was a further pause as Dugger seemed to lose himself in contemplation of whatever piece of Troy Stolle's handiwork it was he'd found. An "exceptional wooden armoire," perhaps, clicked into being years before with virtual saw and lathe. Or maybe a full suit of agapite plate mail, hammered out at the forge downstairs.

I interrupted Dugger's reverie to ask him why he'd wanted to buy such a massive house.

"For one thing it's a status symbol," he replied, giving the question some thought. "In the game you start out, you buy your first house. And normally you buy a small house first. In no time at all you have the amount of stuff that house can hold. So it's

< 52 >

time to get another house. And you try to move up in houses all you can. The last house I had was a large L-shaped and it had ten chests in it that you can secure down—well, they were full. And my banks were full. And a tower is three stories with a roof that you could put stuff on.

"And a friend of mine has a tower, which I thought was always excellent. You go by people's towers, you kinda wonder, you think, well what do they do? How do they get their money? How do they live? What do they do in the game? Who are they? Are they good guys, are they bad guys? Are they with a good guild, a bad guild?

"It's just like everything else in life. You want better. You want to get bigger and better. And it's the same thing in the game. You just want to go for the bigger and better."

After Dugger logged off, I stuck around, walking Alhinud through the rooms of Stolle's tower again. Eventually I stepped outside, into the wooded clearing Stolle had chosen for his building site. The graphics of the game were even then well dated: no fluid 3-D first-person perspective; the view was what the industry calls two-and-a-half-D; the character seen from about twenty feet overhead, dead-center in a curiously foreshortened orthographic landscape. Experienced gamers, even UO fans, tended to snicker at the aesthetic crudity, but I was charmed. "It's like you're inside the Bayeux Tapestry or some other epic Medieval vision of things," I gushed to a friend several weeks later, when my interest in the game had proceeded far beyond the merely reportorial. "It's like: Of course. If you're going to build a world based in a fantasy of the middle ages, this is the perfect perspective for it."

Outside the tower, a small local population of low-level ogres, serpents, and other monsters strolled ("moderate spawn," as I would learn to call it when advertising properties of my own). Dodging them, I wandered over to the nearby mountainside and

< 53 >

took a few swings with my pickaxe: iron ore, iron ore, nothing nothing, iron ore, nothing. I definitely needed to work on my mining skills. Blacksmithing, too. Good thing I'd bought a horse, in any case. It was a long way back to my hometown of Minoc from here, and I only had a few minutes left to get back there and do some skilling up before I had to log off.

Does an addict ever know exactly when he crosses the line from curious to hooked? Maybe there never was a watershed moment, some instant before which the precise configuration of desires that could build and buy and sell a Britannian large tower was someone else's mystery and after which it was my own. But if there was, I'm pretty sure that moment was behind me now.

< 54 >

PART FOUR

Springtime in Luna

CHAPTER 8

Two months later I sat on the warm wood floor of a handsome, elegantly furnished Victorian in one of the lovelier neighborhoods of San Francisco, thinking again of John Dugger as I watched my two-year-old daughter play at nothing in particular and feeling, with a sudden pang, a mournful envy of them both.

Not that I had much to complain about myself. After several years chasing after writing assignments from the bland remoteness of South Bend, Indiana, I was living in the most beautiful city in North America under circumstances a freelance writer could normally only pray for. Almost out of the blue, I'd been awarded a year-long fellowship at Stanford Law School's Center for Internet and Society, with a comfortable stipend and minimal obligations. I was to co-teach (with the noted legal scholar Lawrence Lessig) a single, one-day-a-week course on virtual worlds and the law; I was to make myself at least a semiregular presence in and around the corridors of the law school; and I was otherwise to do as I pleased, pursuing whatever research interests most inspired my passion.

That these interests, for the time being, consisted largely of slaying lizard men for their hides didn't trouble me as much as perhaps it should have. I had spent my entire career laboring

< 56 >

under the peculiar anxiety of the freelance life—the unrelenting sense that any daylit minute not directly devoted to generating income was a minute sinfully wasted—and now that that anxiety had melted in the warmth of a guaranteed monthly paycheck and an office with my name on the door, I was in no rush to question whether I was spending my time productively enough. Besides, I had a passable cover story to tell myself or anybody else who happened to wonder what exactly I thought I was doing. My compulsion to play Ultima Online at every available opportunity, after all, had arisen naturally from my initial fact-finding visits to Britannia, and it was arguably just a continuation of that research. The course on virtual worlds was to begin in late January, just a few weeks away, and it seemed not only excusable but altogether responsible of me to acquire as in-depth an experience of this canonical virtual world as possible before presuming to lecture anyone about such things.

Comforting though this story was, however, I could feel myself beginning to resent the very comfort I derived from it. On the floor before me now sat Lola, with her toy car and her squishy ball, engrossed without alibi in a game of her own devising—her highest calling in life precisely this undivided self-abandonment to play. She needed no excuse; why then should I? Could a grown man never hope to give himself so wholly to a game? Could unadulterated play, among adults at least, ever count for more than a diversion—more than a brief exception to the productive (and reproductive) pursuits that are supposed to give life its meaning and its weight?

I imagined it could, actually, though it wasn't the more obvious examples I thought of now—not the Michael Jordans and the Maria Sharapovas and all the other well-compensated professional players, whose play in fact is all work and whose work it is to perform for us the fantasy that modern economies place

< 57 >

any value whatsoever on play in and of itself. It was here, rather, that I thought of John Dugger, who valued play at not less than the $750 he'd paid for Troy Stolle's tower and the hundreds of hours he'd devoted to Ultima Online in the solitude of his garage. There was little that mattered to him more than the game, I sensed. His kids, certainly. But his position with Wonder Bread? That, I felt certain, was just a day job. Dugger's *vocation* was UO.

And yes, at that moment I envied him his calling, as I envied Lola hers. And no, it wasn't that I'd lost my grip on the order of things. I understood that Lola was an infant; that Dugger, by most contemporary standards of achievement, was a lost cause; and that the world I lived in by and large recognized just two kinds of activity: production and distraction, the latter being generally synonymous with marginality, self-indulgence, and childishness. But far from soothing my envy, this recognition of the facts only made me sadder, more sullen. It wasn't fair, I thought. Put it to a universal vote, I suspected, and at the very least a sizable minority of the human race would choose to organize its relationship to play along less ascetic lines.

Oh I was in a childish, self-indulgent sulk, all right, but as it happens, I was also right: Seen from the perspective of a great many human beings living and dead, the stark distinction between work and play the rest of us take to be a universal fact of life turns out to be nothing of the sort. Or rather it appears no more or less a universal fact than, say, the internal combustion engine, which it resembles chiefly in being an invention of the modern West—irresistible and increasingly ubiquitous in the way so many products of modernity have been, but an invention all the same, and a fairly idiosyncratic one at that.

Ethnographers, for instance, have catalogued a number of human cultures in which the line between work and play fades

< 58 >

almost to insignificance. The Kpelle people of Liberia, to name one, scarcely make the distinction at all, allowing for a difference between arduous "forest work" and lighter "town work" but generally avoiding all work that can't be done playfully, amid song and dance and jest. It's not that they're slackers. On the contrary: Diligent rice farmers, they organize their lives around the constant activity of cultivation. But when government advisers pressured them to switch from dry rice farming to more productive paddy-based methods, they resisted—not because they had no interest in making more money (they'd happily taken up cocoa as a cash crop on the government's advice), but because they had no interest in working joylessly. The techniques of paddy-rice farming might be more efficient, the anthropologist David Lancy has explained, but they would reduce the Kpelle's daily activity to "just plain work," bereft of "the vital leavening of gossip, singing and dance" that makes Kpelle work worth doing.

Even the history of Western culture reveals, at its roots, a surprising intimacy between play and the culture's more earnest pursuits. In his classic study *Homo Ludens*, completed in 1944, the Dutch cultural historian Johan Huizinga uncovered an archaic cultural past in which the role of play was much more prominent than it is now. Sifting through the classical Mediterranean origins of Western law, religion, war, and other deadly serious traditions, Huizinga found the themes of play—of contest for its own exciting sake, of self-conscious and flamboyant make-believe—so closely woven into the fabric of civilization that they effectively defined it. "[C]ivilization is, in its earliest phases, played," Huizinga wrote. "It does not come *from* play . . . it arises *in* and *as* play, and never leaves it."

Yet if civilization could never leave its roots in play behind, it was clearly, by Huizinga's day and long before, doing a pretty

< 59 >

good job of repressing them. That Huizinga could even find the heart to go on digging for those roots under the circumstances in which he finished *Homo Ludens* (living out his second year of confinement in a Nazi internment camp, he would die there soon after, just three months before the war's end) says a lot for his faith in their depth and strength; but even he could not deny, in the end, that play had had a very great fall from grace. "More and more," he wrote, "the sad conclusion forces itself upon us that the play-element in culture has been on the wane since the eighteenth century, when it was in full flower. Civilization today is no longer played, and even where it still seems to play it is false play."

What had gone wrong? How had Western culture led itself, and now the world, away from its once more ludic path? Huizinga, it seems, was too morose about the whole development to attempt a proper explanation. And so, for the definitive account of play's decline into marginality, we must look elsewhere—to a text in whose 183 pages the word "play" hardly appears. Max Weber's *The Protestant Ethic and the Spirit of Capitalism* (1904) is best known for establishing the concept of the work ethic as a hallmark of modern economic culture, but it's better understood as an unveiling of that culture's theological foundations. Here Weber documents the origins of our notoriously materialist modernity in a paradoxically spiritual source: the austere yet rigorously productive "worldly asceticism" of early Protestant Christians, the Calvinist or Puritan variety in particular, who believed in profitable work as a calling from God, sacred insofar as it served to discipline, and not to gratify, the fleshly appetites.

That the Puritans had no patience for the playing of games, in which there was neither honest profit nor grim self-denial to be found, comes as no surprise. "[A]s a means for the spontaneous expression of undisciplined impulses, [sport] was under suspi-

< 60 >

cion," writes Weber in his one, brief passage on the subject, "and insofar as it became purely a means of enjoyment, or awakened pride, raw instincts or the irrational gambling instinct, it was of course strictly condemned." In this, as in other ways, Puritanism differed little from the many asceticisms that had come before it, in an ever-present line of religious thought stretching back no doubt to the dawn of human culture.

In Weber's view, however, two things combined to set the Protestant version of asceticism apart: its embrace of productive labor as a sanctifying principle rather than a necessary evil, and the spectacular economic power that resulted from that embrace. And it was this power, in turn, that resulted in asceticism's unlikely transformation from a perennially cranky rejection of the material world into the material world's now-hegemonic organizing principle—capitalism. Naturally, the asceticism that shapes our lives today is not the Puritans'. But Weber shows compellingly how certain core features of the Protestant ethic— its veneration of efficiency as an end in itself, its essentially irrational attachment to rationalism, and perhaps above all, its curious injunction to acquire as much wealth as possible and enjoy it as little as possible—jump-started the modern economic system and remain its motivating forces, driving even now the furious technological innovation, relentless standardization, and vast accumulations of capital by which we recognize it.

And there, in Weber's grim narrative, the story ends. Bequeathed a living, guiding framework of Calvinist beliefs, we dwell now within the cold and soulless structure that remains of it, trapped inside what Weber famously calls an "iron cage" of rationalized existence and unmotivated toil:

> . . . material goods have gained an increasing and finally an inexorable power over the lives of men as at no previous period in

< 61 >

history. Today the spirit of religious asceticism —whether finally, who knows?—has escaped from the cage. But victorious capitalism, since it rests on mechanical foundations, needs its support no longer. The rosy blush of its laughing heir, the Enlightenment, seems also to be irretrievably fading, and the idea of duty in one's calling prowls about in our lives like the ghost of dead religious beliefs. Where the fulfilment of the calling cannot directly be related to the highest spiritual and cultural values—or on the other hand need not be felt simply as economic compulsion—the individual today generally forgoes the attempt to find meaning in it at all.

Yet if this iron cage was founded largely on an exaltation of work as everything that play is not—productive, rational, efficient—might we not find our way out of it in a countervailing exaltation of play?

For Huizinga, this was perhaps a bit much to hope for. Between the alleged frivolity of his subject and the blazing calamity of world politics at the time he wrote *Homo Ludens*, it was challenging enough just to take play as seriously as he did, never mind discerning its potential to redeem us from the soul-sucking gloom of everyday life under advanced capitalism.

But in Huizinga's successor Roger Caillois, the French sociologist and author of *Man, Play and Games* (1958), the hope could clearly be seen to glimmer. Where Huizinga had left his definitions of play loose, slippery, and not especially pointed, Caillois was systematic in defining it in opposition to the social machinery of production. It was Caillois, for example, who called play "an occasion of pure waste," and it appears he meant it as a compliment. The vitality of play lay precisely in its uselessness, he argued, and it withered as the pursuit of profit came to taint it. As play survived the modern economic regime intact, on the

< 62 >

other hand, it posed a standing threat of subversion. Among other French intellectuals of the day, the authenticity of the rebel was very much in fashion, but Caillois placed as much stock, it seemed, in the inauthenticity of the player: Play's capacity for simulation, he wrote, was "in principle and by nature in rebellion against every type of code, rule, and organization."

But Caillois was a poseur compared to Huizinga's most excitable disciples, the celebrated pan-European cultural anarchists who called themselves the Situationist International. "The central distinction that must be transcended is that established between play and ordinary life, play kept as an isolated and provisory exception," they declared in the brief essay "Contribution to a Situationist Definition of Play" (1958), which like most Situationist writings teetered between red-Crayola manifesto-speak and a nuanced grasp of higher social theory, in this case a guardedly utopian analysis of the emergent postwar, postindustrial society of leisure combined with a Weberian critique of capitalism's machinelike reshaping of the everyday. That is, "Ordinary life, previously conditioned by the problem of survival, can be dominated rationally—this possibility is at the heart of every conflict of our time—and play, radically broken from a confined ludic time and space, must invade the whole of life."

Naturally, by the time the countercultural romanticism of the 1960s kicked into high gear, this sort of talk was sounding pretty good. Indeed, it's fair to say that 1968 was *not* the year to buy stock in the ludic philosophies of either the Situationists or Huizinga, that being the approximate high-water mark for the intellectual currency of both. The subsequent persistence of certain economic realities inconvenient to the founding of a worldwide people's republic of recess—market crashes, oil crises, forty-hour workweeks—was hard on any school of thought that smacked of liberation ludology.

< 63 >

And so it was that by the time I found myself alone with my sullen thoughts and my laughing daughter on the floor of a Haight-Ashbury sublet, I had only the vaguest notions of what Huizinga and Caillois had accomplished and no idea the famous Situationists had ever spoken straight to the heart of what preoccupied me now. Had I known, of course, I would have welcomed them all into my thoughts as wise old veterans of the struggle I was just beginning to engage.

But soon enough I would have recognized, as well, the one key difference separating their intellectual enterprises from the project that even now was dimly taking shape somewhere inside my head: They had all set out too early in the history of play to know the mystery of Stolle's tower, and to know that mystery— and the curious configuration of productive energies that had brought it into being—was to see a possibility they never would have understood.

Between me and a life at play (the life of Lola, of John Dugger) stood the Protestant ethic, but there were chinks in its formidable armor now. For long years it had managed to convince us all, even the defenders of play, that play was pure waste. But now there were virtual economies, and virtual economies presented the single counterexample necessary to destroy the Puritan hypothesis: an example of productive play.

And that made all the difference, didn't it? It meant that an escape from Weber's iron cage did not require a revolution, after all. It meant that all I had to do to make my getaway was tap into the system of production that had built Troy Stolle's tower and, as it were, start building towers of my own.

And all I had to do to wake up to the fact was make that one late-night lizard-man run too many that introduced me to the instructive humiliations of death by Energy Bolt. Which I believe I did about a day or two later.

< 64 >

CHAPTER 9

"I ween thou art new in crossing this land. Might you rest here a while, young travelling friend? Shall I proffer a warm meal and song? I implore thee to pause and rest until dawn. My fire and my song shall be thine for an eve. Which of these gifts wouldst thou gladly receive?"

The words were those of Sedrik the Amicable, apprentice to the Britannian court composer, a fictional character invented by some anonymous OSI employee for the purpose of relating, on a Web page buried deep within the Ultima Online news and information site, a strange and mythic tale yclept "The Ballad of the Shattered Stone."

For lo: "Long before the Stranger ever entered the lands of Sosaria and the four continents within—the Lands of Lord British, the Lands of Danger and Despair, the Lands of the Dark Unknown, and the Lands of the Feudal Lords—there arose a young wizard named Mondain. As Mondain grew in age and knowledge, so grew his unquenchable thirst for power and discontent with mortal life. He became obsessed with transcending mortality and gaining perpetual life. Eventually, he learned of the treasured Gem of Immortality, which grants unimaginable power and everlasting life to its owner. Surely, you have heard of this?"

< 65 >

A hunger for the gem corrupted Mondain, who in the fullness of time arose to slay the its guardian—his own father—and take it for his own. Within the gem there dwelled a captive image of all the lands that blanketed the world, and through it Mondain bent the people everywhere to his dark and shadowy will, until the day came when the Stranger arrived to free Sosaria from the evil sorcerer's rule. The Stranger smote the wizard, yea, and gave a mighty smiting as well to the source of all the wizard's rule, the Gem of Immortality, so that it shattered in a thousand pieces, each one of them, the legend says, containing the same universal image of the world. Only the most careful of efforts by the guardian spirits of the land kept the universe from disintegrating altogether in this great rupturing of the cosmic unity: "They seized hold of the fabric of time and space and re-wove the fibers of Sosaria, which today we call Britannia."

But the pieces of the gem itself were scattered, lost forever. "No mortal has yet found the means to find or reassemble these fragments," Sedrik said (or perhaps quoth). "Would I not give but my very life for a spell to reverse the flow of time to unveil this bit of history! Perhaps one day, another Stranger will arrive—one similar to yourself—who has the wherewithal to answer such questions."

It was uncanny, really, the way Sedrik seemed to be speaking directly to me, as if an ill wind had lifted me up unto the very heavens and deposited me, lo, within the same nightmarish gathering of the Society for Creative Anachronism that the speaker plainly inhabited. But if Sedrik honestly believed I had come to carry on the great unfinished work of the Stranger, then he was sadly mistaken, for I was on a somewhat less ennobling quest that day.

The Age of Shadows was upon us: the first full-fledged expansion of the UO commercial package in many months, now set to launch in a matter of days. With it, a brand new continent was

< 66 >

going to open—the virgin territory of Malas, a lost land said to be floating in space high above the established realms of Britannia—and I was on the prowl for any advantage I could secure for myself in the inevitable rush for unclaimed house plots that would follow.

Already I had got my hands on a coveted advance copy of the Age of Shadows installation discs. I'd wangled it from UO's publicist on the suggestion, let's say ("promise" is such an unforgiving word), that I would be reporting a feature article on the launch from the angle of its implications for virtual real estate. The truth of course was that I had no intention of writing about the land rush or any other facet of the expansion. In fact, the only aspect of it that I really wanted to investigate was the possibility of claiming a choice housing plot or two for myself, flipping them on the real estate market for the quickest profit possible, and skimming the proceeds for enough gold to buy the starter home I'd been hankering for since I started playing the game in earnest.

And since it seemed to me the quickest, fattest profit would logically be found where demand for housing was highest, I was doing a little background research now into the mechanism that, more than any other factor in UO, defined the shape and size of its local markets: The shard.

In UO mythology, a shard was any of the thousand bits of broken reality that survived the Stranger's long-ago shattering of the Gem of Immortality. Just about anywhere else people played computer games online, it was called a server. Any of a number (dozens, sometimes hundreds) of high-end, networked computers running the game in parallel, each shard was home to around 10,000 players, whose characters resided there and nowhere else. This was a congenial arrangement for game developers, who much preferred the manageable challenge of designing game

< 67 >

content for 10,000 players at a time to the impossible dream of doing it for hundreds of thousands. And though it had its awkwardnesses for players themselves, the strictly segregated populations gave rise to economic divergences a clever player could sometimes turn to advantage.

And so it was that I'd made my way to the UO Web site in search of information on the workings of the shards, found only Sedrick's mythical origin story, and decided that once the Age of Shadows came online, I might as well just focus on the server I had made my home: the popular Great Lakes shard.

In the meantime, though, the advance disc gave me early access to the test server, which gave me an edge in scouting out the best locations for house placement. But when my own server finally went live with the new lands, it wasn't like I had my pick of spots. Malas was overrun with land-grabbers within seconds of its opening, and if I'd had to waste ten minutes deciding where to place the two houses my two user accounts entitled me to, I would have ended up with a couple of shack-sized plots out in the spawn-infested boondocks, if that. Instead, I was able to grab two ample sites inside the walls of Luna, a bright-lit, sandstone city that my gut told me was destined to be a prime real-estate location.

My gut was right. *These will go for as much as $600 each*, Bob Kiblinger IM'd me after dropping by my Luna spots a few days later. *And I guarantee you if you hold onto them for a while they'll go up higher than that.*

Six hundred dollars each. A thousand dollars' profit at least. And just two days into my new career! If things kept up at this rate, I'd be banking six figures before a year was up. And even if they didn't, a solid grand was a fine bankroll to set out on my adventure with, and I intended to set out with nothing less.

A funny thing happened on the way to my capital gains, though. Putting the first of my two house plots up on the market

< 68 >

was easy—I just typed FOR SALE, ICQ 154304668 on the plot's built-in signpost, for all passersby to see—but when it came time to list the other one, I found I couldn't bring myself to do it. Situated just inside the city gates, the plot was a perfect location for a "vendor mall," a sort of in-game retail emporium that was said to be an ungodly source of gold for those who owned one (one legendary mall operator on the Great Lakes shard, a player named Ultima, was rumored to possess no less than a third of the shard's entire gold supply). What if running a mall—or a chain of them—turned out to be my path to riches? And even if it didn't, wouldn't an established retail site end up selling for a lot more than this empty plot?

Even as I asked myself these questions, though, I saw them for the rationalizations they were. Deep down, there was only one real reason I didn't want to let go of the property: It was uber.

I remembered John Dugger looking at the biggest houses in the game, the towers and castles, and wondering about the people who lived in them—who are they? how do they live? how do they get their money? are they good guys, bad guys?—and it struck me how much I wanted to be one of those people, too. I wanted to make strangers wonder about me. I wanted to be noticed. I wanted to be envied. And though I'd long thought I would be more than satisfied owning a one- or two-room cottage far from the beaten path, now that I was sitting on a tower-size plot in a tony, urban location, I had my doubts.

But was I really willing to give up $600 in exchange for a bit of fame and status inside a video game? I had my doubts about that, too. But it couldn't hurt, I supposed, to spend a few days improving the property while I decided whether I could bear to sell it. And so, using the new housing-design feature introduced with the Age of Shadows expansion, I set about building the mansion of my dreams—a three-story Gothic-Moorish fantasy in

< 69 >

sandstone, with high-peaked towers and a broad, inviting grassy courtyard.

And on the second day of construction, as I was applying the finishing touches, a stranger approached on horseback. He wore a black hooded robe, which might have looked sort of edgy and distinguished if not for the fact that everybody else was wearing the same thing just then (the robe was a bonus gift for players who'd upgraded to Age of Shadows and could be bought by anybody else for as little as 750,000 gold pieces down at the West Britain Bank).

u interested in selling this place? he asked.

I stopped my design work and moved closer to the stranger. I thought about his question.

no, I said.

And so it was settled: the house and all it signified, I had evidently decided, were worth at least as much to me as the average monthly mortgage payment in Middlebury, Vermont.

but i have another plot i'm selling, I quickly added.

same size?

yep

how much?

I steeled my nerves and asked for the equivalent of $600 in gold:

30 million

good god man. i should slap u, said the stranger. *come on, be nice.*

We rode down the street together to look at the property. It seemed to meet his approval.

do u know who I am? he said finally. I didn't, but when I clicked on his profile to see his name, my mouth fell open.

you're THE ultima?

:-)

< 70 >

In theory, of course, the information that I was dealing with the richest man on the shard should have emboldened me to stick to my price. But in fact, it had the effect Ultima probably intended it to: Thrilled to learn that my wealth had been both noticed and coveted by a local celebrity, I softened. By the time the bargaining was over, I h3ad agreed to give up the property in exchange for 20 million gp and a rare polar bear rug, worth 4.2 million according to Ultima. We closed the deal then and there: A few mouse clicks brought up a transaction window, the house deed appeared on one side of it, and into the other Ultima dragged and dropped the rug and twenty checks for 1 million gp each. He clicked the confirmation box on his side and waited for me to click mine. I took a deep breath and clicked—and in an instant more Britannian wealth than I had ever seen in my life was safely stowed in my backpack.

A few days later I sold 18 million of the gold and my two black robes to Bob for $400, which he sent to me via PayPal, for a final payout, after transfer fees, of $388. The polar bear rug, it turned out, was worth about half what Ultima had claimed; as he himself no doubt knew when he made the deal, a recent change to the game design had inflated the rug supply and crashed the market. I decided my new mansion needed some classy furnishings anyway and kept the rug. As for the cash, I made a strategic decision not to plow it back into the business as planned but to invest it, instead, in impressing my wife with the productive potential of the enterprise. On a family trip to Disneyland a week later, I blew the $388 on a nice hotel room.

Thousand-dollar bankroll, indeed.

I did have a killer house now, though.

< 71 >

CHAPTER 10

⬇ **Tuesday, March 11, 2003**

So It Begins

I made my first eBay sale today: a runebook, mapping the best mining spots in the mysterious new land of Malas. It went for $1.99 to a person from Florida who said she would be online all day today. This is not a school holiday as far as I know, therefore I conclude that my first customer was a grownup. This pleases me for reasons I can't quite determine. I'll give no further details as to the customer's identity. Bad for business.

After eBay and PayPal fees, I estimate my profit at about $1.05.

This, the first entry in my blog, marked the public commencement of the Play Money project. It was not only a beginning, however, but a culmination: the fruit of two weeks' prospecting for precious metals in the caves and mountains of Malas.

< 72 >

It had been tedious work, but I didn't have much choice. I needed startup cash, and having pissed away my first chunk of revenue, I saw no other way to get it but the hard way. A bolder entrepreneur, I suppose, might have gone the time-honored Internet start-up route and maxed out his credit cards for the money, but I had made it a rule not to risk a penny of my existing assets on this venture. The whole project was questionable enough without staking my family's financial health on it, and besides, where was the challenge in buying my way into the market? Though the business model itself depended entirely on the willingness of UO players to buy advancement with out-of-game cash, I wanted—perversely perhaps, but sincerely—to be able to say I'd built my business from the Britannian ground up.

So off I went into the hills, clicking on rocks and dirt for piles of ore. Mostly I hit iron, but here and there lay more valuable finds: rarer metals such as copper, bronze, and gold, to say nothing of the mythical agapite, verite, and valorite. The ore itself had some value to me, but it wasn't really what I was after. I was harvesting information: Every time I found a vein of rare ore, I stood where I'd found it and marked a page in a magic "runebook." Later, casting a spell on the same page would bring me back to that spot, sparing me the hassle of hunting around for that particular metal again and, more important, allowing me to mark another runebook with the location. Once I'd filled a runebook with sufficiently bountiful locations, I would have a product—an endlessly renewable one, at that—that my fellow miners might pay good money for. Real money, even.

Whence it came to pass that on or about the fifth of March, 2003, I listed my first eBay offering ever: a handsomely organized runebook entitled "Malas for Miners," available for a limited time only at the incredible "Buy It Now" price of just $1.99. It sold a week later, as noted above, for the asking price.

< 73 >

CHAPTER 11

A word now about that aspect of MMOs that market research has consistently shown to be the primary draw for most players: Camaraderie. Fellowship. Conviviality. The bonds of friendship formed among fun-loving people joined in adventure. The company, in short, of other players.

I didn't care for it.

I recognized of course the essentially social nature of the game, and of my goal in it. But from the outset I was sort of hoping to keep my fellow player at a safe remove, in contact with me only through the arms'-length channels of the market. Customers I wanted, sure; companions, not so much. God knows I didn't want a roommate.

But God knows better, generally speaking. And one day late in March, while I was smelting ore at the forge on the second floor of my house, an eager player showed up on my front steps and hailed me. I had placed a row of vendors there, five of them, dressed in understated earthtones and matching gray capes, and when I descended, the visitor asked if he might place a vendor or two alongside mine. The idea had its merits. I hoped eventually to fill the courtyard with vendors but didn't yet have enough goods to stock that many, and letting other players fill the place

< 74 >

in the meantime would be good for traffic. The guy seemed to have a marketable line of goods, in any case—low-end power scrolls, enchanted weapons—and it wasn't like I couldn't boot the vendors anytime I felt like it. I let him set up shop.

We'll call him Radny. Not Randy. Radny—a normal American name deformed, apparently, by a typo committed when he created the character. And this was the first thing that started to bug me about him. The second was the tacky neon green clothing in which he dressed his vendors. But worst of all, I suppose, was his mere presence, which from the moment he placed his vendors was more or less constant. He'd been away from the game for a while, he explained, having sold his old house on the way out, and he just needed a place to log in and out till he got back on his feet. And did I mind if he stashed some stuff here? And hey, he had an idea, what if we set up a box that he could drop his loot in and I could enhance it with my smithing skills? And listen, could he maybe have a room where he could put some chests and do some decorating?

I acceded to all his requests. I'm not sure why. I liked my solitude, and I began to cringe slightly on logging in, wondering if Radny would be there to greet me with a *sup* or a *hey bro* or an observation that some ill-designed aspect of the game was *gay*. The house was no longer entirely my own, and though I still had final control over it, including the ability to banish Radny at the drop of a mouse click, I saw no good enough reason to do so. The best I could do was remind him not to get too comfortable and point out that the price of a new house was dropping fast since the Age of Shadows release.

He showed no signs of taking the hint, however, and in the end I was glad of it. Because eventually we turned a sort of corner, Radny and I. It started one evening around 5 p.m. my time. Radny was downstairs working on his tailoring, cutting, and sewing the same shirt over and over again, when I breezed

< 75 >

through on my way to logging out, giddy with the purchase of a +10 magery power scroll. I had bought the scroll for a reasonable 500,000 gold pieces, but it was an extravagance nonetheless. My magery skill had reached the Grandmaster level, the maximum 100 points, and couldn't get any higher now unless I used the power scroll to raise my skill cap to 110. I'd convinced myself that raising magery would make me a more efficient runebook maker, since my teleportation spells wouldn't fail quite as often. But in fact, it wasn't efficiency I lacked so much as dedication. Halfway through the Felucca ore-book project, the tedium of prospecting was wearing me down, and I longed to get back to the Ice Dungeon spawning grounds for the thrill of casting deadly Energy Vortex spells at Arctic ogre lords—and the satisfaction of watching my magery inch slowly upward by the kill. The power scroll was my ticket back to the hunt. And who else could I share my excitement with but Radny?

We got to talking. He told me he'd been making big cash with a rares vendor at Ultima's new vendor mall, built of course on the site of my former property.

made 3 million this weekend, he said, adding that he'd sold 2 million on eBay to pay his subscription fees for another few months. *i had enough to move out on you :)*

oh? I delicately inquired. *why didn't you?*

becuz i love you man lol

And besides, he added, *i still have a lot to teach u*

Which it turned out was not entirely untrue. Radny proceeded to explain that if I wanted to make real money, I should start trading rares:

go to the Majestic Oaks auction wed sun and mon nights. buy some things to sell. you have to know a little about prices. but with a vendor at Ultima's you can pretty much put any price and you will sell out over the weekend. every time.

< 76 >

I liked the idea, but I pointed out that the auction in question—a live affair conducted in a large old house just outside the city of Britain—always took place right around the time my daughter came home from day care. It really wasn't an option for me to attend. He thought about that, then asked: *how much do u have in the bank?*

uh oh here it comes, I replied, only half joking. Just a few weeks earlier I would have stopped listening at this point, sure I was about to be scammed. But now I felt almost ready to trust Radny. *u give me some money to invest,* he said. *I'll buy things at auction with it and sell on my vendor. I'll guarantee your principal but keep 20 percent of the profit. deal?*

Deal. I went to the bank and brought back a check for 500K, then logged out to go pick up Lola. The auction was set to start in twenty minutes.

When I came back on later that night to water the plants I was growing on my rooftop (a fairly elaborate process that in a week or two, depending on how carefully I watered, fed, fertilized, and bug-sprayed my charges, might produce a handsome set of ponytail palms for the courtyard), Radny said he'd already turned a small profit for me. He'd beat someone for a 400K clothing bless deed, then turned around and sold it to the very same loser for 430. I liked this, and at last, genuinely, I liked Radny.

We hung out for awhile, doing our various tasks (from the desktop speakers came the gurgly sound of my watering, while Radny's tailoring produced an incessant *snip-snip-snip*) and talking both in-game and via ICQ. I told him I was forty years old; he said he was fifty-two. *whoa,* I said, *i thought i was the old man around here.* But he was kidding, of course. Radny was a teenager and immediately started acting like one, razzing me about my ancientness: *hey i got a question for you—can you still get it up?—cuz u know i'm 17 and when i tell it to tuck it rolls—*

< 77 >

just kidding!!! Or this: *hey you were alive in the 70s, did you smoke pot?*

Which turned out to be a serious question. Radny was interested in marijuana, and his interest was apparently more than academic. I told him I didn't like it much but didn't deny I'd tried lots of drugs.

And suddenly I felt very cautious about what I should be saying, being the responsible adult in the conversation. I said as much, and Radny laughed: *'But Mommy its okay to do drugs this guy on the internet told me so!'*

lol, said I, and for once I actually *was* laughing out loud as I typed that. I felt a little dizzy with the complexity this relationship had taken on in the course of an evening and still wasn't entirely sure what to make of it. Mentor, business partner, kid brother and roommate, Radny was now most of all a puzzle.

< 78 >

CHAPTER 12

By Friday, April 11, I had sold a total of ten ore books on eBay, for a net profit, after fees, of about twenty-two bucks. Or to put it another way: My new line of business had earned me the dollar equivalent of a little over 1 million gold pieces.

And having made my first million, I found myself at a crossroads. Cash out or reinvest? I could move my $22 out of PayPal and into the family bank account, as I had done with my real-estate gains, or I could put it back into the UO economy—find some undervalued item on eBay, say, and wring some more profit out of it, or even buy a million gp and do some reselling inside the game. It was a business decision, of course, but it was also, in a sense, an existential one: Was I still only playing the game, bringing home the occasional winnings by way of prize money, or was I finally going to take that first decisive step toward making the game my living?

By the time I made up my mind, further sales had increased my cash reserves to $37. I had decided to reinvest the money, and after some thought (and close study of a brief downloadable "manual" entitled "Make Ultima Online Your Job," which I had purchased on eBay for $9.99), I had decided just how to do it.

The first step was to turn my dollars into gold, not the easiest thing to do at the time if, like me, you were hoping to pay no

< 79 >

more than $18 per million. The best I could find off the bat was a 1 million gp lot selling for $18.50 on eBay. I won the auction, PayPal'd the money, picked up the check from one Isis of Eden at the bank near my house, then went in search of my broker.

I found him hanging out at Ultima's new vendor mall, around the corner from my place. The conversation went something like this:

Who's my hoe?

sup radny?—listen, i have 1 million i'd like to invest with you—at the usual 20% commission on profit of course

of course :)

I gave him the check. Some chitchat about the mechanics of farming Champion Spawns ensued (a lucrative business; champ spawns drop power scrolls that can sell for upwards of a hundred bucks), along with the usual high-toned badinage. I believe Radny at various points called me a loser, if not a candyass.

all right, I said finally. *this isn't working—give me the check back—NOW!*

All in good fun, of course. Radny threw the check on the ground, where any passerby could have grabbed it, and I typed NOOOOOOOO! and LOL'd. He LOL'd, too, and the check disappeared, back into his backpack presumably.

ok give me the check back, said Radny.

lol

no seriously—i just dropped it on the ground for a joke—you didn't pick it up?

lmfao, said I, and my laughter, though genuine, was nervous.

lol, he said at last. Jesus.

Later, I found another million on a UO trading site for $15.50 and gave that to Radny, too. That night, he promised me, he would go to the Majestic Oaks auction and do some buying for me, along with his own. The last investment I'd placed with him, 500,000 gp, had netted me 300,000 in two weeks, for a 60 per-

< 80 >

cent ROI. If he did as well this time, my 2 million gp would become 3.2 million, which with any luck I could eBay for $64, an 88 percent return on my $34.

Eighty-eight percent.

I liked the sound of it.

By this point in the story, the fact that some small portion of the world's population has learned to value imaginary gold as matter-of-factly as you might value the real thing should pose no great challenge to your comprehension. To those of you still struggling to get your heads around it, however, allow me to suggest the following exercise:

Find a ten-dollar bill and hold it before you. Look at the fine-lined curlicues, the fat lettering, the portrait of Alexander Hamilton. Allow the distinctive aura of the bill's purchasing power to suffuse you, its undeniable value to impress itself on your mind. Settle into the reality, solid and familiar, that you are holding ten U.S. dollars in your hand. Now ask yourself: What exactly possesses you to believe those dollars are real?

The paper is real enough; the ink, too. But the dollars? Can you see or feel them in the thing you hold? Can you say what chemical process transforms this particular configuration of paper and ink into the equivalent of an evening at the movies or a pound of rib-eye steak? Or which law of physics allows the same ten dollars to exist in the very different paper-and-ink configuration of a personal check or in the electrons of a bank's online accounting system? You can't, because of course the dollars aren't in the bill the same way the paper and ink are. They're in it the same way Alexander Hamilton is, which is to say: not really. They're a fiction. A social convention. A shared suspension of disbelief no more or less delusional, finally, than the conceit that a few yellow pixels on a computer screen are valuable pieces of gold.

< 81 >

Still not buying it? OK then, picture this: You're at the firing line of the Action Gun indoor pistol range in Melbourne, Florida, on a balmy afternoon in April of 2001. Next to you a man named James M. Ray stands calmly firing round after Glock nine-millimeter round at a photocopied image of Adolf Hitler. You're aware that Ray supplied the target himself, that he purchased it at the Web site of one of his favorite nonprofit organizations (Jews for the Preservation of Firearms Ownership), and that its ideological content is not exactly subtle: Against the background of a standard ring target, the Fuehrer stands in full Sieg-heil mode, his arm up high and his sternum right in the bull's-eye, above a caption that reads, "ALL THOSE IN FAVOR OF 'GUN CONTROL' RAISE YOUR RIGHT HAND." By the time Ray has had enough of the Glock, you note, the target is nicely perforated. And then he picks up his .44 Magnum hand cannon and you watch, with slack-jawed fascination, as he commences blowing the target pretty much to bits.

Or maybe you don't. But I did. And I hasten to add that the purpose of the visit was not so much to marvel at the destructive power of the modern hand gun (that couldn't be helped) as to investigate the purchasing power of a curious alternative to the dollar: an online currency called e-gold, privately owned and operated by a small company for which Jim Ray worked as "lead evangelist." Almost everything we consumed that afternoon—the bullets, the Hitler target, the shooting-range time, even the .44—was acquired with payments denominated in e-gold's basic unit of currency: the gram. And every gram spent was backed, like all e-gold in circulation, by an equivalent amount of solid gold held in one of e-gold's private vaults in London and Dubai.

At the time, there were over 200,000 user accounts in the e-gold system holding a total of about $15 million worth of assets and

< 82 >

generating over $1 million a day in transactions (both figures have more than quintupled since then). And while the very existence—let alone the vast circulation—of a private currency dreamed up and managed by a retired Florida oncologist might seem improbable, it was, all things considered, nothing of the sort. Launched in 1996, e-gold was just the oldest of a half dozen private metal-backed currencies then circulating online and elsewhere. And these metallic currencies themselves represented but a fraction of the home-brewed monetary start-ups then and now in circulation—a proliferation of amateur and semi-pro "play monies" without precedent in the annals of finance.

They come, these days, in every shape and size and ideological flavor. There is the soft socialism of "time-based currencies" like the Ithaca Hour—a paper currency launched in 1991 in Ithaca, New York, each unit nominally backed by an hour of local labor and designed to strike a blow against the forces that, in the words of its inventor, "community economist" Paul Glover, "make us increasingly dependent on transnational corporations and bankers." There's the hardwired libertarianism of crypto cash—cryptographically secured, hopelessly untraceable digital money first proposed by mathematician David Chaum and embodied, mainly, in a plethora of half-finished, underfunded projects mounted by a lively subcommunity of finance geeks. And there's even a currency for the artsy crowd: Boggs bills, the creation of conceptual artist J.S.G. Boggs, who rides a line between minting money and mocking it that's so thin he's been dragged into court more than once on counterfeiting charges. Boggs has made a career out of drawing whimsical near-replicas of legal-tender notes, persuading merchants and sales clerks to accept them as desirable art works in lieu of monetary payment, and then selling the sales receipts to avid collectors—who, in the final turn of the conceptualist screw,

< 83 >

track down the recipients and purchase the original Boggs bills for many times face value.

We live, in short, in an age of money hackers—a curious by-product of financial deregulation, digital technology, and contemporary culture's diverse and sometimes contradictory fascinations with the workings and meaning of money. Political convictions, artistic impulses, religious beliefs, entrepreneurial ambitions, and the eternal urge to tinker all variously inspire both the inventors of new currencies and the enthusiasts who put their faith in them. But underlying all these motivations is a single enabling cultural development: a growing willingness to recognize the collective act of make-believe required to establish monetary value.

The economic anthropologist Keith Hart has proposed, in his remarkable treatise *Money in an Unequal World*, that this curious turn of events may point the way toward a more humane redistribution of global wealth and power—a democratic, postcapitalist financial order in which the impersonal monolith of high-modern money gives way to something more intimate and multiple. "I suggest," he writes, "that money will eventually take as many forms as the plurality of associations we enter"—and that the ultimately crippling logic of capitalist finance, in which money seems to live a life of its own, growing fastest where it feeds only on itself, will cede ground everywhere to the more empowering recognition that it's we ourselves, as a community and as many intersecting communities, who make money and have always made it.

Hart's vision is a compelling one, but I'm not out to convince you of anything quite so grand. I point to the florid creativity of the money hackers merely to suggest you see it as a kind of cultural backdrop, against which the faith of a couple hundred thousand video-gamers in the enduring value of the Britannian gold piece should begin to look somewhat less bizarre.

< 84 >

And if that helps at all, I might ask you additionally to consider, once again, the particular case of e-gold. Consider, in particular, the implicit longing of its users for the late–nineteenth-century glory days of the gold standard—when a real dollar was, by federal law, a coin containing exactly 23.22 grains of gold, and a ten-dollar bill was just a contract binding a bank or government to give ten of those coins to whoever showed up with the bill in hand.

And now imagine, if you can, asking someone so enamored of solid gold money to judge the realness of the Britannian gold piece. That it's just a cartoon image of a golden coin will be obvious enough to your gold fanatic. But whereas even the flimsy paper dollar of the post–gold-standard era has at least the solid political weight of being printed by the most powerful government on Earth, the currency of Britannia, you must now explain, is minted by a bunch of nerds running around virtual reality slaying arctic ogre lords and mongbats. No, really: Every time a player kills a monster in the game, she's rewarded with a small number of gold pieces added to the database on the spot, and that is pretty much the only way new currency enters the funhouse economy of UO. There's no government deciding how many banknotes to print up. No Federal Reserve board keeping an eye on the broader money supply. Just a couple hundred thousand free agents pumping gold into the system more or less for the sheer fun of it. And if this sounds like a recipe for endless supplies of funny money to you, what would you think it sounds like to an advocate of the gold standard?

You might be surprised. Alter that description of the Britannian monetary system in just a few particulars, and it sounds like nothing so much as the global monetary system of the late nineteenth century. For in the days of the gold standard, the global gold supply effectively *was* the global money supply, and hence the only people who truly added money to the system were the

< 85 >

people who dug it up—the prospectors, mine operators, and thousands of other free agents who pumped gold into the system more or less for the sheer profit of it. And while most economists today will tell you the gold standard was ultimately not a great idea, few would call it a recipe for funny money.

Indeed, die-hard fiscal conservatives to this day grow weepy reminiscing about the rigor of the gold-backed dollar, governed as it was not so much by the notoriously flexible political will of nation-states as by the iron law of supply and demand. Too much gold in circulation meant its value went down, which in turn meant people lost interest in hauling it up out of the earth; too little in circulation meant the value went up, which in turn spurred people to dig for more of it. Thus was the money supply kept lean and tight—not by Alan Greenspan's delphic wisdom or even George Soros's predatory second guesses, but by Adam Smith's invisible hand. And so, too, in loosely analogous fashion, is Britannia's money supply designed to keep itself in sync with Britannia's productive capacity, growing faster or slower according to the number and energy of economic actors out scouring the monster-hunting grounds for loot.

So whether or not you can accept, finally, that the Britannian gold piece is every bit as real a currency as the U.S. dollar, perhaps now you can understand how some people might actually come to think of it as, if anything, slightly realer.

Failing that, you can at least now understand the peculiar mix of wonder, dread, and vertigo I felt the day I first laid eyes on Richard Thurman's twenty-bot gold farm.

< 86 >

PART FIVE

The Gold Farmers

CHAPTER 13

Hello fellow merchant—just read some of your UO selling tra-vails—I was laughing my ass off at some of it :)

I blinked. It was an IM from Bob Kiblinger. I hadn't told him about my blog or my business plan, and I frankly wasn't sure how he'd react to my aspiring to join his competition. But apparently he kind of liked the idea.

If you need any help or advice about what sells, etc—just give me a shout—the door's always open to you, said Bob. *Like I said, I don't do this to get rich—I just enjoy the freedom it allows me :). We are having a baby in July—so I am going to need it.*

well yes, I replied. *i'm sure i'll come running for advice more than once :) and gratz on the baby! that is great!!*

I sat there basking in the warm collegial glow for a moment, and then Bob typed *Hey take a look at this.* A link in the message pointed me to an image file. It was an Excel chart tracking the average selling price of Britannian gold on eBay over the previous month or so. The price line wavered like a seismograph, but a long, straight trend line knifing through the squiggle showed plainly where the price was headed: south.

This didn't surprise me. High inflation rates, it turns out, are a standard feature of virtual economies. For although in theory the

< 88 >

loot-based monetary system I described above is a tightly wound, self-managing piece of economic clockwork (and therefore almost universally adopted by MMO designers), the screws invariably loosen somewhat on the way from theory to practice.

In theory, for instance, players will ease up on their monster-bashing whenever the money supply grows too fast and the value of gold drops, but in practice players go out hunting (or fishing, or mining, or tailoring, or any of the game's other productive activities) not only because it's profitable but because it raises their skill levels or simply because it's fun. In theory, too, designers could counter the resulting gold bloat by either lowering wages (i.e., decreasing the monetary return on hunting and other occupations) or raising taxes (cranking up the price of exotic hair dye, home-building permits, and other much-sought-after "gold sinks"). In practice, however, players resent that sort of direct intervention in their livelihood a lot more than they resent inflation. And forced to choose between an optimally efficient economy and a happy player base, designers will stiff the economy every time. End result: the value of gold, in dollars, slides ever downward while the price, in gold, of the game's scarcest items rises as steadily as a hot air balloon. Every day, every month, all year, inflation is just there, like the sky, and after a while nobody really even notices it.

Nobody that is, except people like Bob. When the amount of virtual gold that yearly passes through your hands gets up into the millions of dollars' worth, you pay very close attention to the way its value moves. You learn pretty quickly to tell the difference between everyday, run-of-the-mill rampant inflation and the scarier varieties. And the graph he'd just sent me was apparently a picture of something decidedly scary.

Gold has dropped from $30 to $20 per million since AoS, Bob explained, referring to the two-month aftermath of the Age of

< 89 >

Shadows launch that made a virtual homeowner of me. Then he pasted another link at me and said, *here is why.*

I clicked on the link and found myself looking at an eBay page. The page listed all the auctions for a single seller over the last thirty days, and the list was astonishing: More than 1.5 *billion* gold pieces up for sale, in lots of 5, 10, 20 million, and priced to move. The seller's identity surprised me, too. It was Ingotdude, the well-known nom de eBay of a guy named Gene who, so I'd heard, worked out of his house somewhere in Georgia, sitting day after day in a swivel chair surrounded by computers, flitting back and forth between a dozen or so miner characters he worked without letup. This scenario went a long way toward explaining how he had become the game's biggest purveyor, by far, of metal ingots, but it hardly accounted for the massive quantity of currency he suddenly had on offer.

supposedly he's sitting on about 20 billion that he's trying to sell, said Bob. Which was nuts. The figure implied not only a real-world payout of more than $300,000, but an in-game fortune of macroeconomic dimensions. The best guesses I'd heard at the *total money supply* of the English-speaking shards put it around 35 billion gp, so if Bob's intelligence was correct, Ingotdude had either cornered more than half of all the money in our little world or, somehow, nearly doubled it. In either case, a tidal wave of cash was preparing to wash into circulation, and the damage it had already done to the price of gold was a love tap compared to the thrashing that awaited.

how does somebody even get their hands on that much gold??? I asked.

well, it's not easy to say for sure, but here's a clue

Bob then e-mailed me another file, this one harder for me to interpret than the first. It was a photograph of twenty-two personal computers attached to a single monitor and neatly arrayed

< 90 >

on three shelves of what appeared to be someone's former linen pantry. I couldn't tell if the computers' running lights were on, but the whole arrangement looked functional enough and seemed to be connected to a cluster of broadband modems.

um, ok, I said. *what is it?*

It belongs to a guy I know, sort of a gold wholesaler.

yeah and?

It's how he gets his gold

???

Bob explained: Each one of those computers was running a copy of Ultima Online. And in each of those copies a character was working hard, just as tens of thousands of other characters did each day. Except that unlike most of those characters, these were not under the direct control of a human being. They were controlled by a computer program, which directed them to engage in some simple money-making task over and over, long past the point where any mouse-clicking human would have given up in an agony of finger cramps. The characters were allowed to break from work only long enough to deposit their earnings in the bank, and the only human intervention required was a quick daily look-see at how the gold was growing and the occasional drop-in to unsnag a character that had run into some unforeseen obstacle and stopped functioning. The characters were robots, in other words, or as the locals generally called them, bots.

but but but—but that's cheating!!! I typed, which was true enough but didn't quite convey the essence of my astonishment. The rules of Ultima Online did indeed explicitly outlaw botting, which they referred to as "unattended macroing." But unlike most other games on the market, UO didn't mind if you let a macro program run your character through some of the more tediously repetitive tasks—raising your blacksmith skills turning ingots into broadswords over and over and over again—as long

< 91 >

as you sat and watched it run. And which of us hadn't occasionally left a character in macro mode while we went to the bathroom for a few minutes or out to lunch for an hour or, well, why not, off to bed for the night? Cheating, thus defined, was as common among UO players as mage characters.

This, however, was cheating of an entirely different order. It was cheating so ambitious it transcended the category of cheating. It was cheating as art form, cheating as civil engineering, cheating as renegade social policy. It was fucking awesome.

how much u think a setup like that produces?

Bob couldn't say, but a few days later he told me about a new post on one of the message boards of UO Stratics, a popular fan site for UO players. According to the message, it was possible to earn 350,000 gp per hour buying bolts of cloth from a certain type of NPC vendor, then using basic tailoring skills to cut the cloth to bandages, then selling the bandages at a profit to the nearest NPC healer. There were a few other ways to make that much gold, but none nearly so simple, or so easily automated. Programmed into a gold farm the size of the one in the picture, the bandage-cutting method could conceivably turn out more than 175 million gp (about $3,500) per day. And at that rate, piling up a 20 billion gp mountain of gold wouldn't take longer than four months.

Here at last was a plausible explanation for Ingotdude's egregious new wealth. But the explaining wasn't quite over.

My source says Ingotdude is just a front man, said Bob. *The gold is coming from somebody behind the scenes*

just who is your source anyway?

lol, it's the same guy who gave me that picture

and would that same guy be ingotdude's supplier by any chance?

lol, no. definitely not

< 92 >

who's the supplier then?

Take a look at the post

Bob pasted me the link, and I followed it. The message was headed "How to make 350k gold per hour. no joke," and it had been posted under the username InTheKnow. I skimmed the contents and stopped short at the last line, where I was surprised and, I confess, not entirely unamused to see the name of some long-lost acquaintances:

"Blacksnow Interactive."

< 93 >

CHAPTER 14

Some days passed in which I awaited the total collapse of Ultima Online's economy. I drew some solace from the fact that I now understood a little better the nature of Blacksnow's operations. Whether or not they were still employing their Mexican workers, it was clear to me now that the job had probably consisted, in large part, of babysitting a highly automated but finicky mechanism for exploiting economic loopholes like the bandage bug. There was as well, I guess, a fleeting sort of narrative pleasure to be found in the notion that Lee Caldwell et al., having screwed me out of a story, were now about to screw me out of business.

Yet it was far more satisfying to hear at last, from Bob, that Blacksnow's latest get-rich-quick scheme had come to ruin. Even before the tell-tale message went up on Stratics, it seemed, an inside tip had led UO's de facto police force—the in-game customer service reps known as game masters, or GMs—to Blacksnow's bots. Every single Blacksnow account was canceled, along with everything in them, which naturally included their ill-gotten gold. Ingotdude was shut down, too, his accounts wiped and his appetite for the virtual-items trade spoiled for good. A notice on Ingotdude's Web site, once among the most heavily trafficked in the

< 94 >

business, curtly announced his permanent retirement. With the banishing of these rogue traders and the deletion of their assets, the powers that be had effectively swept billions of inflationary gold pieces from the money supply—and averted an economic cataclysm that could have cost Electronic Arts thousands of customers, if not the game itself.

I hurried to my blog to post the news. And along with my report, by way of illustration, I put up the gold-farm photo Bob had sent me. A few days later some player caught sight of it and posted a link on Stratics, and the next day I came home to a loud and urgent message on my answering machine. "This is Rich Thurman," the voice growled, all but ordering me to call back at the first opportunity. "You have a photograph of mine on your Web site. We need to talk about it."

I called and barely made it through hello before Rich Thurman was demanding I tell him who had given me the picture.

"I can't tell you that," I said, feeling very Woodward and Bernstein. "I'm sorry."

"Then I can't let you publish the photo. I took it, it's my intellectual property, and I demand that you remove it."

"Well, look . . . OK," I said, feeling my journalistic resolve begin to crumble. "But first, maybe you could tell me a little bit more about it?"

And with that, it seemed, I had spoken the magic words. For as I quickly learned, Rich Thurman liked to talk. A lot. And talk he did, recounting for the next hour or so the tale of his career as a $4,000-a-week UO gold farmer.

"I started doing this a year and a half ago, while I was waiting for my second son to be born," he said, with a slight West Texas accent. "I'm thirty years old, I work full-time as a software engineer, and I'm married with two boys, a three-year-old and a one-year-old. I used to play UO hardcore. I played it two years

< 95 >

straight, right from the start of the game back in '97, until my wife started complaining that the only way she could socialize with me was to play UO.

"I was what you might call a griefer. I played a thief, and I stole tons of things. I used to like to steal people's houses. You could do that back then, just steal their key and cast a recall spell on it, and there you were at the front door and the house was yours. One time I broke into this house that it turned out was a guild house, for this big PK guild, and all the members kept their house keys in there. I just went from one key to the next, taking all those houses. And then when I finally quit the game, I just gave it all away. I'd find people who looked new, and I'd go up to them and say, 'Here, here's a tower.'

"Then later I heard a friend had sold his stuff on eBay for a thousand dollars, and I was pissed.

"So I decided to start playing again. Only this time the idea was to at least make back the money I'd spent on the game the first time, which was about $400. I started researching what people were buying on eBay. I saw that there was a million-dollar market here, if not more. And I got working on carto."

I interrupted Rich's monologue to ask him what, exactly, he was talking about.

"Cartography."

I still didn't get it. As UO skills went, cartography was a backwater, an obscure art that had something to do with the drawing and deciphering of treasure maps. Making use of it was a first, partial step in the treasure-hunting process, which was itself a long drawn-out affair that tended to pay out more in entertainment value than in gold. But as Rich explained, the best gold-farming bugs were often the most easily overlooked, and carto, it turned out, harbored one of the more profitable bugs the game

< 96 >

had seen. By making and selling maps to certain vendors, and automating the process through the use of a high-powered macroing program called EasyUO, a dedicated gold farmer could amass gp at a rate of about 35K per character-hour. Rich quickly got himself up to speed with the technique, then figured out a way to boost its productivity to 60K an hour.

"I started with three machines," Rich told me. "Then I went up to five. Then fifteen. Then five more for a total of twenty. By that point they were drawing so much power I had to run a separate line to the circuit breaker for them. And that little room they're in gets hot, too, shoots right up to 110 if the A/C goes out. So I had to rearrange the setup for better ventilation."

By his sixth or seventh month of operations, the gold farm was a well-oiled cash machine. "I went away on vacation for a month, up to Coeur d'Alene to see relatives, and I decided to leave it running. For the first two weeks it worked beautifully. I would check in on it with a remote-admin connection; even managed to sell off some of the gold that was piling up, on eBay. But then one day I logged in and found my accounts blocked. Every one of them. Why? Well, a new version of the game had come out. Before that, no one had been doing cartography. Barding was what all the gold farmers were into. And then publish sixteen nerfed barding, so everybody moved into carto, and when that happens, things start to get very cut-throat. So naturally the competition went and paged a GM on me."

It was Rich's first bust, and it hurt. He lost twenty-eight accounts and a nice pile of gold. And after that, he started to think more strategically. He stopped retailing his gold on eBay — too time-consuming—and built up a reliable stable of wholesale buyers, who bought from him at 40 percent off the average retail price. And he started to build defensive measures into his bots.

< 97 >

"Paging a GM on somebody is easy. I can tell now just by looking at a character whether it's macroing or not, and I could go around shutting down competitors like that if I wanted—but I don't, because I believe in karma. So the trick is to be ready for when a GM does come try to bust you."

Naturally, Rich explained, any gold farmer worth his salt had basic GM-dodging maneuvers built into his macros. Typically, these took advantage of the fact that GMs usually tested for macroing by directly interrogating the character under suspicion. This made it relatively easy to program a bot to recognize a GM's presence and make a canned but plausibly human response along the lines of *hold on a sec gotta take a leak*, to be followed by an immediate logoff. Or the bot might sound an alarm on the farmer's PC and spout random pleasantries long enough for the farmer to get to the keyboard and take over his end of the conversation. The GMs had gotten wise to these tactics, however, and adopted countermeasures of their own.

"They'll come up to your character and hold up an orange or blue stick or whatever and say, 'What color is my stick?'" said Rich. "You can't macro an answer to that. And by the time you get to your keyboard, the jig is up. So what I did is, I programmed the bots to send me an instant message at work anytime a GM showed up, and I could start IMing answers back to the GM right away. Or if I wasn't at work I would set it to forward the IM to my cell phone, and I could send text messages to the GM with my cell phone. So even if I'm at the movies, it's not a problem. I'm right there, ready to have a nice chat with any GM that wants to prove I'm not there."

I was speechless. Not that I'd been doing much talking, of course. But the degree of technical sophistication in Rich's setup was beyond anything I would have guessed. And there was more:

< 98 >

"You know that A.L.I.C.E. bot software?" he asked. I did. A.L.I.C.E. was, at the time, the reigning champion of the annual Loebner Prize competition, a contest to determine the computer program most capable of carrying on a convincingly human conversation. It was also available for anyone to download and customize for different contexts.

"Well, I was thinking I would try to route my bots' IMs to A.L.I.C.E. in case I didn't answer," said Rich. "Can you picture that? A GM talking to a character they suspect might have some little macro behind it when they're actually talking with a program that can practically pass the Turing Test?"

Rich paused to allow me to picture it, and for the first time since he'd picked up the phone, there was a moment of silence.

< 99 >

CHAPTER 15

Various computer games, of variously ancient vintage, have been declared the first ever invented. Among the strongest candidates, however, is a game that has rarely, if ever, been nominated. Designed by Alan Turing in 1950, it was a variation on "The Imitation Game," a party amusement in which a man and a woman, hidden in separate rooms, take written questions from the other guests and send typewritten answers back, each competing to convince the questioners that he, or she, is the woman. In Turing's reworking, a computer programmed for conversation replaces the man, and the computer wins if its answers either convince the questioners of its femininity more often than the man did or—in the simpler and better-known version of what's come to be called the Turing Test—convince them that it's human at all.

The main reason the Turing Test tends not to appear in histories of the computer game is that it was a purely hypothetical invention—a thought experiment proposed by Turing as a way of addressing the question "Can machines think?" without resorting to metaphysics. But it is a computer game nonetheless, played regularly nowadays in settings as rigorous as the Loebner contest (in which no computer program has yet fooled a human) and as ad hoc as AOL's adult chat rooms (in which male users are rou-

< 100 >

tinely lured away to commercial sex sites by convincingly flirtatious girl-bots). And if you survey the field of digital innovation prior to 1950, you'll find no computer-game inventor with a greater claim than Turing's.

Unless, perhaps, it's Turing himself. For he didn't only invent the Turing Test, of course. He also invented the computer, more or less, and in a sense, too, he was the first to see it for the game that it essentially is.

It was in 1936, a decade before the first modern digital computers were built, that Turing's brief paper "On Computable Numbers, With an Application to the Entscheidungsproblem"— a watershed in the history of mathematics—staked out the logical foundations of what he called "the computing machine." As with his later reformulation of the Imitation Game, his aim here was not so much practical as theoretical. He was seeking a solution to one of the deepest and most vexing mathematical problems of the time—seeking, in effect, to locate the farthest limits of calculation and proof—and the abstract machine he conjured up was just a prop to help him get there.

But its design was meticulous, and its details were easy enough to picture: An infinite ribbon of paper, infinitely divided into little square sections, is fed into the machine one square at a time. On each square a symbol is inscribed, 1 or 0, and for every square that enters, the machine consults a single line of instruction—one of many coded into its inner mechanisms—and makes three simple choices as instructed. First: change the symbol or let it stand. Second: move the paper left or right. Third: look up a new instruction, which becomes the rule for handling the next square on the ribbon. In a machine with forty-five instructions, for example, instruction twelve might say, "If the square reads 0, change it to 1, move left, and look up instruction 44; if the square reads 1, let it be, move right, and look up instruction 5."

< 101 >

No instruction is ever more complicated than that, and the essential operation of the machine is indeed as boneheadedly simple a loop as is thus implied: Look at the rule, look at the input, turn the input into output, look at the new rule, do it all again.

But don't let the minimalism fool you. Turing's point, which he established with sweeping mathematical rigor, was that this simple machine was capable of all the complexity an inventor could possibly hope for in a mechanism. Given enough instructions, it could, in Turing's dry formulation, "compute any computable sequence." And by this he meant, basically, that it could do anything. Or rather, that it could represent in the stream of its symbols the workings of any system, logical or physical, that could ever be known or imagined. "It can be shown," Turing later elaborated, "that a single special machine of that type can be made to do the work of all. It could in fact be made to work as a model of any other machine."

Now think about that for a moment. In the intervening decades, many a metaphor has competed to define the way we understand computers: Massive calculators, electronic brains, ethereal engines of productivity, the world's most powerful printing presses. But when Turing first beheld the computer in its abstract essence, stripped to its mathematical core, what he saw wasn't a brain or a printing press at all, though it could of course model those things and more. What Turing saw was, rather, a simulator—or what he called a "universal machine." A machine for creating imaginary replicas of any real or possible system, using logically expressed rules to define the interaction between user and machine that brought these replicas to life.

And what was the precedent for such an invention? If you wanted, you could could count the orrery—a clockwork model of the solar system popular in the early days of modern astronomy—or similar gimcrackery scattered about the history of science and technology. But to even begin to match the versatility,

< 102 >

the complexity, and above all, the defining interactivity of Turing's invention, you need to look much farther back into human history, or even pre-human history, to the origins of games.

Two puppies at play, some animal behaviorists will tell us, are engaged in structured simulation—building an imaginary dog-fight shaped by simple rules forbidding only the too-sharp bite and the menacing growl. But even ruling out all games prior to the origins of language and tools, we arrive very early in human evolution at the first relevant examples: games of chance, played with shells and sticks and sheep's-knuckle dice. Board games, like the ancient Egyptian Senet, dated to 3,500 BC and said to be a racing game not unlike backgammon, or the similar Mesopotamian Royal Game of Ur (2,600 BC), or the ancient Chinese battle game Liubo (1,500 BC).

That these games could usually be understood as modeling recognizable real-world activities—horse races, wars, the workings of fate—is hardly the main point of comparison with Turing's simulation engine: The representation was often so abstract as to defy easy recognition. But in a sense the abstraction was itself the point: You wanted to simulate the mind-riveting unpredictability of fate, not its burdensome consequences; you wanted the strategic challenge of battle, not the blood and guts.

And so it is with computers. Which is why when you look down from a certain level of abstraction at any board game you can think of—at any turn-based game at all, in fact—you find that its workings are essentially no different from those of the abstract machine Turing described: Take user input (a dice roll, a chess move), evaluate according to a particular set of explicit instructions (the rules of the game), return the evaluation as output ("advance your piece five spaces," "no, that's cheating!"), then do it again, and again, until the sequence reaches a halting state ("you win") or proves to have none ("draw").

< 103 >

It is this endlessly repeatable collusion of freedom and determinism—the warp and woof of fixed rules and free play, of running code and variable input—that sets both games and computers apart, together, from the larger universe of information technologies they inhabit. The printed page, the painted picture, the film, and the photograph—no more or less than computers, they all design to represent the world in ways both richly particular and highly abstract. The abacus, slide rule, and other predigital tools of calculation likewise prefigure the computer's extraction of complex information from the simplest of rules. But only games share the universal machine's thoroughgoing commitment to the principle of recursion: the chained repetition of simple operations, each building on both the input of the moment and the outcomes of the preceding steps. And only games, therefore, come close to capturing that precise mix of unpredictability and inevitability that makes the computer such a powerful simulator of our lived experience of the world.

I won't push the point much further. Personally, I'm convinced historians of technology will one day recognize no essential difference between the ancient board game and the modern computer, just as paleontologists have come to think of birds not as the dinosaur's closest surviving relative but as its living representative. But you don't need to follow me that far to recognize the unique affinity of games and computers.

Just consider the history of the computer game. Even ignoring the Turing Test's claims to prior art, the first applications of gaming to computers weren't long in coming. As early as 1952, a program called Noughts and Crosses, written for Cambridge University's EDSAC machine by doctoral student A. S. Douglas, was playing tic-tac-toe invincibly against human opponents. Six years later William Higinbotham, a former Manhattan Project physicist working at the Brookhaven National Laboratory, cre-

< 104 >

ated a proto-Pong that used the screen blips of an oscilloscope to represent the ball and paddles of a table tennis game. All of which was prelude to the invention, by MIT hackers in 1963, of the legendary rocketship duel Spacewar!, which engrossed programmers there as no other program had and later became one of the first arcade video games marketed.

And then came Pong proper. And Space Invaders. And Donkey Kong and Mortal Kombat and Sonic the Hedgehog and, in time, a $7-billion-a-year industry that at this point drives the evolution of computer hardware more than almost any other sector, pushing the limits of what the microchip can do and ensuring a steady stream of revenue for the entire computer business.

But all that is only the more visible face of a symbiosis that runs much deeper—into the heart, soul, and imagination of the hacker culture that created computing as we know it. For while it's obvious that the computer is a consummate vehicle for games, what's less widely recognized is that games have long served programmers as a kind of ultimate reference point for understanding the inner workings and broadest possibilities of the computer. It's no accident that many of the first hackers came to computing straight from the ranks of MIT's Tech Model Railroad Club, where they had already whetted a taste for complex, playful simulation. And in time hackers would come to recognize the connection between programming and play almost as a matter of course.

Indeed, by the time journalist Tracy Kidder wrote *The Soul of a New Machine*—his Pulitzer-winning profile of a late-'70s corporate computer-design team—his subjects could think of no better way to show him what it was like to write code than to sit him down in front of the pioneering text-based computer game Adventure and let him play. Framed as a quest into a dizzyingly complex cavern full of treasures, trolls, and other Tolkienesque thrills, Adventure challenged the player to find a way through its labyrinthine,

< 105 >

branching structure by typing in one line of simple commands after another ("go left," "go up," "get bird," "kill dwarf"). "Each 'room' of the adventure was like a computer subroutine, presenting a logical problem you'd have to solve," Steven Levy later explained in *Hackers*, his epic history of coder culture. "In a sense, Adventure was a metaphor for computer programming itself—the deep recesses you explored in the Adventure world were akin to the basic, most obscure levels of the machine that you'd be traveling in when you hacked assembly code. You could get dizzy trying to remember where you were in both activities."

Should it come as any surprise that Adventure was the direct and founding ancestor of the online role-playing game genre to which Ultima Online belongs? The genealogy is well-established: Adventure went forth and multiplied, giving rise to a host of knock-offs from whose single-player template there emerged, at last, the momentous, many-player MUD ("multi-user dungeon"), which in its turn brought forth a multitude of similar text-based games and, in the fullness of time, the 3D graphical universes of EverQuest, World of Warcraft, and all the others.

And along the way, directly and indirectly, this same lineage of games has continued to shape the minds that shape the digital landscape. Computer scientist and science-fiction author Vernor Vinge, for example, plainly had the Internet's earliest role-playing games in mind when he wrote his 1981 novella "True Names," a weird tech-thriller wrapped around the central, luminous conceit of the Other World—a vividly immersive, globally networked virtual reality populated by hacker wizards and shapeshifting FBI agents. Vinge's game-inspired vision paved the way for a genre's worth of literary cyberspaces—including both cyberspace itself, the star attraction of William Gibson's novel *Neuromancer,* and the celebrated Metaverse depicted in Neal Stephenson's anarcho-capitalist fantasia *Snow Crash*.

< 106 >

The term "cyberspace," of course, went on to broader circulation as the name a generation of mid-1990s Internet virgins gave to the alternate dimension they couldn't help sensing they stepped into every time they went online—a revealing and almost hilarious shorthand in retrospect, given the distance between Gibson's cyberspace (a dark, sleek "consensual hallucination" jacked into via fiber-to-the-brainstem cranial delivery ports) and the dial-up CompuServe screens we were all geeking out about. Since then, the buzzword crown has passed to "Metaverse," which has become the rallying cry for an insurgency of hacker virtuosos and venture-capital visionaries who find in *Snow Crash*'s networked otherworld—a virtual planet with twice the square acreage of Earth, where fortunes are made and lost in unreal-estate speculation and the consumer classes spend most of their time and money—a magnetically attractive target for their aspirations to construct the ultimate human-computer interface.

Projects explicitly aimed at this target range from the noncommercial Open Source Metaverse Project—a stab at free and open standards for building and connecting 3D worlds across the Internet—to the above-mentioned There, with its planet-size dimensions and corporate cross-marketing deals. Another commercial venture directly inspired by *Snow Crash,* the fast-growing Second Life, has perhaps the starkest Metaversal ambitions of the bunch. With its wide-openness to user-created architecture, objects, and other in-world content, and its whole-hearted embrace of the real-money trade in virtual properties, Second Life is striving mightily to leave the games market behind and become, instead, the next- and perhaps final-generation desktop—a globe-spanning virtual realm in which everything from social lives to business plans to artistic movements unfold.

It may get there. It may not. Maybe none of these aspiring Metaverses will succeed beyond the level of boutique attractions. But

< 107 >

even in their present, embryonic forms, they gesture strikingly toward a technological endpoint that has beckoned since the moment Turing recognized the computer as a universal machine: the fusion of every replicable real-world system into a single, endlessly replayable simulation. The reduction of the whole world to a game.

Would we even recognize that virtual cosmos as the game it would remain? On one level, of course we would. As unlikely as the simple cocktail-conversational criteria of the Turing Test are to convince anybody that a computer has attained true sentience, a simulated universe—complete with replicas not only of chatting party guests but of everything else on earth—would surely have an even harder time passing itself off as genuine.

But the Turing Test gives other, and perhaps more relevant, answers to the question as well. Philosophers have wrangled through the decades over the validity of Turing's argument, but I would argue that its historical importance lies not so much in what it says about intelligence and computers as, ultimately, in how it thinks about computers and authenticity. At bottom, it asks a single, brilliantly rhetorical question: If you find yourself having as scintillating a conversation with the computer behind door number one as with the grad student behind door number two, then why require that the computer have a conscious subjectivity as well? This is a party, remember? Not a marriage. The Turing Test, in other words, assumes that whether it's conversational intelligence or rush-hour traffic or nuclear reactions you're seeing modeled in digital form, it is always just that: A model. And that therefore it's a waste of precious time and creativity to wonder whether the model is the same, on some deep, ontological level, as what it simulates. The question, rather, is whether it's the same *in every way that matters for the purposes at hand*.

Call it the virtual turn, this mode of thinking. Or you could call it, as the social psychologist Sherry Turkle has, "taking

< 108 >

things at interface value." Either way, there's no escaping it these days. For though it may seem heretical to apply its skin-deep logic, in Turing's provocative fashion, to such profound questions as the nature of human thought, any practical use of computers pretty much requires it. Go to the "productivity" section of your local software store and what will you find? A dazzling variety of products all amounting, in their technological essence, to the same mind-bogglingly arcane thing: A string of 1s and 0s, the encoded rules and playing pieces of a fantastically abstract board game. A turn-based simulation somewhat more complex than but formally no different from a war gamer's hexgrid reenactment of the Battle of Austerlitz—and utterly useless, of course, unless you adopt something like the gamer's suspension of disbelief and accept that a particular tool or process can, for a particular set of purposes, be replaced by a computer game.

That word-processing program, for instance, will do nothing for you unless you stop pondering the unbridgeable gap of ontic difference between a real typewriter and its reflection in 1s and 0s and accept that the simulated typewriter can do the job as well or better. The tax software in your hand is, at best, an obscenely complicated description of the tax-filing process until you accept its practical equivalence to your accountant and start playing the game it encodes. For every new digital application we adopt, the same decision must be made, consciously or not: to affirm that some make-believe replica or another is, for all pragmatic intents, as good as real. The broad, historic project of computerization, in other words—the daily integration of the digital into more and deeper aspects of our lives and economies—is in effect the ceaseless replaying of a stripped-down, generalized variation on the oldest computer game there is: the Turing Test.

With the computers winning more rounds all the time. And while it will likely be a long, long time before they can adequately

< 109 >

fake full consciousness, other significant features of human existence are sure to prove more easily gamed. Already the complex computer systems that constitute the world's MMOs have passed a significant Turing Test of sorts: When Edward Castronova declared their economies indistinguishable, for the purposes of economic analysis, from their real-world counterparts, he brought them one major step closer to deserving to be called virtual worlds. As the universal machine continues to replicate more and more of the real world's subsystems, with more and more of the real world's compelling subtlety, it will surely just get easier to fall into the habit of accepting our digital "other worlds" and "second lives" as functional equivalents of the originals.

Personally, though, I'm working on another habit, and as I write this I realize I've been working on it ever since I first glimpsed the UO auctions on eBay. Whenever I see some online phenomenon that sets the metaphysics spinning in my head—the big, hairy questions about what's real, what's virtual, and what could possibly connect the two—I try to close my eyes and imagine the computer as Turing imagined it in 1936. I see the paper ribbon, and the ribbon feeder, and the simple motions of the feed. I see the rules that govern those motions, and the symbols that invoke the rules. And finally, in the interplay of motions, symbols, rules, and ribbon, I see the game at the heart of the machine.

And I guess that's why, when Richard Thurman told me of his plans to pipe the A.L.I.C.E. engine into UO through his bots, it fairly took my breath away.

As I'd been listening to him talk, I could feel his story tugging at me in a warm, inviting way. Partly it was the call of easy money. Some gold farmers, Bob had told me just a few days before, *are probably making upwards of 1 mil per year real money—all from doing nothing. I mean I work my ass off—like 14 hours per day. These guys are on the beach while their macros run inside.*

< 110 >

Even without running bots themselves, retailers like Bob—like me—could get a piece of those fat profits by making volume buys straight from the farmers, at the cheapest wholesale rates around. Not that there was much difference, of course, between cheating and profiting from the profits of cheaters. And Bob had made it clear he would do neither. *I do not buy from them,* he'd said. *That is the ugly side of UO—a side I prefer not to get involved with . . . These guys are serious people—it is like a UO mafia—LOL . . . I would love nothing more than to see all of them rot in prison—but I would fear for the safety of my family if they found out I told anyone—lol.*

Sure, he conceded, you could never entirely avoid buying farmed contraband: *Joe Schmoe comes to me wanting to sell 100 million gold—he says he sold his castle—but I really have no clue where he got it :(—neither would anyone else.* But the point for Bob, it seemed, wasn't so much to avoid contact with the farmers' tainted gold as to steer clear of their tainted attitudes: *I don't care about the money like those guys do. They look at it as a cut-throat business—and they do not play around . . . I am not in it for the money. I am doing this so I can live close to my family and raise my children in a good place. It sounds romantic—but mixing chemicals [for Procter & Gamble] the rest of my life was not appealing—no matter what they paid me.*

But as Rich Thurman talked, and talked, I got the feeling he, too, was not just in it for the money. Clearly, Rich's enterprise was not a noble one, yet between the lines of his narrative I'd been catching glimpses of something verging on transcendence, something I'd been unable to put my finger on until the moment Rich mentioned the Turing Test and lit it all up for me. Ultima Online was a game, of course, but beneath it there were levels within levels of another game, the game of virtuality that Turing invented and refined. We were all playing it on one level or more,

< 111 >

but the breadth and intensity of focus that Rich's work seemed to require—the obsessive attention to everything from the minutiae of UO's server code to the broad trends of its macroeconomy—had brought him closer to the core of that deeper game, I sensed, than the rest of us could ever hope to go.

And so, between the sheer, loopy audacity of Rich's A.L.I.C.E. implementation and the flock of insights it sent fleeting through my brain, is it any wonder I required a moment to collect my thoughts?

But not a long moment.

"Dude," I said, "that I have got to see."

Rich gave a short, bitter laugh. "Don't hold your breath. My accounts are gone. Every last one got banned. I am dead in the water right now, and frankly, dorking around with chat AIs is very, very low on my to-do list."

I won't say I was crestfallen, but if technological history was to be denied its first-ever Turing-testable gold-farm bot, I needed a fuller explanation than that, and Rich was naturally delighted to oblige. There followed the long and turbulent story of the events that had led to the hosebagging of Rich's operations and, per-force, the indefinite suspension of Project A.L.I.C.E.

And I was not the least surprised to learn it all began with a message from Lee Caldwell.

< 112 >

CHAPTER 16

It was a common foe that brought Rich and Lee together: A deadbeat customer had defrauded them both, buying gold from each of them on eBay and then, after making payment and taking delivery, telling PayPal he'd never got the goods and having the payments reversed. It was the dread "chargeback" scam, bane of RMT retailers everywhere, and it left Lee screwed to the tune of $260 and Rich for $800. Neither was aware of the other's predicament—or existence—but a mutual acquaintance in the farming scene put two and two together and alerted them to their shared problem. Soon thereafter Lee contacted Rich by instant message to knock around ideas for persuading the scammer to return their money.

There was no shortage of options to consider. Rich, it emerged, was partial to legal threats and hacking attacks. Lee, on the other hand, had something a little more old-school in mind: a visit to the young man's home address in Downey, California, which as Lee pointed out was just an hour's drive away from his own. Rich, a resident of Flowermound, Texas, but handy with MapQuest, pointed out that the address was also just a few blocks from Compton, a place he had heard of in gangsta raps

< 113 >

and was not eager to set foot in. Lee (or as his IM handle identified him, Destiny) was not dissuaded:

fuck i dont care, i used to live in long beach right in the heart of the riots, i dont give a fuck, said Destiny. *i will go packing too*

Lee typed those words at 2:44 p.m. Pacific Standard Time on October 19, 2003, and the reason I can tell you this with such precision is that Rich—who, as I may have mentioned, enjoyed a good conversation—also enjoyed sharing the records of his conversations. Not long after our own first talk, he made available to me an apparently unedited log of all his IM exchanges hitherto with Lee, and it is a remarkable document: the narrative in chat of a relationship that grew from that first day's ad-hoc plans for revenge (which came to nothing much, in the end) into a cagey awareness that between the two of them they held potentially controlling sway over an entire economy's money supply.

Not that either of them was individually so very powerful, but on Lee's side the Blacksnow-Ingotdude coalition and on Rich's a loose international affiliation he sometimes referred to as "the cartel"—half a dozen highly skilled coders, all intimately involved in the shaping and maintaining of a popular macroing program called EasyUO—probably produced as much gold, in aggregate, as the rest of the player population combined.

And that was just in lean times, which the Age of Shadows was not. Although the AoS expansion had effectively nerfed cartography, till then the farmers' mainstay, the gold-farm business was booming nonetheless, riding high on a wave of newly discovered dupes that included not only the cloth-bolts-into-bandages exploit ("Bandaids" or "Bolts," as the farmers called it) but a bug that instantly transmuted dirt-cheap Bulk Order Deeds into 4,000 gp worth of commodity iron at a pop ("Ingots"), as well as an obscure method of profiting from the purchase and preparation of raw poultry ("Birds"). By May, some market watchers

< 114 >

were estimating that 90 percent of new UO gold was being introduced by the top farmers, and it was clear to both Lee and Rich that the time had come for them to start thinking big.

What follows is the record of their most ambitious attempt at doing so, an IM sitdown of sorts between the representatives of two formidable but illicit economic blocs. I have lightly edited and intermittently annotated the text, but I invite you to imagine yourself reading this passage as I first read it, coming upon it after plowing through the first several hundred lines of Rich and Lee's otherwise banal IM relationship like a bleary-eyed FBI agent babysitting a wiretap, surrounded by the donut crumbs and paper coffee cups of a hundred hours' useless surveillance, who suddenly finds himself listening in on negotiations for an underworld merger of historic proportions. For the gold farmers of UO, this was a shot at unprecedented power—at more control over the game, perhaps, than even the game developers maintained—and this is how they took that shot.

May 20, 2003, 2:21 A.M.

Destiny

so how ya been

Rich

good . . . busy . . . and too stressed out

Destiny

lol i know that feeling its been a crazy 3 months here lol

Rich

tell me about it . . . and everyone is freaked out because of Ignotdude and his auctions . . .
although I realy didnt see a drastic drop in price till everyeone started copying him

< 115 >

Destiny

yeah it was a pretty dramatic statement

Rich

what was intersting is that no one noticed until like the 3rd week he was doing it

Rich

and by that time I could already see that he was only causing a 50 cent drag on the over all avg ebay price

Destiny

yes it was definitely the copiers that had the overall impact.

Rich

but like any market . . . one drops . . . they all drop . . . like dominos

Destiny

agreed. we have spent alot . . . and i mean ALOT of time studying the market the competition, the corporation [Origin Systems Incorporated, or OSI, the EA subsidiary in charge of the game's development] *and the entire situation as a whole*

OK, things have already gotten a bit Kabuki here. What exactly did Lee mean, calling Ingotdude's market-crashing sell-off a "dramatic statement"? Was the whole thing some kind of muscle-flexing on the part of Lee and co.? A demonstration of how ugly things could get if the cartel declined to join forces with Blacksnow? And was Rich's minimizing of the damage Ingotdude had done a similarly pointed rejoinder, a sort of "Message received, and shrugged at"? In any event, it was time to cut to the chase:

< 116 >

The Gold Farmers

Rich

so . . . whats this all about?

Destiny

well i think we can really and seriously benefit from a strong association. i am not talking about some candyass bullshit association, i am talking about the type where we are willing to fly and meet you guys to seriously hammer out some important decision, details everything

Rich

when you say WE . . . who do you mean? if I may ask?

Destiny

:)

Rich

cant say? I understand . . . I couldnt say either . . .

Rich

but the "we" behind me is a loose contingent of individuals.

Destiny

a loose contingent of individuals is at best difficult to manage and at worst impossible

Rich

you have noooo idea

Destiny

i can in fact shut ebay down for sales, literally

Rich

so can I . . . but why?

Destiny

to affect a more reasonable adherence to a pricing structure

< 117 >

Rich

it wont happen . . . there are too many yahoo's with onesy twosy out there.

Destiny

there is no such thing as a pricing agreement if there are no controls or even better . . . repercussions for not adhering to the agreement

Destiny

i feel much more confident that i could control the ebay price by far

Rich

your forgeting something though

Rich

it is really easy to move the price down

Rich

but once it is down . . . you cant move it back up because your customer segment will expect the lower price

Destiny

well as long as full bore supply leak is going on that is true. but lets talk about PRODUCERS as opposed to sellers.

Destiny

we are producers and sellers. but if the REAL producers . . . you and us . . . were to begin working together, i mean really working together not bullshitting, we would literaly control the entire supply, that coupled with extreme prejudice on the pricing structure you would see a dramatic increase in the price. if you guys could even do half of what you say, shit just 1/4 then i could personally guarantee an ebay price of 30 per

< 118 >

million within 60–90 days and an increasing price after that.

Rich

I would love to see that . . . and tried that once before . . . but then there was the ignot bug . . . you found bandaides . . . etc . . . there is always goign to be somehting else that really breaks the foundations of agreements . . . plus mistrust among the producers . . . etc

Rich

we tried this once before

Destiny

well like i said honor among thieves is very historically overrated

Destiny

without enforcment of an agreement, an agreement is basically worthless and unnecesary to begin with

Rich

can we talk voice?

Destiny

calling

And here, as when the mobsters on the far end of the wire decide to step out of their social club for a strategic walk around the block, we encounter a maddeningly suggestive one-hour-and-forty-two-minute gap in the transcript, during which the negotiations apparently proceeded fast and furious by telephone. A best guess at their content, arrived at only by painstaking cross-reference with subsequent remarks and other transcripts, suggests that Rich, having staked out the high ground of reluctant skepticism toward Lee's overture, now played his hand. And that Lee, in turn, overplayed his.

< 119 >

it wont happen, Rich had IM'd, but in fact a true cartel of all the major gold producers, an OPEC of the farming underground, was just the sort of thing Rich would have loved to bring about. He considered himself not only a manipulator of the gold supply but a caretaker, responsible for keeping market prices sound and stable as much as for keeping retailers in stock, and more than once I heard him compare his role in UO's economy to that of Alan Greenspan in the United States's. But in truth his own efforts at responsible restraint were pretty useless without a global price-control regime to back them up, and maybe this proposed "association" was the chance to make it happen.

When Lee made his conditions known, however, the deal evaporated. Blacksnow had organization and discipline, the cartel had programming skills, and if Lee was going to bring his group's strengths to the table, he wanted Rich to pony up a share of the cartel's. Specifically, he wanted access to a closely guarded piece of code called exevents.dll, a routine that penetrated deep into UO's code to open up a world of profitable farming options. The answer was no. And no matter how many ways Lee rephrased the demand, the answer was still no. Exevents was the creation of the cartel's ranking UO hacker, a Swiss kid called Cheffe, who had made its operation dependent on server calls only he controlled. Even Rich himself couldn't use exevents if Cheffe didn't want him to, so all he could offer as Lee hammered at the question was Cheffe's well-known hard line: No outsiders get exevents.

Apparently Rich managed to make the point diplomatically enough, however, and the final words of their exchange that night, after they'd hung up the phones and gone back to IM, gave no hint of animosity:

Rich
thanks for the chat . . . I really think we can co-exist

< 120 >

Destiny

so do i, good luck and nice talking to you

Therewith commenced the peaceful co-existence of Blacksnow and the EasyUO cartel, which was to last almost a full fourteen hours.

May 21, 2003, 5:58 P.M.

Destiny

hey you there?

Rich

yes . . . hows it going?

Destiny

someone has started calling alot of gms today [i.e., sending in-game messages to game masters reporting unattended bot characters], *i believe i know who it is and that its not you guys, but could you confirm for me that it is not you*

Rich

no . . . it is not me . . . hang on

Destiny

the characters are on atl and LA [the Atlantic and Lake Austin shards]

Rich

all of us were banned today

Rich

arround 2pm cst

Rich

who is it [that's calling the GMs]*?*

Destiny

its the fucking angelius motherfucker

< 121 >

Destiny

they actually got one of our atlantic guys, fucking
gm silvani even though we were there

A common complaint among bot farmers: Technically, of course, the GMs weren't supposed to ban you for unattended macroing if you could establish your attendance, but it happened, and in the face of such rank injustice it was sometimes hard for the poor farmer to remember he was still guilty as sin.

Destiny

angelius is just atlantic and LA he usually does
like 5 packhorses through a gate

Destiny

he is pissed because we are kicking his ass

Destiny

atlantic and la were the two shards where he called
gms we defended all the la ones and most of the
atlantic ones but lost one just because silvani
[the GM] felt like it

Rich

well they got all my bots and my main char

Rich

how the fuck they linked them is beyond me

Or not. After previous bannings, Rich had taken to running his bots and his delivery characters on separate accounts, with separate IP addresses, so he knew in fact that there was really only one way the GMs could have connected them all: A snitch. A fellow farmer, no doubt, with an axe to grind. Maybe someone whose ambitions he had frustrated, say, sometime in the last twenty-four hours.

< 122 >

But Lee had suspicions of his own, provoked by the apparent activities of cartel member Rain Dog, also known as Josh:

Destiny

not that i am saying your lying but could you explain how all your accounts got banned but at least one of josh's [characters] *on atlantic is still running, john i think it is*

Rich

everyone in my group has been blocked.

Destiny

not everyone, josh is still running, let me go double check but 5 mins before i icq'd you josh's char on atlantic was still recalling away [i.e., using the Recall spell to teleport a character from one spot to another]

Rich

I dont speak for Josh, you will have to ask him.

Rich

Josh doesnt Recall btw [by the way]

Destiny

hmmm then i am a bit confused because the person recalling is definitely using exevents

Rich

I woudnt make that assumption

Rich

Cheffe just pulled exevents today because of this

Rich

are you there?

Destiny

yes talking to my partner on the phone, something is up and i dont like it

< 123 >

Rich

explain?

Destiny

*we had a wave of gms, you had a wave of gms, i am
  sure there is mistrust on both sides,
  unfortunately you are, or rather one of your
  members are still going and you are telling me
  that you guys are completely down*

Destiny

*so i am talking with my partner to try to see what
  is going on because i tend to fly off the handle
  and he is more reasonable*

Destiny

*are you saying that this might be because of
  exevents? i am not sure what your saying*

Rich

*I am saying that at this moment exevents doesnt work
  as Cheffe informed me that he turned it off for a
  while.*

Destiny

*ok but that doesnt help us for who is doing the
  calling of gms on such an organized scale or
  rather should i say dedicated scale on two
  different shards.*

Rich

*I was hit by a GM on Cats [the Catskills shard],
  Atalantic, Chessy [Chesapeake], and Sonoma, and GL
  [Great Lakes]*

Rich

more then just 2 shards

Destiny

hmmmm we were only hit on 2

< 124 >

The Gold Farmers

Destiny

*we are not running on cats atm [at the moment] i
think*

Destiny

*but we are running on those others, but we are doing
bolts and you are NOT doing bolts, correct?*

Rich

*that is correct afaik [as far as I know] none of us
were doing bolts*

Rich

*its official . . . if John is recalling and is in
Skara [Skara Brae, one of Britannia's main cities
and a common farming spot] I do not know who it
is.*

Destiny

*well then there is definitely a very organized person
attacking us and we need to find out what is going
on*

Destiny

*hmmmm then there is someone else with exevents or
something similar, go watch him and you will see
what i mean*

Rich

I cant . . . no characters ATM [at the moment]

Rich

when i say I lost it all . . . I LOST IT ALL.

Destiny

*:(well dude i swear to god on everything i am worth
and my kids that i did not nor did anyone even
remotely connected with us in any way call gms or
do anything untoward you guys*

< 125 >

Rich

*no worries . . . I'll be back in a day or two . . .
the part that sucks is losing the main account . . .
not having a [grandmaster] mage on each shard is
going to make it very time consuming to get set up
agian . . . not to mention having gold to buy
suplies.*

Destiny

*i must say your taking this a hell of alot calmer
than i am and i only lost one account*

Destiny

*so if i go look at chickens you guys are going to be
buying. is that a fair statement?*

At this point, it seems, Lee had entered into a parallel conversation with the aforementioned Josh, and apparently he didn't like what he was starting to hear:

Destiny

*ok either you are lying to me about who has
exevents, you are lying to me about what you guys
are doing with it or there is something out there
that can do the exact same thing. on eof those
three are the possible answers and i am beginning
to feel like i am being played and when it comes
to my rent and my food being paid for i dont like
to be played*

Destiny

no you motherfuckers are in for it, its fucking on

Destiny

fucking lying sacks of shit

< 126 >

Rich

yes I am calm because getting all freaked out doesnt help

Rich

like I said, as far as i know, no one is running. Of the people that run in skara, the two I know only one recalls. He told me its not him, which makes sense because as far as i know no one can use exevents. or maybe I am just singled out.

Destiny

yeah fuck you, i just found out from josh the bullshit you two have been running, its fucking on, i will teach you what the fuck its like to toy with someones fucking income

Rich

news to me

Destiny

yeah fucking news to you. fuck you guys, immature fucks

Destiny

you fucked with the wrong person

Rich

I am not fucking with . . . and you should take a deep breath . . . I have no idea who is doing bandaides

Destiny

dont give me that fucking different subject shit and you can count phil goodbye, that fucker is gone, next char

[The gloves, in other words, were off: Blacksnow was taking "Phil" out, calling a GM in on the character, whom Lee apparently believed was one of Rich's.]

< 127 >

Destiny

when you want to fuck with someone rich, take a bit of advice, be a fucking man and tell them your going to do it, dont be some little bitch about it

Rich

good . . . because I dont know who those people are ban them all

Destiny

goddamn right i will

Destiny

how fucking dare you lie to me

Destiny

oh no one gets exevents

Destiny

you fucking gave exevents to fucking blackmailer?

Ah, so now it was clear: Josh had revealed the sordid little story of Inverted, a blackmailing wannabe farmer who had extorted a certain cartel member into sneaking him access to exevents, threatening to rat him out to the GMs if he didn't cough up. Strictly speaking, then, Rich hadn't been entirely straight with Lee when he'd said exevents was off-limits to outsiders, but the episode hadn't exactly inclined Cheffe to loosen the controls.

Destiny

you really are some kind of fucking bitch

Destiny

i have just put one employee full time on dropping you fuckers off of this game, unless you do shit manually, you wont be able to dupe fucking cloth to make gold

< 128 >

The Gold Farmers

Destiny

wbrit and jhelom [Britannian cities and botting centers both] *count those gone*

Destiny

the first key rich is organization

Destiny

the second key is determination, and let me assure you of something. that fucking sack of bullshit you fed me on the phone for 3 hours could have gone unsaid, but you thought you could have fun

Rich

your funny . . . because your blowing up at the wrong guys.

Rich

I take it your seeing someone doing bolts. bandaides

Destiny

i am seeing people doing the birds dipshit

Rich

where?

Destiny

fuck you, you sat there and lied about exevents period

Rich

no I didnt . . . where are you seeing people running birds?

Destiny

fuck you, just know that i am on the job

Rich

dude . . . if someone is doing birds . . . I would like to know as well . . . give me locations. Personaly I think your seeing someone else.

< 129 >

Destiny

do your own fucking research dumbass

Rich

*either way . . . get them busted . . . do what ever
. . . because its not any of us and I would like
to see them gone too.*

Destiny

*you fucking guys gave a fucking blackmailer fucking
exevents then you come to us and try to act like
fucking equals? your a bunch of fucking pussies*

Rich

okay . . . last chance to calm down and be rational

Destiny

*be rational about what, about how you think your
equal to us in business and you tell us a bunch of
fucking lies about exevents then i find out you
give it to anyone that fucking blackmails you, you
fucking idiots deserve what you got, feeding him
along, fucking stupid*

Rich

who . . . specifically are you talking about?

Destiny

*dont play fucking games with me rich, we work a game
not play one, you want to be a bitch, then get
treated like a bitch*

Destiny

*you can forget about minoc [city of blacksmiths],
that one will be gone*

Destiny

*you can count moonglow [city of mages] goodbye in
about 2 hours, you have that much time before i
will have things set up and then you wont macro a*

< 130 >

single fucking thing else and you can take me for a joke all you want, you should realize by now how fucking organized i am

Destiny

ye there was good old phil right in moonglow that guy is gone

Rich

ohhh Phil!!! yes . . . the beetle guy!!!

Rich

Tom, Tim, etc . . . always on a beetle . . .

Destiny

rich if you believe nothing else, believe that i do what i say i am going to do to a fucking detrimental fault

Destiny

and as for joshs comment that you are going to shut me down. . . . ..omfg roflmmfao [oh my fucking god, rolling on the floor laughing my motherfucking ass off]

Destiny

i do this for a fucking living rich. this is my entire fucking job

Rich

I dont speak for Josh, but all I can say is that I dont depend on this . . . and if I cant run, I cant run. I do know that you have it all wrong and talking to you any further is going to be pointless.

Destiny

how do i have it wrong rich, that you lied to me about exevents? do i have that wrong rich? am i way off fucking base rich?

< 131 >

Destiny

please explain to me how i could possibly be wrong
when you told me you wouldnt give shit to a
blackmailer

Destiny

explain to me how i am wrong that you come to me and
ask for something then fucking lie to my face (or
voice rather) and say its not possible for us to
have what we are asking for when you fucking gave it
to some fucking prick who gave you nothing but peace

Destiny

bye bye serpents hold

Rich

I dont control exevents. if Cheffe gave it to
someone . . . there is nothing I can do . . . as
for Inverted getting exevents, that was a
descision to move forward with minimal trouble

Destiny

no rich, you specifically and unequivocally told me
that exevents was in no way possible no matter what

Rich

yes . . . Cheffe doesnt like to give out exevents . . .
if you know someone that has it, they shouldnt (as
far as I know) and it would be good to know. I
already know that exevents is not working as
Cheffe pulled the plug . . . or atleast MY
exevents doesnt work.

Destiny

oh you are a fucking liar, 3 mins after we got on
the phone you said, let me tell you right now,
there is no way you can have exevents. do you not
recall that statement rich?

< 132 >

Rich

yes I do . . . and I stand by that . . . now if Cheffe *IS* giving it out how am I supposed to know that?

Destiny

yep, play your mindgames rich, you fucked up shit for everyone

Rich

it could be that cheffe is fucking me over the whole time . . . I dunno . . . alll I know is what state I currently am in ..and that is fucked . . . I have no active accounts and I lost my main account.

Destiny

no motherfucker you said there is NO way i could get it, it wasnt going to happen. you didnt qualify, you didnt make exceptions, you made a bold statement that controlled the entire 3 hour conversation and you fucking know it

Rich

to my knowledge that is True . . .

Destiny

you would be a good politician rich, say something direct and to the point then fucking start the covered retreat . . . this is my last message, put me on ignore do what you want. you fucked up, and a war has started. when your ready to give up, icq me or dont i dont care

Destiny

bye bye skara

And so it ended. Or began. Two weeks later, the day I first spoke to Rich, the hostilities were still on high flame. If the reports of

< 133 >

Blacksnow's massive account losses were true, the cartel was giving as good as it got. But Lee hadn't been kidding about his determination. Rich, who'd thought he'd be back in full swing a day or two after those first bannings, still hadn't managed to field a single new character:

"Lee is putting too much heat on me right now. Every bot I try to put in action, he finds it and gets it banned. I'm going to have to lay low for a while till things simmer down a little. And start looking for new bugs to work. With all this exposure going on, all the old ones are getting patched left and right by the designers. But it's always like this. Every time OSI goes in and fixes things, they pop a few stitches somewhere else. And you just gotta go and find them."

I'd heard enough. "Well, keep me posted," I said, easing the conversation to a close.

"Sure thing," said Rich. "And listen, if you're serious about trying to sell things for a living, like it says on your blog, talk to me. I'm glad to help show you the way."

I thanked him for the offer. But somehow, after all I'd now learned, Rich Thurman's way no longer seemed so inviting. When you factored in the overhead of gut-churning intrigue and back-stabbing recriminations, the money didn't actually look so easy anymore. And charmed though I remained at the prospect of touching the mystery at the core of the game and so forth, it weighed very lightly in the cost-benefit analysis against the risk of opening my door one day and coming face to face with squat, blunt Lee fucking Caldwell, packing heat.

I'd stick with Bob Kiblinger's way for now. Hell, the way things were going back in my little corner of the market, I was happy to settle for Radny's.

< 134 >

PART SIX

A Thousand Dollars and a Dream

dude, bad news
??
very bad
sigh—it's about the plant set, right?
right

I'd been waiting for this. Two days earlier, Radny had attached a public notice to his vendor over at Ultima's reporting a major financial setback. According to the notice, he had accidentally priced a full set of rare potted plants at 15 gp rather than 2.6 million (the going price) and was now hoping that whoever had bought it at 15 would please please please return it. The mistake was Radny's of course, but somehow, as soon as I saw what had happened, I knew I'd be paying for it.

you're gonna have to give me a couple weeks to get your 2 million
uh huh
no profit on it—but I'll get you your money back
whatever

I considered my prospects. Best case: Radny was as good as his word, but my money was sidelined for weeks. Worst case: Radny defaulted, and the enterprise was back to square one.

< 136 >

This was not good.

It was almost two months now since I'd announced my intention to get rich selling virtual goods, and I was still struggling to turn a profit on $40 worth of gold. The ore books were still selling, but at an increasingly sluggish pace. My one significant virtual asset—the house in Luna—had recently been reappraised, by Bob, at a mere $300 and in any case was essentially worthless, since I seemed to be unable to let it go at any price.

I resolved to redouble my efforts and expand my entrepreneurial horizons. I took up board farming—a tedious but potentially lucrative business that required I keep an eye on certain cut-rate NPC lumber vendors, buying up all their inventory whenever they had any, buying it all up again as soon as they restocked, then selling the boards in bulk (at a 100 or even 200 percent markup) to players working their carpentry skills. I also took up Bulk Order Deed collecting, a more arcane but somewhat less mind-numbing occupation, which required visiting blacksmith NPCs three times a day to pick up BODs and occasionally striking it rich with a valuable one. And naturally I threw myself with renewed vigor into mapping the Fellucca ore sites.

After a month of such efforts, I had increased my holdings to a total of 3 million gold pieces in my bank box and, in my PayPal account, 11 U.S. dollars. A 50 percent gain, in other words, which if you looked at it that way was a fine rate of return but which, applied to my still-meager capital, meant poverty wages for at least another year and a half.

sigh, I sighed one day, IMing with Bob.

my runebook sales have totally stalled, I told him, and I told him, too, about my laborious board-farming efforts, and about my ambitious but as-yet-not-very-remunerative BOD collecting.

< 137 >

I was hoping, I guess, that he would reassure me it was all worth the trouble. I wanted to hear that I was on the right track, however disappointing my progress so far, and that there was really no way up from my humble economic position except through the hard, productive labor I was already engaged in.

But Bob just chuckled.

hehe, he typed.

The secret to making money with UO is not in doing a whole lot of work, he explained. *If you want to know how to start making some bigger bucks—here is what you do.*

I was all ears. (Eyes. Whatever.)

Buy a million gold, he said. *You can get a million gold for $20 or less.*

In fact—he digressed—*it is easy to get gold at $10 per million—but you just can't look at it directly. You go to ebay and buy yourself a trammel tower for $400, and then sell it for 40 million. That is what I have been doing for years. It takes a little more time, but if you know where to go to sell it, the time is minimal.*

I told him I'd keep that in mind the next time I had $400 to invest and the remotest clue where to find someone who would pay 40 million gp for a tower. Meanwhile?

Buy a million on ebay for $18. Buy a spined runic kit in game for 1 mil. Sell the spined runic kit on ebay for $30. Rinse. Repeat. You can buy things with gold, and then sell the item for more than the gold is worth in most cases. Esp with runic sewing kits. That's the big thing right now. Spined is a guaranteed $30, horned a guaranteed $50, barbed a guaranteed $75.

This sounded promising. But even so—a *guaranteed* $30? Bob had an eBay feedback rating approaching 10,000; mine

< 138 >

was still in the low sixties. How could I expect to command the same prices he did?

Bob said nothing for a while. For all I know he'd left his computer for a bathroom break, or gone to the kitchen for a beer. I like to think, however, that he remained seated, quietly pondering my situation.

I'll tell you what, he said finally, and that was when my situation began to change.

< 139 >

CHAPTER 18

Buying 100% LRC SUIT!!! Paying 1.5 MILLION!!!
Buying 100% LRC SUIT!!! Paying 1.5 MILLION!!!
Buying 100% LRC SUIT!!! Paying 1.5 MILLION!!!
I stood outside the West Britain Bank on the Lake Austin shard, spamming the crowd for all I was worth. I was on a horse, wearing a wizard's robe, while around me other players shouted out similar appeals. *selling fel 7x7, 500k!*, cried one (offering a small house in the low-rent Felucca region at an acceptable but not especially attractive price). *someone res my beetle pls???* yelled a bald, kilt-wearing character leading the ghost of a large blue beetle (a handsome mount, badly in need of resurrection by a master veterinarian). At the edge of the crowd sat the usual clutch of veteran players on their swamp dragons, trading gossip, talking about last night's *Survivor* episode, taking in the scene.

I enjoyed the Brit Bank scene too, but it wasn't generally the first place I came looking for LRC suits. I was only here because Bob was desperate for a Lake Austin LRC and nobody had responded to the ad I'd placed on Tradespot two hours before. Otherwise I would have back-burnered Lake Austin and focused on less labor-intensive pursuits.

< 140 >

Not that I was complaining. Why should I? In the two weeks since I'd started working as a supplier for Bob, my holdings had increased fivefold, to nearly 17 million gold pieces. He'd started me out easy. Added to his IM contacts list of Great Lakes buyers, I would get an alert whenever he needed something on my shard (a runic sewing kit, a polar bear rug) and do my best to get my hands on the commodity in question at a price lower than Bob's. It was usually easy enough. Bob bought his gold cheap and sold his items dear, so it was no problem for him to pay me well above market rates. Caught short by a late-night order for a $75 barbed runic kit on Great Lakes, he might send out a distress call to his GL list (*Paying 3 million for barbed kit! Got one?*), then I'd go out and post an ad offering a generous 2.3 million or find one selling for that or less, and in short order some lucky BOD collector would pocket a couple million and change, I would clear nearly a million reselling to Bob, and Bob, having acquired the 3 million he'd paid me at a bargain price of about $45, would net $30 at his end of the chain.

After a few days of this I got a promotion: Bob made me his go-to supplier for a popular new item, the 100% Lower Reagents Cost suit of armor, better known as the 100% LRC suit. At $60 a pop, these were selling faster than Bob could restock them, and no wonder: After years of having to keep themselves supplied with spell-casting reagents (running out of blood moss or black pearl in mid-battle, teleporting off to the mage shop to resupply, coming back to find the fighting done and the corpses looted), mages could finally just throw on an LRC suit and forget about reagents altogether.

Simple though the solution was, however, the suit itself was as complex a commodity as had ever hit the UO market. Comprised of six pieces of armor, a ring, and a bracelet, each contributing a small percentage of reagent-cost-reducing magic to the 100 percent

< 141 >

total, a typical LRC suit took weeks of hunting and crafting to assemble—and the patience of a CPA to purchase. Each suit was a unique puzzle in basic arithmetic and market lore, requiring meticulous examination to make sure the numbers added up and our retail customers' needs were met (mages demanded fully "medable" armor, for instance, their crucial meditation skill being subject to a massive penalty the instant they put on any gear not made of leather, bone, or certain specially enhanced metals). Bob wanted a steady supply of them on hand—two on every shard, twenty-two total—but he had better things to do than waste time, sanity, and eyesight clicking on endless, crumb-size images of mage-wear.

So the job went to me. Every few days Bob would send me an update on his LRC inventories (*atlantic 1, baja 2, catskills 0, chesapeake 3 . . .*), and we would do the rounds, logging in wherever he needed suits, one shard after another, meeting at Brit bank usually, occasionally at a bank in Luna or Skara Brae, where I would give him what I had in stock and, in exchange, he would give me 2 million gp per suit. Then I'd go out shopping for replacements. Eventually, Bob assured me, I would build up my own IM contacts list of semi-regular suppliers further down the food chain, but for now my first resort was to the open market of the Tradespot forums. Shard by shard, on the Atlantic forum, the Catskills, the Pacific, as supply levels required, I would scan the lists of items for sale. If I saw a suit offered at 1.5 million gp or less, I snapped it up. If I saw one selling for more, I offered 1.5 and hoped for the best. If there was nothing to see, I planted my standard one-line ad: *Buying: 100% LRC SUIT (no wep, please; must be medable)—paying 1.5 MILLION!!!* And then I waited for the offers to come in.

They always came, sooner or later. They didn't always pan out. More often than I liked, I would arrive at the designated

< 142 >

meeting spot, locate my seller as instructed (*back room of bank, wearing shroud, riding swampy*), and discover that the goods on offer were simply not acceptable. Sometimes the errors were easy to forgive, as when my inspections turned up slight miscounts (*hrm, sorry, I'm getting 98 percent here*) or skimpy bikini-style "breastplates" amid the manlier apparel (*yes, i'm aware the female armor functions exactly the same as the male—yes, i know most mages wear robes that totally conceal their armor anyway—no, i honestly don't understand why the girl stuff is so hard to sell, but ty for getting in touch and do feel free to q me again if u ever put an all-male suit together, k?*). Other sellers were more exasperating, ignoring the ad text completely and showing up with, say, a full-metal, plainly non-medable piece of 100 percent crap or, for God's sake, a 93 percent LRC suit rounded out with a 7 percent LRC weapon of some kind ("Jesus, what part of 'no wep' didn't you understand?" I would think as I politely declined the item).

All things considered, the job was a pain in the ass. But I was loving it, frankly. The steady income didn't hurt, of course—after spending months amassing my first 3 million gp, the suits business alone was earning me that much in a week—but more than the money, what thrilled me about the work was something I can't help calling, for lack of a less-improbable word, the grandeur of it all.

What to compare it to? The first time I watched a chick pecking its way out of an egg, perhaps. The moment I first grasped the logic that transforms two simple numbers into the oceanic complexity of digital information. All I know is that my new job had planted me smack dab in the middle of a profound and universal process I had only ever seen from the outside, dimly: the process by which a thing becomes a commodity, the network of transactions that connects

< 143 >

the warriors and smiths who produce the pieces to the hustler who puts the pieces together to the broker who buys the assemblage to the eBayer who buys from the broker to the player who pays, finally, $60 to own and actually use the suit.

It was a supply chain, in short, and there was nothing unusual about that except for this one very unusual thing: I was right in the middle of it, where I could see it whole, from end to end. You businesspeople, who live your days in this same, central region of the economy, do you realize what a foreign place it is to the rest of us? I don't think I realized it. But I could see now just how incomplete the consumer's perspective on economic existence is— how infantile it is, really, to go through life expecting products always magically to arrive on the shelves, never seeing and therefore never quite acknowledging the enormous social machinery that connects the jobs we do to the things we buy.

Which isn't to say it can only be illuminating to inhabit this space. The deeper I plunged into the markets of UO—the more time I spent moving through them, as through water, studying for shifts in the currents of desire and supply—the stranger it seemed to me that people did anything else in this game. Or that they could conceive of their silly, nonproductive activities—their guild wars and their chit-chatting and their home decorating—as anything but ancillary to the all-encompassing activity of the markets.

It was a strange and novel way to think. Emboldening, too. As I sat outside Brit Bank on Lake Austin that night, I realized it was time for me to start taking this business seriously. The school year was over. My wife had left town the day before for a three-week project, taking our daughter with her. I had twenty-one days now, therefore, in which to do nothing but ply my trade. Where would it get me?

I staked a guess and ramped up my commitment.

< 144 >

A Thousand Dollars and a Dream

⬇ June 17, 2003

A Momentous Day

Yesterday I put my wife and my two-year-old daughter on a plane and watched them fly away for what will be three weeks apart. I haven't had real solitude like this in a while, and I like my solitude in general, but to my surprise this has so far been as much fun as a punch in the gut. I ended up crying off and on all day, missing those girls.

Today, though, I'm resolved to make the most of it. Family and work have, to date, been the only things keeping me from throwing myself body and soul into this project, and as of this moment I am constrained by neither. Today the project begins in earnest.

Let it begin, then, with these two concrete resolutions, in token of my seriousness:

1. By the time my wife and daughter return, July 8, I will have amassed $1000 (or the equivalent in gold pieces) from UO transactions alone.
2. By the time the IRS comes calling next year, April 15, I will be able to report that selling UO goods is my primary source of income, and that I earn more from it, on a monthly basis, than I have ever earned as a professional writer.

That is all.

Ahead warp factor 5, Mr. Sulu.

< 145 >

CHAPTER 19

My forced march to profitability began auspiciously enough. On the day I announced the thousand-dollar challenge, there were 5.6 million gold pieces in my various bank boxes and $11.81 in my PayPal account. A week later my holdings had doubled twice over, to 29.2 million in Britannian gp and $38.95 in PayPal funds—over $500 worth of gold pieces and legal tender, and more than halfway to my three-week goal.

Market conditions looked favorable as well. Total sales of UO items on eBay that week amounted to $159,078, up $41 from the previous week and headed toward an annual market of over $4.1 million. And though Britannian real estate appeared to be in free fall (the average price of an 18x18 house plot in the upscale Malas region was down $35.93 that week, to a record low of $162.39) the gold piece was holding strong against the dollar at $16.72 per 1 million gp, up 18 cents over the week before.

I had calculated these figures myself, the *Wall Street Journal* having not quite woken up yet to the significance of fantasy commodities. Bob had hipped me to a sophisticated piece of eBay-tracking software called DeepAnalysis that made the calculations push-button simple. All the top sellers used it, he said, sifting

< 146 >

through the numbers for any hint of competitive advantage. But to me it seemed too glorious a tool to use so selfishly, and I'd begun the week before to publish, on my blog, a weekly report tracking the market numbers' moves.

I was happy. The UO items trade was now, at last, my full-time occupation. Mornings I woke up and sometimes went straight to work, still in my underwear, a cup of coffee my only breakfast. There would be instant messages to check—from prospective sellers, mostly, but sometimes now from eBay bidders who had purchased one of the small lots of 100,000 gp I was beginning to sell. Evenings were the busiest times; players getting home from school and work would start to churn the markets, posting items for sale on Tradespot or pestering Bob for items they wanted. If I managed to pull myself away from the screen for dinner, I usually ran down to Haight Street and back for takeout, sometimes eating at my computer while I scanned the trade sites for deals. If I stayed home instead, chances were I went to bed still dressed in the same T-shirt and briefs I'd woken up in.

The house felt lonely, of course, and it concerned me somewhat that I was spending nearly every moment of a beautiful San Francisco June cooped up in a small, windowless room peering at a computer screen. But the rhythms of a fledgling enterprise hitting its stride have a beauty of their own.

And besides, it's not like I was alone in that room.

hey bud

hey radny what up

man, back in the day, were you a player? asked Radny. *I need some advice*

a player? lol ah, you don't even know what that means

sure i do--like with the leh-dehs?

yeah

um. not rilly

< 147 >

so i went to the prom on Saturday with this college freshman,
he explained, *had a blast afterwards*

but now--

No. Enough. Suffice it to say the poor kid was having girl trou-
bles and had chosen to pour his half-broken teenage heart out to
me—not so much for advice really but just because, as he told
me, he *needed to talk to someone about it.*

But why me? And what to make of the trust he placed in a 40-
year-old half-stranger he happened to share an imaginary mansion with? I marveled at it, and at the trust I placed in him. And
mostly what I marveled at was that the currency of this trust
turned out to be, by and large, not emotional—not the sort of
unexpectedly intimate personal revelations chat rooms have become famous for—but economic. The most significant token of
Radny's trust in me was not that he told me about his love life
but that he kept his every virtual possession in my house, from
which I could at any time, if I so chose, banish him bereft of all
his stuff. In turn I showed my trust by placing 2 million gp with
him for safekeeping, and I would have had to reveal some very
personal stuff to him to top that for intimacy. Frankly, I preferred
sharing assets. And though I wouldn't have minded getting my 2
million back with a little more dispatch, Radny seemed to be
doing the best he could:

*i'm still working on it. i got a million back have to sell the rest
of my powerscrolls to get the rest give me a week.*

I gave him a week. I gave him a few, in fact. But I don't recall ever
getting the rest of the gold—or ever seeing Radny again, for that
matter. Not that this diminished my trust in him. On the contrary,
if anybody was skipping out on our partnership, it was me. My new
success kept me constantly on the road, as it were, moving from one
shard to another to close my deals. When I did log on to Great
Lakes now, I almost always went straight to a bank in one of the

< 148 >

major cities—Britain, Skara Brae, Haven, Luna—picking up gold from Bob or delivering purchases to a customer. I hardly showed up at the house anymore, and if Radny was spending more time there now, or less, I wouldn't have had the slightest way of knowing.

I was learning, in short, that the relationship between virtual community and virtual economies is a complicated one. An economic system can strengthen the bonds between people online; it can provide some of the social stickiness missing from computer-mediated communities and reinforce the importance of social networks online (indeed, sociologists have noted the marked similarity in this regard between MMO guilds and that other essentially economic virtual community, the mafia). But at the same time, as I invested myself more and more in the economy of UO players, I could feel myself drifting further and further from their community. The universal solvent of money, which reduces all things to abstraction, was going to work now on the things that had once defined the game for me and still defined it for most players: the dungeon quests, the crafting trades, the big houses and the little chunks of fame that came with owning one.

I had little time for any of them now, and more and more I wondered what the point had been. My memory still teemed with images of midnight visits to the dark lair of the lizard men, but the feelings that had brought me back there again and again were getting harder to remember. It was therefore something of a jolt to come across, one day amid the busy second week of my sales campaign, a brief essay that reconstructed those feelings with a vividness my own powers of recollection weren't up to anymore. The essay, by Swarthmore history professor and hardcore gamer Timothy Burke, was called "MMOG of My Dreams," and it captured so effectively the hypnotic and, if you like, tragic appeal of games like UO that I pasted a big piece of it onto my blog:

< 149 >

Many MMOG players glimpse in the form an impossible possibility and that mere glimpse is enough to drive them almost mad. I include myself in this charge.

What is it that they see? Simply put, they see the enrichment of life itself through its fusion with fiction, a true Dreaming, an almost-sacred possibility of communion with imagination. A novel as capacious as life, a fiction unlimited by the labor time or mastery of its author. Life 2.0, with all of what makes life organic, surprising, revelatory, but always coupled to joy, fun, excitement, adventure. Dramatic conflict without tragedy, narrative motion without the boredom of everyday life, defeat without suffering. A fiction that one does not merely consume but always creates, where you can find out what happened next and where you can see what is happening beyond the frame of the camera or the page of the book.

Unreal, of course, and unrealizable.

Yes, that was it: Unrealizable. And that was exactly the difference, I decided, between the game that had first drawn me into Britannia and the one that was beginning now. There were strange, compelling pleasures to be found in wanting a thing you couldn't have, especially a thing as lovely as a "fusion with fiction, a true Dreaming." But what I wanted now was nothing so impossible as that. It was $1,000 profit by the eighth of July, and it was lovely in its own way, too.

< 150 >

CHAPTER 20

By July 3, I had over a hundred dollars in my PayPal account and more than 20 million gp in my bank boxes—roughly $500 in cash holdings, nicely rounded out by some 40 million gp worth of unsold inventory, and sure to grow even more in the five days remaining if profit rates held steady. But as I'd learned from my conversations with Bob, it was never wise to forget that any or all of your assets could vanish, at any moment, with the flip of a bit. And that night a stranger on the other side of the world was good enough to help me learn the lesson all over again.

It started with the kind of bargain you pat yourself on the back for noticing. A sweet deal, posted on the Tradespot UO trading site, but not quite too good to be true:

selling 110 smithy, paypal verified only for $14

To hear for yourself just how those words spoke to me, you don't have to know the first thing about the nature and function of a 110 Blacksmith power scroll. All you need to know—all I needed to know—was that Bob was paying me 2.5 million every time I brought him one. Which meant that if I bought the scroll on offer, I would effectively be buying 2.5 million gold pieces at

< 151 >

a 66 percent markdown off the exchange rate—and turning $14 into $40.

Why would anyone be selling so low? You never knew for sure. This was the mystery that kept me and Bob in business and that seemed, for that matter, to lie at the heart of market economics.

Once again it had been an epiphany for me. The childlike, magical thinking of the consumer mind looks at price tags and bar codes and imagines—I don't know—some celestial database containing the One True Price of every product under heaven. But from where I sat now I saw that things were otherwise. For any given good, there is no single price. There is, instead, a chaos of them—hundreds or thousands or millions of price points at which the market's various players would be willing to trade at any given moment, some exorbitantly high, a few shockingly low, most clustered around an average number in the middle that may, for convenience's sake, be thought of as the commodity's "actual" price.

My job, though, was not to find that center. It was to find the outliers: buy low, sell high. That's what a trader does. But somehow now that I was doing it, I didn't really feel like a trader at all. I felt instead like a certain mythic little creature I remembered from my high-school physics textbook: Maxwell's Demon. Perched between two chambers full of roiling, gaseous molecules, the imaginary imp of James Maxwell's famous thought experiment (designed as a challenge to Maxwell's own Second Law of Thermodynamics) sat studying the chaos around him, opening and closing a frictionless little door between the chambers at just the right moments, until all the fast-moving molecules ended up on one side, all the slow-moving molecules ended up on the other, and a rudimentary heat en-

< 152 >

gine stood ready to work. The point, for Maxwell, was that this was a theoretical impossibility—an overall increase in energy at the cost only of a little quick-wittedness. A something for nothing.

And the point in my case, I guess, is that just as Maxwell's Demon could never have opened his door in time if he'd had to pause and ponder the history of events that gave each molecule headed his way its particular speed and trajectory, so I could only do my job if I didn't give too much thought to the reasons a person might be offering a 110 Blacksmith scroll for $14.

So I didn't. I IM'd the seller and went about my business. When the reply came five hours later, I could barely remember what the message was about. But it all came back quickly. The seller—he called himself Eval—wasn't sure he still had the scroll; he'd have to check first. But before we traded there was one thing he needed to know:

are you verified?

Of course I had a verified PayPal account, I told him. I was glad he'd asked, in fact—it implied that he was just as wary of the dangers of trading for dollars outside of eBay as I was. Not that I wasn't going to insist on security measures of my own:

can i see the scroll first?

Eval didn't have a problem with that.

what is your email? i will send you a money request
oh, cool--julian@juliandibbell.com

sent, said Eval. *pls check your email for the money request. i will meet you at Main brit bank vault room once you have made the payment. my character's name is Andy*

I checked my email, and there was the payment request, as promised. It looked very official and offered me a login form to get to my PayPal account—but strangely, when I entered my

< 153 >

username and password it just redirected me to PayPal's home page, without logging me in at all. I tried twice without success, then finally just logged in directly through the home page and prepared a $14 payment, ready to transmit at the click of a button.

Ah, but I'm no dummy:

tell you what--i have the payment ready to send--i'll send it when we meet, k?

hold on dont send yet. my little one making noise.

A minute went by.

i am in the vault room whenever yr ready

More minutes went by.

sorry. my son is having stomach ache. i am sending him to hospital. IM you tomorrow morning before i get to work

ok--sorry to hear it--talk to you tomorrow

I *was* sorry, too. I found I always melted a little when someone on the other end of a UO conversation mentioned child care—it was such a relief just to know there are other adults out there.

And then, fifteen minutes later, PayPal sent me a note advising me that someone had been trying to log into my account from "a foreign IP address" (Malaysia, it turned out), and suddenly I realized just how sorry I was. The login form on the money request hadn't been broken, of course. It had merely, quietly, been sending my PayPal username and password to "Eval."

My heart raced as I rushed to log in to my PayPal account and change the password. When I finally got to my balance I expected to see nothing but zeroes. But it was all still there, all $121 of it intact. I thanked God for the very existence of computer security and for whatever sliver of His wisdom He had seen fit to grant the network watchdogs at PayPal.

< 154 >

Still, I had to give props to Eval, too, however grudgingly. He had a slick little con going there. He was offline, of course, when I finally called up his IM window again, and so, for the little it was worth, the last word went to me:

nervy bastard, I typed. *nice line about the kid though*

< 155 >

CHAPTER 21

The days passed, my assets grew, and finally it arrived:

⬇ **Tuesday, July 8, 2003**

The Moment of Truth

In less than an hour I will be leaving for the
airport to pick up Jessica and Lola. As announced
three weeks ago today, their arrival is my deadline:
either I have acquired $1,000 worth of gold pieces
and PayPal dollars--or I have failed the first,
modest test of this immodest proposal of mine.

It could still go either way, believe it or not.

And that was the truth. In some ways the experiment had been
a clear success. At the very least I had proved to my satisfaction
that I could throw myself into this profession without immediately turning into a total no-life geek. Solitary and obsessive
though this interlude had been, it had not become quite the spec-
tacle of bachelorish dissipation many expected it to be, myself included. I have somehow found time every day to bathe. I had

< 156 >

shaved regularly. I had on occasion left the office, and even the house, on errands not related either to UO or the barest biological necessities. And though I suspect some near and dear to me may have laid wagers to the contrary, I never—not once in all that time—ate cereal for dinner.

But the wager I had made with myself three weeks before remained uncertain. With $295 in my PayPal account and 33 million gp in the game, my cash holdings, valued at the previous week's exchange rate, stood at $839—a solid $141 short of the $1,000 goal. The only thing keeping hope alive was my 40 million gp or so in inventory, and in particular the 20 million gp worth of LRC suits Bob had promised to buy. If I could close that deal with him, I'd be at 53 million gp cash and almost certainly in the clear.

But where was Bob? I hadn't been able to reach him on IM all day. The minutes were trickling away, and I was beginning to despair. In the midst of this dilemma, Rich Thurman happened to IM me and, apprised of the situation, offered to try to find another buyer for my suits. For a brief moment I was tempted. But in the end I knew the score: a deal is a deal—even, or maybe especially, when what you're dealing in is make-believe—and I had to say no.

And just as I did, Bob's screen name lit up on my IM panel, telling me he was back online.

I had maybe fifteen minutes to unload the suits, sock away the gold, and get out the door to the airport. In the end, I managed to move only 16 million gp worth of the suits before I hit the stairs running. With 49 million banked, plus the $295 on PayPal, I was good for $1,103 at last week's exchange rate.

But was that good enough? The price of the Britannian gold piece, as I'd learned, could move pretty quickly. A 15 percent drop from one week to the next was hardly out of the realm of

< 157 >

possibility, and that would have been all it took to drop my net worth back under $1,000. The final tally, then, would have to await the verdict of the next day's market numbers.

And the verdict was:

The gp held firm (crept upward 9 cents, in fact), and I made my goal with $108 to spare.

I took the day off.

< 158 >

PART SEVEN

Bone Crusher,
Tax Dodger, Gold Broker

CHAPTER 22

Emboldened by the success of my three-week sprint to glory, I rolled up my sleeves, steeled myself for the long, hard run ahead—and settled into an extended period of slacking off.

Virtual slacking off, that is. Back in the real world, I was busy again—living a family life, preparing for our imminent move back to Indiana, closing a deal with *Wired* for a year-long contributor's contract. The contract was something of a devil's bargain. In exchange for a less-than-liveable monthly fee, it required me to write a barely manageable number of articles—just enough of them to merit me the money, but not too many, I hoped, that I'd have no time to grow my virtual trading into a reliably profitable business.

For the time being, I had just enough time to keep my hand in. Bob was still relying on me to keep his supply of LRC suits steady, but the crash course in wheeling and dealing that I'd just put myself through had turned me into a suit-trading machine, and I was able to meet Bob's demands with just an hour or two's work a day. In fact, I was piling up LRC suits faster than Bob could sell them, so I started eBaying them myself, underselling my top client by about 40 percent yet barely denting, even so, his colossal sales figures. The gold Bob paid me for the suits I con-

< 160 >

tinued to sell in 100,000 gp lots, my eBay rating inching closer to the magical triple digits with every sale. And by the end of July I'd started dabbling in 1 million-gp sales as well.

Three weeks after the close of my thousand-dollar campaign, my cash holdings had gone up nearly another thousand, by $850, and without nearly as much effort on my part. It was an encouraging performance, and God knows I appreciated the kinder, gentler pace. If nothing else, it gave me a chance to stop and ponder some of the more puzzling aspects of the job at hand.

< 161 >

CHAPTER 23

OK, so maybe I was getting ahead of myself, but the question nagged at me: What, exactly, was I going to tell the IRS next April?

By this, I don't mean the amusing but ultimately trivial question of what I was supposed to put down as my job category. (Gold Farmer? Vaporware Vendor? Merchant of Dreams?) This was a tougher one, with rather more substantial implications both for me and the Ultima Online economy in general. It was the big question, in fact, the heart of it all, the only datum, finally, that the tax man was really interested in: What, precisely, was my income?

And as a cursory examination of the IRS's official definitions of income showed me, this was a question much easier posed than answered. You might think it would have been a simple matter of counting the dollars in my PayPal account, but you would not, in that case, be thinking like the IRS. For the government, it appeared, didn't just want to know how much sovereign currency I'd acquired in a given year—it wanted to know how much value I'd acquired. Fair market value, to be precise.

< 162 >

This meant that as a matter of law it mattered not whether the payments I received for good or services rendered was in dollars or in donuts. Either way, I had been paid, and no amount of pleading the incalculably particular ding-an-sich-ness of a given donut would undo that fact. The donut's dollar value was easily enough established by a visit to the nearest Krispy Kreme—and would be, if push came to audit.

More to the point, this meant that while you were free to live outside the cash economy if you so choose, the taxable economy was not so easily escaped. The IRS is very clear about this. Consider, for example, the agency's remarkable IRS Publication 525, "Taxable and Nontaxable Income," in which a brief but thorough section on the cashless exchange of goods explains that "[y]ou must include in your income, at the time received, the fair market value of property or services you receive in bartering."

Helpfully, the section includes various real-world examples, among them the hypothetical case of an artist who gives you, the owner of a small apartment building, a work of her own art in exchange for six months' rent-free use of one of your apartments. This sounds like a lovely arrangement, doesn't it? Rather glamorous—possibly even amorous. Here are the IRS's feelings about this lyrical situation of yours:

> You must report as rental income on Schedule E (Form 1040) the fair market value of the artwork, and the artist must report as income on Schedule C or Schedule C-EZ (Form 1040) the fair rental value of the apartment.

I assume you see where all this was leading me: If I was obliged to declare as income a work of art—that is to say, an object of

< 163 >

highly subjective value that might never do anything more for me than hang in its frame on my bedroom wall—then how in the world was I not also obliged to declare the readily salable Britannian gold pieces I was piling up, whether or not I ultimately sold them for eBay's fair market value?

The case, it seemed to me, was clear: I must declare those gold pieces as and when I received them, quarterly if possible, and never mind how many of them I had managed to convert into U.S. dollars. And if this was what a correct interpretation of the rules entailed, I frankly didn't have a problem with it. Already I was keeping close track of the gold as it came in, mentally converting it into dollars long before I got around to actually doing so.

But here's where things started to get weird: What about all those people who were actually just, you know, playing the game? All those teenage boys and stay-at-home moms and hardworking weekend warriors who were buying and selling their silver vanquishing katanas and their south-facing polar bear rugs outside the West Britain Bank without any intention of ever cashing in the gold they make, without even a shred of respect for those who do—were they also required, under federal law, to report as taxable income the eBay market value of the imaginary riches they were thus acquiring?

And what about the gold and other valuable goods they acquired without ever entering into exchange with anybody else—the stuff they got by killing monsters and stealing treasure chests? No barter there, but the IRS would seem to have that one covered nonetheless. Pub. 525 again: "If you win a prize in a lucky number drawing, television or radio quiz program, beauty contest, or other event, you must include it in your income . . . Prizes and awards in goods or services must be included in your income at their fair market value."

< 164 >

OK, well what about the fact that OSI, the company that produced UO, could make a fairly defensible claim that all the goods to be found in the game remained its property, and that the eBay market was thus at best a form of mass delusion and at worst a collective trafficking in stolen goods? The IRS, apparently, could not have cared less. Here, in my very favorite section of Pub. 525, the IRS gives voice to tax law's serene indifference to certain aspects of property that lesser forms of the law can get so uptight about:

Illegal income. Illegal income, such as stolen or embezzled funds, must be included in your income on line 21 of Form 1040, or on Schedule C or Schedule C-EZ (Form 1040) if from your self-employment activity.

It gets weirder. Pub. 525 makes repeated mention of a phenomenon known as barter exchanges—organizations set up to facilitate the trading of goods and services among large groups of people, typically issuing barter credits in the form of scrip to help streamline the flow of trades. And as I thought about this description a bit, I began to realize that it rather nicely fit OSI itself (for scrip, read: gold pieces). Did this mean, then, that OSI was required, like every other barter exchange, to send out yearly 1099-B forms to all its members and, in certain cases, even to withhold taxes on the fair market value of goods exchanged?

Please, if anybody reading this is a tax lawyer, say it ain't so. Until I hear otherwise, however, I'm going to assume the IRS means just what it says—and that sooner or later some clever IRS functionary is going to read Prof. Castronova's paper on the $143 million GDP of EverQuest, put two and two together, and start initiating some very interesting audits.

< 165 >

The questions just strained harder at the limits of common sense, until I felt obliged to air them on my blog on the off chance some reader would explain to me the flaws in my interpretation of the tax rule. I posted the entry with some trepidation, actually, wondering what hornet's nest of controversy and financial woe I might be stirring up. But the response proved negligible: I heard neither from tax lawyers, which disappointed me, nor IRS agents, which did not. The questions remained unanswered, while others quickly crowded in to take their place.

< 166 >

good grief, I typed. *here's a dilemma. of the ethical variety*

I was IMing at Bob, and if there was anyone on the planet better qualified to judge the dilemma in question, I couldn't think who.

ok, remember that Bone Crusher i was asking you about?

He did. And so I explained:

It had come to my attention that a person calling himself Jammaster (pseudonym changed to protect whoever) was looking to sell an exceedingly powerful magic mace known as the Bone Crusher, one of several UO "artifacts" so rare that only one or two of each kind were thought currently to exist. The reason I knew Jammaster was selling his Bone Crusher was that he had IM'd me, pretty much out of the blue, asking if I would post it for sale on Tradespot for him, as he was temporarily unable to do so himself.

my web browser is broke, he explained.

This struck me as odd. I barely knew the guy. On the other hand, I knew an opportunity when I saw one. I quickly IM'd Bob to ask how much he would pay for a Bone Crusher ("15 million") then IM'd Jammaster asking how much he wanted for his.

i mean, i can post it for you, I added, *but maybe we can make a deal right now and save us both some hassle :)*

< **167** >

The reply, curiously, came a day later: *How much will you pay for it? To save us some hassle.*

The question flustered me, a bit. I was hoping to pay no more than 10 million, but I really didn't know what the going price was. Fidgeting, I called up Tradespot on the unlikely chance that a similar item might have been advertised recently so I could get a rough price check—and lo and behold, there before my blinking eyes was a sell notice for yet another Bone Crusher, posted just an hour or two earlier by one Harcourt (name changed again). The asking price was 10 million.

i was thinking around 8 million, I wrote to Jammaster, then quickly to Harcourt: *you still have that bone crusher?*

oh, Jammaster answered, *I had a bid of 9 at bank yesterday, I was hoping to get 10 mill even, so I can purchase a home*

no, Harcourt answered, *scammed :(*

Me: *scammed? how?*
Harcourt: *i was gonna sell it to this guy. i had it locked down in my house. the guy came to my house and waited outside while i went in to get it. the second i unlocked it, it disappeared. i guess he snuck in somehow.*
Me: *i'll be damned*
Harcourt: *yeah. sucks.*
Me: *when did this happen?*
Harcourt: *about 30 mins ago*
Me: *what was the guy's name?*
Jammaster: *If you can pay 10, ill meet you anywhere right now =)*
Harcourt: *Jammaster*

Oh.

< 168 >

So there it was: Jammaster had stolen the artifact from Harcourt, burgled it right out from under his nose. And there I was: stuck between a dirty deal and a quick 5 million gp profit. I'd been stolen from in the game before, and I knew how much it hurt. Players can use hiding and thieving skills to slip into your house right under your nose and walk away with everything they can carry. It's not just impoverishing, it's humiliating, and I wasn't eager to be part of any such business. That Jammaster had lined me up as a fence a full day before committing the crime didn't help—anybody that calculatingly predatory was plainly nobody to get mixed up with.

And so, vexed, conflicted, and, finally, stumped, I turned to Bob for advice. I IM'd him the details and sat back to await his response. There was a nice long Solomonic pause, and in it I realized I was expecting, and half hoping, that Bob would advise me to walk away from the deal. As categorical as he'd been about the ethics of trafficking with gold farmers, I felt certain he would tell me now that in the long run my reputation, karma, and conscience were far more important to my business than any quick killing at some poor burglary victim's expense.

But virtual reality is a funny place, and here is what Bob replied instead:

Well—to be honest—stealing in game is not unethical to me. Rogue/thief is a player skill—so I would have no problem with that. Now, if it involved real life theft—real money or out of game scamming—that is a totally different story. But using stealth/stealing in game is totally acceptable in my mind

I shrugged and laughed—and quickly closed the deal with Jammaster. Then just as quickly I resold the Bone Crusher to Bob, and as I counted up my profit, I couldn't help sharing a wink and a chuckle with the thief who had made it possible.

< 169 >

good luck with that house you're buying, I IM'd to Jammaster, *and be sure to lock it up tight when you get it :)*

why?

lotta thieves around :)

There was a pause, then finally: *lol. i know what ur hintin at*

just an observation, I replied, *about this wicked wicked world we live in ;)*

Yeah, I was pretty pleased with myself. But since then the amusement has faded, and despite Bob's serene advice, the ambivalence remains. Was it all just business, fair and square—or did I in fact buy that Bone Crusher with a piece of my soul?

Reader, I'll let you be the judge.

< 170 >

CHAPTER 25

⬇ Saturday, August 9, 2003

Enough Already

Do you mind if I ask a personal question? What are you doing here?

I mean, it's the second week in August. If you were European, you would already be halfway through your annual six-week vacation. Do you really think reading this blog on the sly at work even remotely resembles a break from the misery of 21st century, productivity-obsessed American capitalism? (And if you are European, why are you here and not passed out face down in the sand outside some beach bar in Ibiza or Phuket or wherever it is you're supposed to go to pretend to escape the meaninglessness of 21st century, welfare-state EU capitalism?)

Enough already. Go away. And if you don't, don't come here looking for more excuses to stay planted. As of this evening I will be on the road with

< 171 >

Jessica and Lola, headed east and homeward--after a
glorious year in San Francisco--to somewhat-less-
than-glorious South Bend, Indiana. This will be my
last entry for at least a week, maybe two.

You'll survive, I promise.

We drove eight days, through northern Nevada, Wyoming, South
Dakota, Minnesota, Wisconsin, and Illinois, without so much as
a peek at our e-mail inboxes, and we arrived in South Bend to
discover that I had become an international celebrity. BBC News
Online had run a brief article on my project. *O Jornal do Brasil*,
a daily newspaper in Rio de Janeiro, had run a longer feature and
even reprinted one of my blog entries in its entirety. And soon I
was invited onto National Public Radio's "The Connection," a
call-in show, where I was joined by MIT professor Henry Jenk-
ins, noted advocate of video games and gaming culture, and
Wonderbread delivery man John Dugger, current owner of what
had once been Troy Stolle's large tower.

The show was pleasant enough, though I was more or less pil-
loried by the callers, who tended toward the opinion that my customers were cheaters by definition and I, at best, their willing ac-
complice. A few days later I found myself on the phone with one
Marcus Eikenberry, aka Markee Dragon, who'd been a top seller
in the UO market for years and wasn't the least surprised to hear
I'd been given such a hard time. The controversy about our line
of business, he reminded me, had been there from the beginning,
and from where he sat, it wasn't hard to guess which side of the
argument NPR's typically left-leaning listeners would come
down on. "It's like there's two kinds of people in the world, the
ones who think this is unfair and bad for the game and all that,
and the ones who think it's just fine and nobody else's business,"

< 172 >

he said. "And it's probably Democrats on the one side and Republicans on the other."

Being a life-long left-leaner myself, I found the comparison more than a little irksome, not least because I couldn't see any obvious way Eikenberry was wrong about it. Nor was I much inclined to argue with him anyway, considering the circumstances: He had called to offer me a job.

Eikenberry worked full-time for the U.S. Department of Energy somewhere in Oregon, but in his off-hours he ran what was perhaps the best-known Web site in the UO retail business: Markee Dragon Brokers. Staffed by a cooperative of six or seven high-volume gold sellers, the site offered a variety of goods and services, including cross-shard gold transfers (players quitting one shard to start life anew on another could give their gold to a Markee Dragon broker on the old shard and trust him or her to deliver the same amount, less fees, on the new), sales of game-time codes for gold (allowing players without credit cards, or even real money, to pay their monthly UO subscription fee in gp), and of course straight-up gold sales. The brokers were free agents, more or less, setting their own prices, handling their own deals, but their collective marketing power was greater than the sum of its parts. The Markee Dragon brand name attracted customers for the brokers, and in turn, the reliable, round-the-clock sales force that the brokers represented kept the brand name attractive.

When a broker quit the team in mid-summer, therefore, Eikenberry didn't wait to put the word out: he needed a replacement. Bob, already a member of the team, gave him my name and email address, messages were exchanged, and in short order, to my astonishment, I was on the phone with Markee Dragon, sitting for a job interview.

"To be honest, if it weren't for your blog and the publicity it's getting, I wouldn't even be considering you for the position,"

< 173 >

said Eikenberry. "Your sales volume and depth of experience aren't nearly up to the level I usually look for."

Fuck you, too, I thought, knowing full well I had no right to. Eikenberry was right, after all: International celebrity or not, I was still a noob, and to this day I wonder whether he made the right decision offering me the job. But offer it, at last, he did, and I accepted gladly, marveling at the speed with which I seemed to be moving into the charmed inner circle of UO professionals.

Nor was this the only good omen I received that week. The day after the NPR interview, John Dugger sent me a friendly email and a proposition I could hardly refuse:

"Now to the heart of the matter, if ya might be interested in buying my account on UO, the one with the tower, if ya think you can make a profit on it. I have stopped playing uo and went to swg [the newly launched Star Wars: Galaxies]. if interested just mail me back, I know yer pretty busy."

I could hardly believe it: Dugger was offering me the chance to be the next owner of Stolle's tower. It was all I could do not to ask him how much he wanted and offer double, but I forced myself to think like a trader. Breaking out the assets bundled up in Dugger's accounts—characters, houses, assorted loot—I roughed up a guess at the total resale value and offered a little less than half: $250.

"Sounds good," he wrote back.

And that was that. The nine-room, three-story stonework house that once helped teach me what it meant to own a piece of unreality was now my own.

< 174 >

CHAPTER 26

Now surely, it seemed to me, I had arrived. Well-known and well-connected, a credentialed gold broker with my business name ("PlayMoney") in boldface HTML at the top of Markee Dragon's site, I sat back and waited for my ICQ panel to light up like a Christmas tree.

I tried to keep my expectations realistic. I was not yet a full-time pro, after all. Hoping to get a running start on my contractual obligations to *Wired*, I was spending most of my work week researching and pitching story ideas. The virtual-goods trade was taking up most of what remained: an hour or two of Tradespotting to keep Bob's suit supply topped off, an afternoon session every Wednesday to get my ten-day eBay auctions listed, a shorter one Sunday evenings for the seven days, and ten- to fifteen-minute delivery runs whenever auctions closed or repeat customers IM'd me with an order. It didn't add up to a whole lot of income, but now that I was getting exposure as a Markee Dragon broker, it was bound to start adding up to more. Between direct gold sales through the site and links from it to my eBay auctions, revenues would probably triple, I figured, but who knew? Perhaps they would do no more than double.

< 175 >

In the end, however, they did nothing at all. The success of my eBay auctions fluctuated within the same range as ever, and when I found time to man my post at Markee Dragon (a small little icon on the site's front page lit up letting buyers know when Play Money was available for business via instant message), the few orders that came my way rarely added up to a statistically meaningful difference.

The weeks went by, and the sales stayed slack, and I was obliged, at last, to take a reality check:

⬇ Sunday, September 21, 2003

Bottom Line

Now, you might think, with all the self-congratulatory press releases I've been issuing here of late, that the project is going swimmingly. Think again. If this were just a bid to attract attention, I'd be breaking out the champagne, definitely. But lest we forget, this is supposed to be a business, and as such, it's a travesty.

In the three months since I began trading in earnest, I have taken in about $2,400 in revenues and paid out about $850 in costs ($450 to buy accounts; $400 on eBay, PayPal, and other transaction fees). Of the remaining $1,550, I'm holding about $800 in reserve, for operating funds. That leaves $750, which I have generously ceded myself by way of the occasional transfer from my PayPal account to the joint checking account. $750. Three months. Need I point out that in the United States of America in the year 2003, $250 a month is not a living wage?

< 176 >

Bone Crusher, Tax Dodger, Gold Broker

Don't worry, my two-year-old is not starving, or even wanting for a new fall wardrobe. My wife remains gainfully employed, and I haven't exactly given up the day job myself (which of course is part of the reason my UO income remains so piddly). But there is more than sustenance at stake here. Indeed I have staked my honor, or something, on the claim that by next April I will be making more at this than I have ever made as a writer. And even assuming I find the courage to kick away the life support and make a fulltime effort of this, the weak cash flow thus far has made me start to wonder if the UO economy is actually capable of taking me where I aim to go.

Well, is it? Time to do some math. Let me come right out and say that it won't take a huge income to beat my best year writing: I could do it with less than $60,000. The question, then, is this: How many people actually make that much wheeling and dealing in the UO market? Does anybody?

Let's go to the charts. The DeepAnalysis program I use to crunch the weekly eBay market numbers can also break the figures down by individual seller, and while the sales numbers alone can't tell us exactly how much income the sellers are taking home, educated guesses can be made. A 20-percent profit margin seems to be a safe assumption, for instance, judging from my conversations with other sellers. Additionally, the top sellers tend to have their own online retail . . . where they may do three or four times the business they do on eBay. What kind of eBay numbers do we need to see, then, to infer an

< 177 >

income of $60,000? Well, with a 20 percent margin,
total sales would have to be five times $60,000, or
$300,000. And if eBay sales represent a third of
that, then total eBay sales would have to be
$100,000, which in turn implies a weekly sales figure
of about $2,000.

Who grosses over $2,000 a week? According to the
latest DeepAnalysis figures, only one seller, the top
dog, with $8,433.81 in sales over the last fourteen
days. The next three sellers--with $3,744.60,
$3,662.78, and $3,318.32, respectively--don't quite
make it. But assuming these low numbers reflect the
seasonal slowness of late summer, let's say these
guys are in the $60K club too. That means all I have
to do to meet my goal is claw my way up from 65th
place into the Top 4 of the 800 or so merchants
currently plying the UO trade.

Heh. And to think I was afraid this might be
difficult.

The note of desperation in my analysis must have been sharper
than I thought, for within a day the "top dog" eBayer I had referred to—Bob Kiblinger, of course—had IM'd to assure me I
was being much more pessimistic than was called for. "For one
thing," he said, "my margins are way more than you're guessing,
overall." Especially when buying and breaking up whole accounts—as he had done with Troy Stolle's and as I now hoped to
do with John Dugger's—his rates of return could still easily get
into the triple digits.

Besides, he added, I was thinking too narrowly. There were
lots of ways to make real money in addition to the simple buy-

< 178 >

low-sell-high model I seemed to have committed to. "I have one gold supplier who runs big vendor malls on about a dozen shards," he said. "He just goes around keeping them stocked and collecting gold all day, I guess." Another supplier led the biggest guild on one of the game's most popular shards and had worked out a sweet little racket for himself: Having effectively monopolized the best hunting spots on the shard, the guild required its rank-and-file members to pass along choice cuts of whatever loot they bagged to the aforementioned leader, who sold them to Bob in a steady, income-producing stream.

In time I would learn of other, equally robust business models: the house-camping specialty, perfected to the tune of $35,000 a year by a Canadian player who roamed the Britannian countryside looking for and cataloging "condemned" properties (houses marked for deletion unless their absentee owners logged in within the next five days), then laying claim to the valuable plots as soon as they went vacant. Or the BOD-collection business I heard about from a family team in California, who sent a veritable army of blacksmith and tailor characters out each day to gather Bulk Order Deeds, filling the rarest of them and selling off the rewards for gold, which they in turn sold for dollars.

From all these enterprises I drew a measure of encouragement, heartened to see just how hardy a variety of gainful occupations the UO economy could sustain. But in all of them, too, I recognized the critical importance of a resource I was finding it miserably hard to come by: time. Bob's beloved whole-accounts trade, in particular, filled me with an acutely gnawing sense of futility. Having now bought three accounts myself and done some cursory assessment of their assets, I had come to the sad but ineluctable conclusion that the additional work of sorting, listing, and selling them all would take every spare hour I had between then and Thanksgiving.

< 179 >

I couldn't afford to leave my profits locked up in product for that long. Until I could devote more time to the business, I needed to focus on commodities with a much quicker turnaround. I stopped listing my runebooks, stopped looking for accounts to buy, began to realize that even LRC suits were too labor-intensive a product for the kind of growth I aimed for. Efficient though I'd grown at sniffing out the best suit deals and counting up the LRC points, why was I wasting the precious little time I had on all that shlep work anyway? I needed, for now, to zero in on the one product in my line that more or less bought and sold itself.

Gold.

I hesitated to make the commitment. Nothing I'd been up to so far was what most people would call honest work, of course, but even in the unreal context of the UO economy, the gp market seemed particularly distant from anything like real production. Buying gold with dollars and dollars with gold, cycling endlessly from one to the other—what did that have to do with life in Britannia? I thought I'd left the seductive fictions of the game behind, but as I contemplated a retreat into the gold market, I felt with a sort of dull ache my attachment to the stories that had given rise to every account, every house, every little piece of armor I might handle: the quests and characters, the crafting careers and guild politics, the histories rarely revealed to me but always implied. I didn't want them pushed aside now by the much more abstract story money always tells.

In the end, though, these sentiments didn't count for much. What counted was a late-night IM from someone who'd seen my name on Markee Dragon and made the reasonable if mistaken assumption that I was a major player in the gold-piece market:

< 180 >

looking for 100 million by next week. 10 million each on 10 shards. what is the best price u can give me?

I didn't know what to say. This was ten times bigger than the biggest order I'd ever gotten and quite a bit more gold than I'd ever possessed at any one time. I wasn't even sure I could come up with the full amount on all ten shards in less than a week, let alone at a price I could profit by. But I wasn't about to let this one get away.

$14 per, I answered, giving a steep discount off my standard $18 per million. I wasn't able to buy gold much cheaper than $12 per at the time, but I could live with a margin that slim as long as it landed me a deal this fat.

we're going to need it cheaper than that, he said. *this is a longterm operation that will be buying a LOT of gold on a regular basis*

The whole thing was starting to sound fishy, but the buyer promised to pay up front, by Western Union money order (good as cash), so I took the bait and let myself get talked down to $12.50 per million.

What I did next is not something I have any very clear recollection of, but I know it happened, because I couldn't have pulled off the deal otherwise. And besides, PayPal records don't lie: On September 30, 2003, I transferred $500 to the notorious gold farmer Richard Thurman and received, in exchange, 10 million gold pieces each on the Atlantic, Pacific, Chesapeake, Catskills, and Napa Valley shards.

It was a desperate measure, but it paid off. My buyer wired me $1,250, I delivered, and thanks to Rich's cut-rate prices, a $50 profit turned into something closer to $200. The buyer, as it happened, never contacted me again, and I'm sure I told myself I'd never buy from Rich again either. What would Bob think if

< 181 >

he found out? What would Markee Dragon and the other brokers say if they knew I'd jeopardized the reputation of the team this way?

But again, PayPal doesn't lie: By the end of the year I had bought gold from Rich another eight times, for a total of $3,690 in purchases. And those deals, yeah, I do remember most of them.

< 182 >

CHAPTER 27

Go Ahead, Scammer, Make My Day

Longtime readers will recall that I once narrowly escaped losing control of my PayPal account to a wily scammer. I was lucky that time, and I guess luck can't hold out forever. Yesterday, PayPal informed me that I'd lost round two: An $80 payment I'd received a week before for 5 million gold pieces was being reversed as fraudulent.

It's just about the commonest scam there is, and generally speaking, the easiest. Most often it's just some teenage miscreant using Mommy's credit card to run up a tab she will truthfully deny having any knowledge of. In such cases, as my old friend and mentor Mr. Big [the *nom de blog* I had given Bob Kiblinger] informed me, the wisest recourse is simply to scare the crap out of Junior with threats legal and semilegal.

So I put on my best Charles Bronson game face and fired off a message laced, I hope, with just that tone of friendly menace that chills the spine of

< 183 >

bit-part punks in 1970s action movies. "Hi," I wrote. "I am writing to let you know something: I buy and sell UO stuff for a living, so I take fraudulent payments very seriously, and I will pursue them to the point of putting you in jail, if need be." If this didn't work, Mr. Big advised, I should ratchet the threat level up to scarier options, like telling the kid's mom and dad on him.

But as Mr. Big and I followed the leads on this guy, it grew clearer that it probably wasn't the typical teenage crank yanker we were dealing with. A quick look at the perp's eBay purchases revealed a buying spree of over $5,000 in the last week, all spent on virtual items from Ultima Online and the sci-fi MMORPG Anarchy Online. (One poor sap lost an AO account worth $2,000.)

What's more, a phone call to the eBay account holder of record put me in touch with a 21-year-old female college student and her mother, both of them exhausted and exasperated from having spent hours sorting through records, filling out bank forms, and otherwise trying to pick up the pieces from what now appeared to be a classic case of identity theft.

I was obviously in over my head now. Either the college student was far too cool a cucumber for my low-grade interrogation skills or she was telling the truth, and I was up against an unknown, semiprofessional identity hacker.

So I finally did what no self-respecting 70s action hero would have done: I called the cops. Surfed my

< 184 >

way over to the FBI's Internet Fraud site and filed a complaint. And then, one by one, I contacted all the eBay sellers the thief had bought from in his week-long spree and urged them to do the same.

Strength in numbers, and all that. And who knows? Maybe the feds will even manage to wrap their heads around the idea that virtual items have real value and come down on our perp with black helicopters and bullhorns.

And maybe, too, the next little schemer who gets it in his head to scam Play Money will stop first and ask himself: Am I feeling lucky?

Well, are you?

Punk?

The FBI never got back to me, nor did the state and local police, whom the FBI's complaint form promised to alert, if necessary. But what had I been thinking anyway? I'd gone and got myself ripped off too early in the history of online jurisprudence. Had I only waited another few months, I could have cited in my complaint the case of *Li Hongchen v. Arctic Ice*, in which a Beijing court ruled, on December 19, 2003, that Chinese MMO maker Arctic Ice owed restitution to 24-year-old MMO player Li, whose arsenal of powerful "bio-chemical weapons" (among other valuable virtual items) had been stolen by a hacker, thanks in large part to Arctic Ice's negligent security practices.

The police had laughed in Li's face when he first reported the crime to them, just as I now imagined the FBI's Internet fraud desk snickering over my complaint. But unlike Li, I still had other potential sources of redress besides the state-sponsored options.

< 185 >

With the law proving an increasingly unlikely savior, I turned to the market, where years of customer complaints about credit-card fraud and nondelivery of goods had prompted eBay and its subsidiary, PayPal, to institute both Buyer Protection and Seller Protection policies, insuring either end of any transaction for the cost of deals gone bad. Scanning the fine print of the Seller Protection Policy, I stumbled over a clause that appeared to void its guarantees in cases like my own, but I felt confident that once I gave the good people at PayPal a richer explanation of my business and its idiosyncracies, they would see fit to cover my loss.

And so I picked up the phone, dialed PayPal's customer service line, and was rewarded with a gift I would come, in time, to value far more than any mere sum of money: a five-minute conversation that I believe will one day take its place alongside Plato's *Lycidas*, Abbott and Costello's "Who's on First?" and other dialectical inquiries into the profoundest conundrums of truth and language, and which I hereby dedicate to posterity as follows:

Upon the Nature of the Intangible: A Dialogue

"Hi, thank you for calling PayPal, how can I help you?"

"Yes, hi. I just had payment reversed on a sale that I made, and I understand that because the item I sold was a virtual item from an online game, that payment is not covered by your Seller Protection Policy, and I therefore won't be getting my money back."

"That's correct."

"So, yeah, so I just wanted to check in about that and for future reference make sure that I understand just what is and isn't covered under clause 5 of the policy, which requires that 'The seller ships tangible goods.'"

"That means anything that isn't tangible isn't covered. Any kind of digitally delivered goods, or a service, like a moving service.

< 186 >

These are not covered because we need to have an acceptable proof-of-shipment like a tracking number from a shipping company."

"OK, I just want to be absolutely clear about this now. So say I ship somebody tickets to a football game—is that covered?"

"Yes, because you've shipped them tickets. That's a tangible good."

"Uh huh. A *tangible* good that gives access to an *intangible* good, right? So now, what if I ship them tickets to a virtual item?"

"What?"

"Say I write down a password that the buyer can use on a website or somewhere to take possession of a virtual item. Say I write that on a piece of paper and ship that piece of paper to the buyer. And then I give you guys the tracking number for that shipment. Would that be covered?"

"I don't think so. You would have to look at it on a case-by-case basis. You would have to wait until you have a situation like that and then come ask us whether it's covered or not."

"But these virtual items are expensive. I don't want to get to where I've already delivered something and only find out then. Isn't there any way you can give me a ruling beforehand?"

"You would have to wait until you are going to ship such an item."

"Well, OK, I am then. I am going to ship such an item."

"What exactly?"

"I'm selling an online account and I'm going to be shipping the buyer a password to the account."

"OK, I can tell you now then that that would not be covered."

"Why not?"

"Because it's a virtual item."

"But I'm not shipping a virtual item, I'm shipping a piece of paper or a floppy disk with a password for the virtual item."

< 187 >

"But you're not selling the password, you're selling the virtual item, which is not a tangible good."

"Well, neither is a football game. Football games are not tangible goods."

"But you're not selling the football game, you're selling the tickets, and those are tangible."

"So is the piece of paper I'm sending to my buyer."

Silence.

"Look, I just can tell you, right now, that the sale you're talking about is not covered."

"Well, why not?"

"It just isn't."

"I understand that. What I'm trying to understand is the reasoning behind why it isn't. Can you tell me what the distinction is between a football game and a virtual item that results in one being covered and the other not."

"I just explained that to you."

"No you didn't. You told me that there is a distinction. Can you tell me why that distinction exists?"

"Yes. Because it's company policy."

"OK. Could you tell me how that policy decision was reached, or can you connect me to someone who could?"

"I already told you, the virtual item you're talking about is not covered."

"I understand that. What I'm looking for now is a different piece of information. Can you please let me talk to someone who can give me that information?"

"I'll connect you to the managers' line."

Three minutes of on-hold music. Busy signal. Dead line.

I never saw my stolen money, needless to say.

< 188 >

PART EIGHT

Lost and Found

CHAPTER 28

⬇ **Wednesday, October 29, 2003**

Lost

I am in San Francisco tonight and lost.

I flew in yesterday and already felt like weeping even as the plane made its approach across the bay. Every street I rode through on my way into the city reminded me of the life we left behind here three months ago.

And then the hotel, and the oddly unresponsive laptop, and the calm voice of technical support telling me the hard drive was surely dead and all the data on it lost, at least for now and possibly forever. I've spent every spare moment since then mentally cataloging all that may or may not be gone, depending on how bad the damage is and how good my last backup was. The best-case scenarios are not that great; the worst are heart-wrenching.

All of which is to say that operations here at Play Money are somewhat in disarray at the moment and may

< 190 >

remain so for the next few days or even weeks. I have no way of logging in to UO, and no way of delivering the items I've sold in the last couple days (thank God for my good friend Mr. Big, who very generously agreed to fulfill the orders for me). It pains me to say also that I have no way of compiling the weekly Market Watch features, which I would otherwise have been posting right now.

I have no idea when and how I'll be able to sort all this out. My travel schedule is getting crazy: SF this week for a roundtable discussion on future directions for the promising young virtual world Second Life; Utrecht, Holland, next week for the Level Up games research conference; New York City the week after that to give a paper at the State of Play conference.

I miss my data. I miss my home. I don't even know where my home is right now.

What the hell was wrong with me? My gloom was understandable, I guess, but really: A hard-drive crash is a set-back, not an existential crisis. And the travel schedule I complained about, while grueling and a distraction from sales, nonetheless appeared to point toward an expansive future for virtual economies in general, which in turn meant good things for the likes of me in particular.

Second Life, for instance—the embryonic Metaverse whose prospects I had flown back to San Francisco to consult on, amid a roomful of software-industry gurus, technopolitical visionaries, and other bright bulbs convened by the improbably well-funded start-up company that produced the game—appeared to be pushing at

< 191 >

all the edges of what multiplayer productivity could be. The company, a bright-eyed team of techie true believers called Linden Lab, had programmed in the physics, the landscape, a currency (the Linden dollar), and assorted other fundamentals of virtual existence, but had left the rest more or less up to the inhabitants, giving Second Lifers access to powerful but simple online tools for constructing the virtual objects and architectures—houses, clothes, vehicles, pets—that they were to live and play with.

Faced with the unusual challenge, for an MMO company, of trying to stimulate rather than rein in its customers' demand for a role in shaping their virtual world, Linden Lab had already made the equally unusual decision to embrace—indeed, to encourage—the real-money trade in virtual goods, counting on economic incentive to lend momentum to the creative impulse. Now the company was toying with the idea of shoring up that incentive with full-fledged property rights, revising Second Life's click-through user agreement to stipulate that all player-created content (the design of a coffee table in someone's Second Life home, for instance, or the text and images in a book lying on that table) remained the intellectual property of its creator, not only inside Second Life, but out of it. This, too, was an almost unprecedented concession among MMOs, which typically require as a condition of logging in that players transfer to the game owner their copyright in any and every expressive act they might commit within it, down to and including the way their avatars wear their hats or the hot elf-on-elf action they improvise in private chat channels.

There are some defensible reasons, both legal and economic, for the far-reaching control most MMO developers exercise over their virtual domains, but if anyone in that conference room thought Linden Lab ill-advised to loosen their grip on Second Life, they kept it to themselves. A tingling and vaguely political excitement was the dominant mood—a sense that distributing

< 192 >

control more equally among the stakeholders of an online world was good not just for business but for society. While PowerPoint graphs of Second Life's population growth and images of its surreal player-made landscape played on a screen above our heads, a famous legal scholar in attendance made the case that Western democracy itself—with its free markets, universal suffrage, and bill of rights—had succeeded mainly because it proved the most efficient and least costly way to manage massively multicitizen societies. Why should it be different for the massively multiuser collectivities emerging online?

I left the Linden Lab offices that day wondering if I would ever again be in the presence of a group of people so convinced of the historical import of digital playgrounds, but a week later I found myself in Utrecht, Holland, amid a crowd whose collective capacity to take video games seriously put the previous week's to shame.

This was Level Up—the first annual Digital Games Research Conference, attended by over 500 academics from both sides of the Atlantic (and Pacific) and branded as a coming-out party for the emergent scholarly discipline of game studies and its newly formed professional organization, the Digital Games Research Association. At this, the "Woodstock of game studies," which *Wired* had sent me to report on, I sat down to a disciplinary smorgasbord of ways to read significance into games: Ethnographers tracked the dynamics of community among Quake modders and EverQuest powergamers; high-theoretical lit-crit types cited Foucault, Derrida, Benjamin, et al. by way of deconstructing the pleasures of Dance Dance Revolution and Knights of the Old Republic; and one keynote speaker, in the conference's most genuinely Woodstockian moment, declared the advent of video games a "revolution" and "one of the most important contributions to human culture that led from the computer."

< 193 >

That this assertion placed Pong and its descendents on about the same level of human significance as the Apollo moon landings, the sequencing of the genome, and other such momentous consequences of computerization, went neither remarked nor contested by any in attendance, myself included. If it weren't true, after all, whatever would we all have been doing there?

And so it was that I arrived in New York City, the following week, convinced that I had heard it all—and almost wholly unprepared for what I was about to hear.

< 194 >

CHAPTER 29

⬇ Tuesday, November 18, 2003

Play Money, Meet Big Money

Brock Pierce looks like a Norman Rockwell 13-year-old, talks like a coked-up 35-year-old, and happens to have turned 23 last Friday. He is either my new best friend or my new worst nightmare.

More to the point, Brock is co-founder and chief executive officer of Internet Gaming Entertainment, the leading purveyor of EverQuest platinum pieces and Star Wars Galaxies credits. Along with a couple of his fellow IGE execs (and me, and over 100 other attendees) he was at a conference this weekend called The State of Play: Law, Games, and Virtual Worlds, hosted by New York Law School and co-sponsored by NYLS and Yale. The conference was, as the kids say, off the hizzook, and I will be digesting its many lessons and discussions for weeks to come . . . But nothing I heard there seared my brain pan quite as memorably as the hallway

< 195 >

PLAY MONEY

conversations I had with Brock and his partners
about their business.

To set things in context, let's review: I am a small
fish in this market. Others are big. But big or
small, the scale of operations never really grows
beyond the level of mom-and-pop. Mostly it's just
pop, in fact, alone at his desktop filling orders and
counting PayPal receipts, even when they add up to
mid-six-figure annual profits.

Imagine, therefore, my surprise upon learning that
in addition to the half dozen executive types
working out of IGE's Boca Raton headquarters, the
company employs another 65 Chinese citizens at its
Hong Kong base of operations, the majority engaged
in 24/7 delivery of virtual goods . . .

And imagine, finally, the shock and awe I felt upon
learning that IGE is now, as a matter of company
strategy, targeting all game-currency markets with a
player-base of 250,000 or more, which as of this
year includes my own Ultima Online.

I swallowed hard and tried not to sound too pathetic
when I told Brock & co. I'd be interested in working
with them in the UO market. "Well, we're always
looking for suppliers," replied Alan Debonneville,
co-founder and COO, grinning sort of like a fox
inviting a hen over for dinner.

And frankly, I wasn't too unhappy to get the
invitation. I could do worse than end up in the
belly of a supply chain like theirs, after all. But

< 196 >

there's no sugar-coating what's about to happen
here: I haven't even had a chance to get my little
five-and-dime up and running, and already the Wal-
Mart is coming to town.

It was worse than that, actually. In truth, I didn't mind so
much IGE's threat to my budding livelihood. It was the threat
to something far more fragile that troubled me. Call it my sense
of professional direction. Call it a reason for living. Either way,
my hold on it had come to feel especially tenuous of late. The
depth of despair I'd fallen into after my computer broke and
left me virtually adrift in San Francisco may ultimately have
had no single explanation, but I was coming to think the explanation was precisely this: I had no idea what I was doing there.
Or anywhere.

I hadn't had much of an idea the year before either, of course,
the year of my fellowship at Stanford. But there at least I'd been
granted the rare freedom to let the question lie—to trust that an
answer would emerge from the free play of my intellectual passions and conversations. Now, though, I was back in the real
world, and the real world demanded something rather more solid
in the way of professional identity. And as it happened, neither of
the two identities I was improvising for myself had yet convinced
me it was up to the demand.

At conferences, presenting myself as a commentator on the socioeconomic and other broadly important aspects of multiplayer
game worlds, I secretly cringed, wondering how long it would
take the others there to see through the scam. Anyone familiar
with my blog and the project it documented would figure out
sooner or later who they were really dealing with: a man obviously more eager to live in worlds of play than to understand
them, purporting to work long hours teasing out their signifi-

< 197 >

cance while really just securing an excuse to spend longer hours screwing around in them.

Not that I really believed in this caricature of myself; but neither, on the other hand, did I exactly *not* believe in it. From the Second Life roundtable on, I felt a steady self-doubt eating away at my ability to join in the discussions with much enthusiasm. By the time I got to State of Play, the fraudulence of my pose was almost palpable to me, and I engaged the relatively heady policy questions on offer there with all the confidence and entitlement of a dog sneaking scraps off the dinner table.

At the end of State of Play's first day I snuck away for beers with Edward Castronova, the economist, and a pair of up-and-coming legal scholars named Dan Hunter and F. Gregory Lastowka, whose first paper on law and virtual worlds had just been accepted by the prestigious *California Law Review*. It should have been a moment of high spirits, and I imagine for the others it was: Two months earlier, the four of us had co-founded a collaborative blog called Terra Nova, which had already become a magnet for game scholars, designers, and other thoughtful observers of the MMO scene, and this was our first meeting in the flesh.

But even here, amid toasts and jokes and the company of new friends, I couldn't help feeling at sea. I was scheduled to speak the next day about the implications of virtual economies for the existing intellectual-property regime—the same question that had fired my imagination when I first encountered it in Blacksnow's lawsuit against Mythic. In the meantime, though, Lastowka and Hunter had persuasively recast the virtual property question as a problem all its own, analogous in legal terms as much to real as to intellectual property, yet ultimately reducible to neither, and my own more hands-on exploration of the facts surrounding *Blacksnow v. Mythic* had in any case confirmed the almost com-

< 198 >

plete irrelevance of copyright concerns to the actual issues involved. I should have found the elusiveness of the problem exciting, I suppose, pursuing it into the briar patch of questions that preoccupied my fellow conference-goers: Should virtual economies be subjected to fiscal regulation? Should the law accord MMO developers all the freedoms of creative authors or hold them accountable as governing bodies?

But all I felt was baffled. And as I drank my beer and laughed with Greg and Dan and Ted (as I now was chummy enough to call Dr. Castronova), I wondered quietly what I was missing: Had these guys really managed to cut through the haze of half-formed deep thoughts that seemed to be the closest I could come to fitting virtual worlds into the greater scheme of things, or were they all just happily deluded as to the ultimate significance of our field of study, not at all concerned, as I was, that its intellectual substance might at bottom be about as substantive as pot smoke? And either way, what business did I have being there?

As if all this wasn't demoralizing enough, there was the flipside of my professional identity to worry about—my alleged career as a virtual merchandiser—and my encounter with the slickly professional boys of IGE presented, naturally, a perfect opportunity for worry. Not that *their* pose was entirely convincing either: A quick bit of post-conference Google work revealed that Brock Pierce (former child actor and co-star, with the comedian Sinbad, of the 1996 *Home Alone*-knockoff *First Kid*) had at the age of eighteen been co-founder and executive vice-president of the Digital Entertainment Network, one of the most notorious figments of smoke, mirrors, and scandal to have pumped hot air into the Internet bubble. Slated for a $75 million IPO in 1999, the company instead crashed and burned amid news that its three top officers, Pierce among them, had allegedly molested underage boys working for the company. Pierce and the others spent the next

< 199 >

few years abroad, conveniently beyond the reach of civil judgments and criminal charges, until police at last arrested them in a seaside villa in Spain stocked with what one report described as "enormous amounts of child porn."

Well, boys will be boys, and besides, though DEN ex-chairman Marc Collins-Rector wound up doing a couple years' jail time, Pierce seems to have beaten the rap. And it's not like any of this information did much to soothe my anxiety anyway. Even assuming Pierce's checkered past had any bearing on his present endeavors, the sheer organizational momentum of the enterprise put the seriousness of mine very much in question.

Who, after all, was I kidding? Rubbing shoulders with the Bob Kiblingers and Markee Dragons of the world, I could at least assure myself that, though my income was barely a fraction of theirs, my circumstances were roughly similar. One-man operations that had started out amateur, half-playing the trade, half-astonished it could turn a profit at all, they had risen almost by accident to the top of the profession—and who was to say I couldn't, too? But now that IGE had arrived to redefine the top, the path from here to there was suddenly harder to make out, and I was left to contemplate the real difference between all the other pros and me: They had all at some point made the decision—unspoken perhaps, or even unconscious, but deep down and irreversible—to stake their futures on this absurd line of business.

I, on the other hand, remained uncertain whether my trading was ultimately just something to write about, whether my writing was ultimately just an intellectual fig-leaf covering the naked philistinism of my urge to trade, and whether my pathetically underpowered resolve would ever permit either line of work to define me once and for all. For the time being I couldn't say for sure that I wasn't just playing at both, and though the blurring of

< 200 >

lines between work and play had sounded great as a research question, as a way of life it so far felt like crap.

The dejection these thoughts inspired brought me close to abandoning it all—the blog, the business, the pretensions to long-range profitability. And had I come to this pass just a week before, I suppose I might have followed through on the impulse. But in the brief interlude between my return from Holland and my trip to New York, I had been granted the blessing of another option. It had come to me in the form of a fax, sent from an exotic-looking international phone number and bearing the following message from a stranger:

Dear Mr. Dibbell,

How do you do?

Let me introduce myself: I am living in Hong Kong and working as coordinator and investor on high-tech projects (mostly biotech) such as vaccines and anti-tumor therapies. All of these projects are for long term and in the mean time I continue to look for good projects that we can work on.

Recently, I read your article "The Unreal Estate Boom" and realized another opportunity that we can collaborate together to make real good money. My proposition is rather straight forward: I will hire as many people as required in China to play various online games such as UO, EQ or SWG and "make" all those virtual products that can sell. You act as my partner in the selling of the virtual products and collection of sale proceed and remit my share of costs and profits to me. Your share of investment is just by providing me with the necessary geared-up accounts (say 5 to 10 accounts to start with). I will invest in buying 10 sets of computers and other hardware and software,

< 201 >

PLAY MONEY

renting a place, putting in telecommunication lines etc., and hire 10 full time workers to play the games, and all you need to do is to sell our products once every week or so and then remit my share to me.

According to my study on the game EQ, the platinum pieces are still selling at a reasonable prices of about US$80–90 per 100K, the costs of making the 100K pp in China is estimated to be about US$35, leaving a healthy margin of $45–55. My proposal is that you share $22 per 100K pp sold. My calculation is that 10 full time workers can generate 2 to 2.5 million pp a week, equivalent to $1,600 to 2,000 sales a week. If things go well I can invest further to scale up the operation so that we can have 50 to 200 workers (certainly, you provide more accounts), within 2 to 3 months, going full time on any games that can make money. In this scenario, we are talking about weekly sales of about $8,000 to 40,000 and both of us are making some good money.

The above explanation is the nutshell of my proposal. It is simple and you have no risk (even the accounts you provided are yours to control and resell if you are not happy with the partnership), except spending some of the valuable time to sell the products that I produced.

I like to work together with my partner on an open and honest attitude even though we don't know each other well yet. I am prepared to email you my CV (certainly yours to me) for reference. There are numerous opportunities around and I prefer to work wholeheartedly together to win rather than playing tricks or cheat to take advantage of others for a short term gain. The online games shall have several years of "haydays" ahead before other forms of entertainment replace it, so we are aiming at

< 202 >

make hundreds of thousands (if not millions) dollars together, we shall treat each other with dedication and respect.

Please keep this message confidential because such operation can be copied by others who have connections in China and become our competitors.

Looking forward to hearing from you very soon.

The message was signed, with "best regards," by Gordon L_____, CEO of _____ Limited, and I carried it with me through every waking moment of the three days I spent in New York. I had laughed out loud the first time I'd read it, and shaken my head, and wondered at the madness of the business world. But the encounter with IGE had subsequently rearranged my notions of entrepreneurial madness somewhat, and heading home to Indiana, I was having very different thoughts about the letter in my pocket, the sum of their various implications being this:

Mr. Gordon L_____ would indeed be hearing from me very soon.

< 203 >

CHAPTER 30

On or about the same day I received the fax from Hong Kong, a 30-year-old unemployed software programmer in Little Rock, Arkansas, walked into his study not long after midnight and approached the computer there with a prayer on his lips. He was praying for a break.

The man's name was Mithra, or at least that's what all the other UO bot farmers knew him as, and like a lot of them he'd been having a rough six months. Through June, July, August, and into September, Lee Caldwell's rain of fire on the EasyUO cartel had not let up. Blacksnow swept the prime bot-farming spots several times a day, reporting any rival bots they found and riding especially hard on any they found running Birds, the cartel's trademark exploit and principal moneymaker. In time they even wrote informant bots to do the policing for them. With all the bannings that were going on, at least one farmer had opened and lost over a hundred new accounts by the time the summer ended. A few cartel members eventually found ways to dodge the daily sweeps, but even so, the time and effort wasted on evasive maneuvers kept production levels far below what they'd been in the booming days before all hell broke loose.

< 204 >

Lost and Found

When Lee at long last tired of his campaign, the cartel breathed a collective sigh of relief and went right back to doing what it did best: Buying three hundred raw birds at five gold pieces each from a butcher NPC, then cooking them for resale to a tavernkeeper at 6 gp each—over and over again, 30 times a minute, 24 hours a day. It was a mindless loop, essentially, but keeping the Birds exploit going at maximum profitability required brain-melting, ass-numbing stretches of deep-level hacking—and paid out in sums well worth the effort. At more than 500,000 gold pieces per hour per bot, running flat out, Birds left all previous farming exploits in the dust, including the infamous Bandaids, whose 350,000 gp per bot-hour had boggled the minds of ordinary players when publicly revealed in May.

Mithra ran Birds, but though he was friendly with most of the cartel's farmers, he'd never been admitted to its inner circle and was obliged to work out the exploit's deepest secrets on his own. This would have taken a while even under the best of circumstances, but with the GMs' constant harassment further slowing him down, it wasn't until October that Mithra finally got Birds working for him at top productivity. The timing was miserable: Two weeks later, the devs announced that the next revision of the game's code—the upcoming Publish 21, due in late November—would include measures aimed at stopping all the most profitable exploits dead.

Which wasn't all that complicated a thing to achieve, as it happens. The technology of macro farming was and always has been a diverse ecosystem of strategies and techniques, but its life blood, at the time, was a single, somewhat brain-dead feature of the UO economy known as static vendor pricing. And to understand why this was so, all you have to do is think about how Birds made money: Buy raw poultry cheap, sell cooked poultry dear, pocket profits, rinse, repeat. As long as you could keep the cycle spinning faster

< 205 >

than an unassisted player could, it was a rock-solid get-rich-quick scheme. Try the scheme in anything like a real-world economy, however, and it would run face first into the law of supply and demand. A butcher suddenly getting 43,000 chicken orders a day would register the rise in demand and raise prices to the sky, while the same number of roast chickens offered to a tavernkeeper would smother the market in supply and push prices to the floor. In no time, you'd be buying high, selling low, and hemorrhaging whatever money you had left. But UO, happily, was not the real world, for there the prices set by merchants never changed, and upon this one simplifying fact the most dependable bot-farming strategies all relied.

And Publish 21 was going to shut it down. From now on, buying huge quantities from vendor NPCs would trigger vendors to raise their prices fast, and selling hugely would drive them down. Simple as that. The days of static vendor pricing were numbered, and the era of "the dynamic economy" (as the devs were calling it) was at hand.

A week or two before Pub 21 was to go live, the devs released it to a test shard so players could kick it around for a while and give some preliminary feedback. By then, the haze of apprehension and despair that had begun to settle in on the gold farmers of UO was just about palpable, and for Mithra the anxiety was especially acute. He'd quit a well-paid programming job two years before to farm full-time, and though he'd earned enough in the first year to get by on, the last several months' adversities had brought him to the brink of destitution. Now Pub 21, it seemed, was going to push him over the edge. Working at an office job did not agree with Mithra—like, *seriously* did not agree—but if he couldn't find a way around the new pricing fix, it was back to the cubicle for him. So on the same day the test shard opened, he rolled a character there and started a relentless hunt for weaknesses in the new design. And three days later, he was still at it.

< 206 >

Lost and Found

This was not one of those roam-the-countryside-in-search-of-quarry type of hunts. From the new-character inn in the center of Britain, he had walked south about two hundred feet, past the main bank, to the little brick-built butcher's shop near the water's edge, where he began to buy and re-buy absolutely stupid quantities of meat. And there he'd stood, ever since, doing nothing else: buying meat, watching how the new system handled the transaction, diddling the code on his end of the client-server connection, tweaking a parameter or two, buying more meat, watching for something to give. Here and there he'd caught a small break, a subtle shift in the vendor code's response to his probing, but nothing that opened the door to even penny-ante macroing schemes, let alone the mighty stream of profit that was Birds.

He wasn't having a bad time, really. In general he loved hard problems almost more than money itself (in college, he'd been a double major in philosophy and sociology). But now it was precisely his ability to go on devoting his workdays to problems like this one that hung in the balance. And so, although he'd never much believed in God, his prayer that night—"Dear Lord, please let me figure out a way to make some money here"—wasn't altogether insincere. All things considered, Mithra didn't see much earthly reason to be hopeful, and as he slumped into his chair, he resigned himself to the the prospect of another long, fruitless night of packet-twiddling.

But then, at about 4:00 a.m., the session took an interesting turn. Chasing a hunch, Mithra made a purchase of 4,000 slices of bacon. This in itself was something of a feat. Players normally weren't allowed to buy more than 500 of any vendor items at a time, but Mithra and other UO hackers had long before figured out ways to bust that cap. Now, though, he was trying to figure out something else. The new pricing system, he had discovered, had a 500-item limit of its own: For every 500 items purchased

< 207 >

from a vendor, the vendor would raise its price by a single gold piece. In principle, then, his 4000 slices of bacon, base-priced at 3 gp per slice, shouldn't cost him the 12,000 gp it traditionally would. Instead, if the new system worked as advertised, the cost would now swing higher in response to the massive size of his purchase. The question was: How much higher? And here, Mithra suspected, lay the key to the puzzle.

It turned out he was righter than he could have imagined: The buy went through at 12,000 gp exactly. The cost didn't rise at all. Somehow, the way he had deployed the cap-busting hack had jammed the dynamic pricing system, and if he could do it again, the Birds exploit was saved.

He clicked on the butcher to make another attempt. But then, when the butcher's sales menu popped up, he saw with some confusion that he didn't seem to have broken the new system after all. The price of bacon had gone up precisely as it should have, from 3 gp to 11 gp per slice. Not sure what to think, he sold his bacon back to the butcher to try another round of buying. And then he saw it: The *buy-back* price had gone up, too, from 1 gp to 9. He had bought bacon at 3 gp per slice and *instantly* secured himself a return of 6 gp per slice.

Mithra sat there for a moment, soaking it in. Then he tried the same trick with a 65,000-slice purchase and instantly locked in a profit of *one hundred and twenty-five gold pieces per slice*. He took a few minutes to think it all through, confirmed to his satisfaction that the implications really were as monumental as he thought, and then arose, ecstatic, to go wake up his wife and tell her the news.

The next day Mithra called the one other person he intended to tell about the discovery: Rich Thurman. Rich wasn't precisely a friend—they had a mutual respect for one another's seasoned coding skills, and they shared a wry self-consciousness of being,

< 208 >

as Rich liked to put it, "practically the only two grown-ups in the gold-farming scene." But above all, Rich had been generous with his knowledge of the UO codebase's hairiest secrets, as the other cartel members had not, and Mithra felt he owed it to him to return the favor.

Rich grasped the nature of the discovery instantly. Indeed, he was one of only a few other gold farmers who'd made much use of the item-cap hacks before, and his own ideas about how to hack the new pricing mechanisms had been running along the same lines as Mithra's. The two wasted no time, therefore, in readying their robot work forces for the coming of Pub 21.

The first order of preparation was secrecy. They needed to keep their operations hidden not just from civilians but also, especially, from other macro farmers. For that, location was crucial, and because the new exploit worked with any vendor-sold commodity, their choice of venues was practically wide open, limited only by the need for a nearby bank to dump the gold into. Mithra opted for remoteness, setting up his bots at what was almost certainly the least-visited banking site in all Britannia: a tiny village—unnamed, unguarded, and accessible only by mountain passes thick with high-level monsters—on the southern desert shore of Lake Flam in the northeast wastelands of the far-off Ilshenar region. Rich, on the other hand, selected the second-most popular bank in the game, right in the middle of Luna, relying for concealment on certain of the bank's more baroque architectural features and on his choice of commodity—bowyery feathers, lightweight and easily hidden.

Their bots in place, they started road-testing, working out snags and timing production runs. From the start, they'd both realized that this was going to be an unprecedented money maker. With its whopping price spreads and its time-saving reliance on a single vendor for both buying and selling, the new exploit had

< 209 >

clear advantages over Birds. But when they finally clocked their top production rate, on the eve of Publish 21's wide release, it was all they could do to keep from telling it to the world. Their exploit didn't just improve on Birds. It was an *order of magnitude* better than Birds: At top speed it would give them not six hundred thousand but *six million* gold pieces per hour for every bot they had running it.

I posted my weekly Market Watch two days later, as ignorant of Rich and Mithra's maneuverings as anyone else in the game. "The numbers look good this week, and why not?" I wrote. "It's the dawning of a new era in the UO economy: The Age of Publish 21." I followed this pronouncement with a brisk summary of the new pricing rules, a blunt assertion that "the golden age of the gold farmer is over," and an utterly deluded prediction that the price of the Britannian gold piece would now—at long last—begin to climb. My closing words, regrettably: "You read it here first."

By that point, the gaping rift Mithra had opened in Britannia's economic fabric had already spilled several billion gold pieces into the money supply. But I suppose it's just as well I didn't know. I was making arrangements now for a gold farm of my own, a project free of all the shady practices I had seen in every farming operation from Blacksnow's on, committed to a policy of playing by the rules and built on a—how had the fax from China put it?—on "an open and honest attitude" and a dedication "to work wholeheartedly together to win rather than playing tricks or cheat to take advantage of others for a short term gain." I didn't need to be reminded just then how much easier it was to go ahead and break the rules.

< 210 >

CHAPTER 31

"So what is your plan?" said the voice on the telephone. It was a calm and not unpleasant voice, wrapped in a paper-thin Cantonese accent that somehow added to the serenity of tone. But the question hardly put me at ease. It was the middle of the business day in Hong Kong but 11 p.m. in Indiana, and I had not remotely been expecting Gordon's phone call or had a moment's chance to collect my thoughts and prepare what might, by the lights of this 47-year-old biotech executive, pass for a plan.

In fact, I hadn't thought much further planning was necessary at this point. By now we had exchanged a few e-mails clarifying how our collaboration might proceed. I had asked for, and received, assurances that Gordon's workers would in no instance be using software exploits or other bannable techniques to acquire their loot. I had explained also that I was in no position just yet to help him with EverQuest accounts, and he had agreed to focus initially on UO.

Realizing, too, that there was no way I could possibly market the amounts of virtual swag Gordon was proposing to produce, I had invited Bob into the partnership. This had been a tricky proposition. I knew how vehemently Bob disapproved of dealing

< 211 >

with bot farmers, and I could only guess what he'd think of factory farming. Technically, of course, it was just a more organized form of RMT, paying hourly wages for "player"-produced goods rather than bidding for them on eBay, so in UO, at least it wouldn't even have been against the rules. But with Blacksnow still the only professionals even rumored to have set up an off-shore loot shop, the practice had a somewhat tainted reputation, and I hesitated to bring it up with him.

But in the end I had to ask:

so hey, i was wondering if i could run a proposition by you

OK--grt--what did you have in mind?

lol. i can barely bring myself to say it

Hehe--are you going to tell me how good looking I am?

lol, that would be easier

I took a deep breath, and typed:

ok, 2 words

And then: *chinese sweatshop*

Ahahahahahaha

After his laughter died down, though, Bob ended up accepting the invitation more enthusiastically than I could have hoped. He was in a period of expansion himself, branching out into games beyond UO and finding that the more recently launched titles in particular—Star Wars Galaxies, Final Fantasy XI—were particularly lucrative. *SWG is just too good to be true . . . maybe $3,000 per month profit,* he'd said, and with ambitious new MMO projects entering the development pipeline every few months, there was no end of virgin territory to be mined. He'd already been thinking he could use a partner on the retail side of things, just to manage all the growth that lay ahead. And with a partner on the production end to help us maximize supply from the moment the next big game came on-

< 212 >

line—well, said Bob, *If we could have done this when SWG started up, we could both retire right now.*

And that, for me, was plan enough: Get in, get rich, and get out quick enough to spend a leisurely second half of my life figuring out what the point of it all might be. But Gordon seemed to be looking for something a little more specific, and as I was eager to conceal from him any hint of doubt about my own seriousness of purpose, I resolved to wing it:

"Well, keep in mind that big changes have come in with Publish 21, and that's going to make the UO market a whole new ball game," I said, improvising what I hoped would hint convincingly at deep reserves of strategic thinking and inside knowledge. I brazened out an executive backgrounder on gold-farm economics and the upcoming pricing fixes, trying to make it all sound as complicated as possible and playing up the supposedly devastating effects on the botting crowd.

"That's advantageous for us, right?" said Gordon, tentatively.

"Um, right," I replied, realizing only as I said so that indeed it probably was. "Granted, it's a thin line between a bannable exploit and an honest living, and some of the money-making routines I'd thought your workers might do well to start out with—like chopping down trees, carving bows out of them, and selling the bows to NPCs—probably depend on the same static pricing the farmer exploits do. But definitely, once your guys' characters are all skilled up to where they can do more productive work like champ spawns, or maybe treasure maps, it'll be nice not to have to deal with competition from the macro farmers. And even if they do figure out a way to get back in business, I'll bet you nine times out of ten it's cheaper to do with your workers than what they'll be doing with fifty computers stacked in a closet somewhere in California."

< 213 >

"Yes, I saw that picture on your Web site," said Gordon, referring, with a certain solemnity, to the photo of Rich's gold farm. "I could not believe it."

"Well, honestly, I sometimes have a hard time believing any of this," I laughed. "I mean, these people you find to whack monsters all day long. What are they, gaming fanatics, or college kids with too much time on their hands, or what?"

There was a pause.

"They are employees," said Gordon, perhaps not getting my point, or perhaps conveying his too subtly for my grasp.

"But I mean, do they enjoy playing games all day?"

"They like having a job," he answered drily. "Unemployment is very high in China."

It was a sobering reply. Gordon's workforce was on the mainland, he explained, where the average annual income amounted to $2,000, and he said he was paying them a better-than-average wage of $1.50 per hour. I supposed that as a lifelong consumer of globally produced goods, I had always borne some responsibility for the incomes of people like Gordon's employees, but now I could see how that responsibility might come to weigh more heavily in the very near future.

"It would be nice if we could meet someday," I said, suddenly smitten with the same curiosity that had led me to wait three futile days in a Tijuana hotel to lay eyes on a functioning offshore gold factory—and dizzy, in a not altogether pleasant way, with the thought that when I finally saw one it might be as a partner in the operations.

Now Gordon laughed. "Well, that's no problem—if we make money," he said. "Actually I would like to see the States again. It's been about ten years since my last visit."

With that, it seemed, the business conversation officially ended, and whatever test Gordon had set me appeared to have

< 214 >

been passed. The partnership was a reality, and in the morning I had new email reviewing the path that now lay ahead of us:

Dear Julian,

I think the figures provided in your email will be quite profitable for both of us.

Based on one player generating $4 to $5 an hour, actually it is worthwhile to work on a large scale, say 100 people in 3 shifts and six days a week. With extract supply that may drive down the price of UO items even by 10%, we will still be quite profitable . . . I will concentrate on bringing you very steady supply of UO items, and you shall do your best to fetch the best prices so as to maximize our return. Your workload will be heavy too. If I can establish a 30 staff team to concentrate on this within a month or two, you will have to sell $1,200 to $1,500 worth of items everyday (your income will be $300 to $375). And I mean to reach that scale for sure. My long-term goal will be to maintain 100 staffs working on this game alone. Don't worry about competitions since every business has competition. Just do our best.

As I mentioned before, one of the very important contributions of yours is to provide us the appropriate accounts and practical guidance on the game. I like to suggest that you send us . . . 8 new accounts to begin with as soon as possible. This will be minimal cost on your part. We will start immediately and hopefully by early December you will have a lot of "GOLD" or other items to sell and we will have a real good Christmas to celebrate, just 33 days away. Within 2 months (or sooner) we shall have 15 active accounts to generate salable items on fulltime basis. I hope you will be satisfied with this scenario. I like to make this

< 215 >

big within a short period of time so that we are strong enough to compete with IGE or Mysupersales.com, possibly in the middle of 2004 . . .

Best regards,

Gordon

I opened an earlier email to which Gordon had attached his résumé and a photo of himself. The picture, set against a background of lush tropical foliage, showed a broad-faced, salt-and-pepper-haired East Asian man in polo shirt and large glasses, his gaze at once serious and friendly. Looking at the photo it occurred to me that, for all our many differences, Gordon was probably the only person I'd encountered in this business who approached it quite the way I did: As a deliberate vocational experiment, a half-committed leap into the dark of an alternative career. I could only guess at his feelings about the elusive vaccines, anti-tumor therapies, and other projects "for long term" he claimed to be pursuing, but if they were remotely as complicated as my feelings about my writing career, then we were practically soulmates.

In any event, he was my partner; and so, too, now, was Bob. It wasn't like I'd found a second family or anything, but it was enough to make me feel, for the first time since I'd abandoned Radny and my home on the Great Lakes shard, that I was no longer in this game alone.

< 216 >

CHAPTER 32

Sales records show that the 2003 holiday shopping season was not a stellar one for the Play Money enterprise. But I took the weak numbers in stride.

The business was in a larval stage, I told myself. I was preparing for the day, now imminent, when Play Money would grow wings and fly into the upper reaches of profitability, and for the time being these preparations were more important than any immediate revenues.

For starters, I needed to expand my online presence. eBay was a perfectly decent sales channel for now, but once the volume ramped up I would want a storefront site of my own, both to cut down the drag of auction fees and to serve as a magnet for repeat business. I could have just bought some off-the-shelf e-commerce software package and been done with it, I suppose, but I wanted the online face of Play Money, Inc., to radiate style. So I contacted an old high-school friend whom I knew to be both a graphic genius and a demon Web-site coder and, for the sum of $100 and 1 percent of future sales receipts, engaged his services in constructing a fully automated, stand-alone Play Money storefront from the ground up.

In addition to expanding, of course, I was going to have to diversify. To which end I made my first forays beyond the familiarity

< 217 >

of the Ultima Online market, tossing up an exploratory handful of eBay auctions for Star Wars Galaxies credits, which Bob supplied me at handsomely discounted wholesale prices. Bob was bearish on UO, in any case, at least as a growth prospect, and he counseled Gordon and me to focus our start-up efforts, instead, on establishing a beachhead in Final Fantasy XI, which had built up a player base of more than 200,000 in Japan and other Asian countries, and was just now entering the U.S. market.

So I bought eight copies of the game, set up accounts for Gordon's alpha team of workers, and began scouring FFXI fan sites for get-rich-quick tips to pass along to Hong Kong. I set up some accounts of my own, as well, for the retail end of things, and found myself charmed by FFXI's soft-edged, anime-inflected aesthetic (as I had not been by SWG's sci-fi world of chrome and plastic).

I created a small fleet of delivery characters, selecting the doe-eyed, childlike Taru Taru race to represent Play Money within FFXI's mythical realm of Vana'diel. And as I walked my characters one by one through labyrinths of winding, bricklaid streets toward the central marketplace of Windurst, the Taru Taru capital city, I felt both slightly seasick (my internal motion processors overloading on the game's immersive, 3D perspective after so many months of UO's comfortably flattened God's-eye view) and sorely tempted by the siren song of a new game ripe for the obsessing, a seduction strong enough almost—though in the end not quite—to pull me from the more serious business at hand: my headlong advance toward early retirement.

Those were hope-filled days. Dark clouds would gather in the distance, now and then, only to dissipate almost as soon as I found time to worry about them. On the message boards of Stratics and other fan sites, rumors started swirling about a colossal dupe spawned by the release of Publish 21—a gold gusher so prodigious it would take years to drain the flood of ex-

< 218 >

cess back out of the money supply. But the predicted economic apocalypse failed to materialize, and I decided to assume that any hoards the dupe had generated had met the same fate as Ingotdude's, deleted without fanfare once the GMs traced the rumors back to their source.

My own sales slowed to a crawl, meanwhile, and finally stopped altogether for a full five days before it occurred to me to wonder what the hell was going on. *Help! What am I doing wrong?* I typed at Bob. But Bob advised me to relax. For some reason it was like this every year, he said: For those of us who catered to MMO fanatics, the weeks before Christmas were a commercial dead zone. *I guess people actually spend time with their family or something,* he mused. *Crazy.*

So I relaxed. And soon enough I made a sale: a $24.99 100 percent lower reagents cost suit, bought by a Wyoming woman as a Christmas present for her "hubby." She didn't play the game herself and seemed a little baffled by the entire process. *I can't believe I'm buying something that doesn't really exist!:),* she said, when I met her at the Luna Bank to make delivery. Her husband played on the Sonoma shard, and I was happy to discover that the one suit in my inventory there was a very nice specimen: all-leather, all pieces dyed a deep cobalt blue. In another nice coincidence, OSI had just given out its holiday gifts for players, the usual crap (a poinsettia plant, a snowman, a snowflake, a holiday wreath), except that they came in a lovely box wrapped in festive ribbon. I cleared the crap out of the box and put the suit in, all nice and Christmas-wrapped for when hubby came to pick it up.

And then I took the rest of the year off, figuring I'd earned it.

< 219 >

PART NINE

A New Beginning

CHAPTER 33

⬇ **Tuesday, December 30, 2003**

Happy New Fiscal Quarter!

Live from the Avalon Hotel in Beverly Hills, California, I'm wishing you and yours a prosperous new year--more prosperous, at any rate, than the one I just completed, which closes with a whopping $3,131.42 in profit accrued from my dealings in virtual items.

I am on vacation now and for the first time in months don't have a single item up for sale on eBay. I suppose I should be using this downtime to strategize and regroup for a more profitable quarter going forward, but I'll save that for my return to South Bend. Meanwhile, don't worry too much about me. I've still got a few tricks up my sleeve, none of which I'm at liberty to disclose just now. Stay tuned, and stay well.

And two days after that, we were back in Indiana—my family and I—our two-week holiday visit with my mother and sister in

< 222 >

Southern California at an end. I sat down now to a more thorough assessment of that plucky new year's outlook (dashed off from the midst of a one-night getaway mini-vacation with my wife, our first child-free night together in years) and took a stab at gauging the exact percentage of bullshit it contained.

Middling-to-high was as close as I got, but it was close enough. "A few tricks up my sleeve"? Sure, there was the partnership with Gordon, but that was hardly proceeding according to plan. Instead of the pile of "'GOLD' or other items" Gordon had promised in time for our "real good Christmas," there'd been a trickle of gil, the Final Fantasy XI currency, and a stream of anxious e-mails describing the difficulties of leveling up characters in that game. Not that I'd put much store in Gordon's projections anyway, but at this rate it could well be long past April 15 before Gordon's workers started adding much to my bottom line.

Nor had my other efforts at diversification made much headway. A week of Star Wars Galaxies auctions, it turned out, had been enough to bring me to the attention of eBay's "Trust and Safety Department," who sent an email that reminded me how sheltered an existence I'd been leading within the warm embrace of Ultima Online's RMT-friendly licensing agreement—and gently apprised me of their intentions to annihilate my eBay account if they found me trafficking in the intellectual property of Sony Online Entertainment again. No biggie, right: I could always sell SWG credits off my own storefront, the same way Bob did. Except that my own storefront was still under construction and looked likely to stay that way for a while, at the rate my designer and I were trading notes on how to proceed. As for Bob's talk of a broad, bright future of joint ventures for the two of us, I didn't doubt his sincerity, but I sensed him holding back now, watching for a bit more evidence of my long-term—or even short-term—commitment to the business.

< 223 >

And what could I offer? *Wired* magazine had its hooks in me deeper than ever. The story about game studies and the Level Up conference had kept me busy all through December and then been killed on its way to print, scooped, more or less, by a *New York Times* feature just a little too similar in focus for anybody's comfort. Consequently, I was desperate now to get my latest assignment underway, a dauntingly ill-defined feature article on the cultural politics of intellectual property in Brazil. Between travel, research, and writing, I would be lucky if I finished it by March and surprise no one if I kept wrestling with it all the way into April.

"A more profitable quarter going forward." Jesus, what a crock. Even the whiff of romantic glamour I'd injected into the post, I now had to admit, was largely fraudulent—the hint at nights of glitz and bliss in a Beverly Hills hotel a thin cover for the wrenching marital misery that actually transpired.

But more about that later. Suffice it to say that the gloom that had settled over me in the weeks before I got Gordon's fax was seeping back now with more determination than ever.

< 224 >

CHAPTER 34

Wednesday, January 14, 2004

Flying Down to Rio

I am on my way to the airport, headed for a week in Brazil . . . It's work, of course, but it could be worse. It's summer down there right now, and I will be spending much of the week in my dear old Rio de Janeiro and in the company of a dear old friend or two.

All the same, it says something about what the Play Money project has done to my mental health that I can't say, honestly, that I wouldn't rather be spending the next week tending my virtual-goods business with the full-time attention I have yet to be able to give it. Instead, I have had to suspend all my eBay auctions again for the week--and probably won't be doing much more than tread water till the article is finished, in another month or so.

Perhaps by then I won't even remember why I wanted to get into this business in the first place. Here's hoping.

< 225 >

In retrospect, I don't think there was even a drop of irony in those closing sentiments. This was as close to a public farewell as I had come, and had my schedule proceeded as projected, I suspect it wouldn't have been too long after my return from Brazil that I announced my retirement from the business.

Instead, though, I returned to the news that *Wired*'s editors were postponing the article—and my deadline—for another three months. Before me, suddenly, stretched a clear, unbroken path from now to April 15—a final stretch of trading time unhampered, if I so chose, by any further writing assignments. I perhaps should not have so chosen: Assignments thus postponed had a way of evaporating on the shelf, and even if I did end up completing this one, it would be a tight squeeze after that to turn around another in time to renew my contract.

But the long-deferred dream of going full-time was too seductive, finally. And the despair that earlier had dragged me toward surrendering the race now seemed, if anything, to be urging me on, as if the likelihood of blowing my contract with *Wired* and the rumblings that had begun to shake my marriage merely hinted at a destiny so spectacularly wretched it could not be missed—some unknowable, inevitable catastrophe that I could only hope, at best, to plummet toward with eyes wide open and the Seven Dwarves' *Hi Ho* in my heart.

And so, though I kept the news from my reading public—and very nearly from myself—I decided to go for it. The decision was its own reward, I guess, but I can't help noting I was soon thereafter blessed with a sale that, bittersweet though it was, proved the single largest and most profitable of my career.

< 226 >

CHAPTER 35

This Is Not My Beautiful House

Here is something I have somehow neglected, in all
the months of this endeavor, to show you: A picture
of the world that makes my business possible. More
precisely, it's a screenshot of my main character
there, the blacksmith Alhinud, in the mansion I
designed and built for him 11 months ago on the
Great Lakes shard.

< 227 >

Take a good look, because you're not likely to see this image again. I sold the house a little over two weeks back, for 60 million gold pieces. I could have had $600 cash, but gold is looking like a solid investment right now, and by the time I sell this pile off it should bring me $800 or more.

That's clear profit, too. I put nothing but sweat equity into that house--camped the login screen for hours on the day the Age of Shadows expansion launched, claimed my plot the instant the new territories opened up, spent another week or so shaping the house itself into the gothic-Moorish palace I'd been dreaming of. I lived there, too, for another many months, plying my craft, talking to passersby, even taking on a roommate, Radny, as those of you who have followed this journal from its beginnings may recall.

But then one day I got serious about making money, which meant that I had to start up characters on all the English-speaking shards and spend my days shuttling from one to another, looking for deals. I spent less and less time on Great Lakes, less and less time in my mansion. After a while Radny stopped showing up, and I learned he'd let his account lapse.

I don't know why I didn't sell sooner. No, I do know why. I didn't want to believe I'd stopped living there. I didn't want to think I'd stopped playing the game and slid into the distant, alienated perspective voiced recently by Gaming Open Market client Kenneth Michael Merrill, a trader in the

< 228 >

currencies of UO, Star Wars Galaxies, and Second
Life, among others:

"I feel like I am above the players of these games,"
Merrill told Wired News the other day. "They are
toiling and investing hours and hours into creating
wealth and building empires and here I am, no
virtual avatar running around and no virtual real
estate, just skimming money off the top."

Must commerce always alienate? Is it by definition
the opposite of lived community?

Maybe so. Still, it warms my heart a little to know
that the buyer I sold my house to was my old friend
Mr. Big, and that he in turn sold it to a player who
makes his living in real life as an artist, who will
pay for the house not in cash but with a portrait of
Mr. Big's six-month-old son.

OK, but seriously now: "it warms my heart"? I don't know
whether the sentiment was insincere or just naïve, but in retrospect, something about it doesn't add up. I mean, can I really still
have cared, at this point, who bought my house or why? I suppose it's possible. Yet I can't help feeling now that a genuinely
honest report on the state of the business would not have left it
at this heart-felt, soul-searching portrait of a deal. For balance,
there would have had to be another five or six dozen snapshots
of the sort of everyday transaction—shallow, calculating, frankly
banal—that represented the vast majority of my trades and the
emerging heart and soul of my enterprise.

Too late now, I guess. But there is room here still, I think, for
me to attempt some small redress—a single case that in its almost

< 229 >

luminously unremitting dreariness may evoke the broader flavor of those weeks in which my business began to find its momentum and its character. Herewith, then, I submit the record of my conversation with one Red, a young adventurer of the Great Lakes shard, beginning with the first message that flashed across my IM screen late one mid-winter afternoon:

SELLING 10 MILLION GOLD $125.00

Yes, so it commenced, our little contredanse—with this brief come-hither coyly blasted out to about a zillion of Red's IM contacts, including total strangers such as I whom he remotely suspected had an interest in this sort of thing.

And my riposte:

what shard?

GL, he said. *wanna buy?*

I considered briefly: Once I would have snapped at $12.50-a-million gold, but now I could almost always find it cheaper.

cant' for that price, thanks though

An IM silence hung between us.

i can go lower, said Red. *lowest i can go is 110*

highest i can go is 100, I answered, quickly, as in: take it or leave it.

fine:/

And here, officially, the deal was clinched. But note the curiously placed colon and solidus at the end of Red's line, which to an eye less trained than mine might have appeared a mere typo, evidence perhaps of a hurried mind impatient to consummate the trade. But I knew better. Red, in fact, had typed the universal emoticon for skeptical unease, a smiley face half-tipped into a frown, and even the missing space between the word and the grimace was no mistake: Red's explicit assent to my price was of a piece with his abiding discomfort with it, and never would the two be separated. That was the message, and from it I deduced

< 230 >

that if I didn't want the deal to blow up in my face, I was going to have to coddle this guy all the way to the goddamned close.

Deduced correctly, I might add.

is there any posible way u can mail it?

"It"? Mail "it"? Oh: the hundred dollars. He wanted me to send it to him, I deduced, in some antiquated, pre-digital form, possibly paper-based.

instead of paypal you mean?

sec, he replied, and then, instead of returning after the indicated one second, he went missing for something more like three hundred, during which I waited patiently for his clarification.

still there? I eventually inquired.

yah

so you want me to mail payment?

yah

ok, i can send money order sure, I said. *but as you probably know, when you sell to a Markee Dragon broker, we get the gold up front*

Ah, the magical Markee Dragon name. This in the end was probably the greatest benefit I derived from being a broker: not having to haggle with customers over which of us could be presumed more trustworthy. Even Red made no complaint about giving me gold before getting paid. He had more important things to worry about anyway.

if u sent a money order would u send it over night? he asked. *i need money for this weekend heh*

i could do that, sure, but i would have to deduct shipping costs
how bout i give u 12 mil and there is no shipping costs heh
then u could send cash $$

Cash? He wanted me to mail him one hundred dollars cash?

lol ok, I replied, forcing out the bland, gregarious *lol* lest any trace of my actual, astonished laughter come through. *but i will*

< 231 >

*send you a money order in any case--you don't want me sending
cash in the mail*

*if u send it overnight it would be secured or somthing cuz its
like 4 or 5 buxs*

no, I said, *they don't insure cash*

they give u a lil box u kno

yes i know

and u can put the cash in an envolope

with paper in there

it will not be secured, I insisted. *and what's wrong with a
money order anyway?*

i need my parents to cash it

then they know how much money i have

oh, I said, beginning to grasp the full dimensions of the situation. *hehe*

And its my b-day this weekend

soo

*well, listen, it's your call--if you want cash that's fine, but if the
money never arrives you're out of luck*

yah ill take the cash but look do this

There was a long silence, during which I could almost hear the
wheels turning inside Red's head, wherever it was.

put it in a cd case

--another thoughtful pause--

and put the cd case in there

--the final pieces falling into place now--

and put a cd in the case but the cash under the cd

--followed by one last stroke of genius:

just a blank cd or somthing

I typed nothing for a moment or two, thanking the Internet
gods that Red could not see the expression on my face just then.

lol, too much expense, chief, I said at last.

< 232 >

ill add another mil

so id give u 13mil

sigh, all right, lol--but what's the point of adding the cd exactly?

so if they do open it lookin for money theyd see a cd

no, they'll see a cd case, I pointed out.

if they don't open the case they don't need to see the cd, I further explained.

And finally: *if they do open the case they'll see the money anyway*

A full minute passed.

bah fuck it just put it in a envolpe and ill give u 12

lol, k

but make sure the envolope is inside the box lol

my dad said they usualy dont steal from over nights

Red now gave me his mailing address, naming a small town in southern Michigan not too far from where I lived.

cripes, I said. *i could drive it up, lol*

really?

Again I thanked God for the limitations of text chat, which in this case permitted me, on the one hand, to cling to the possibility that Red was only joshing here and, on the other, prevented him from seeing me realize he was probably serious: A personal hand delivery of his hundred dollars would suit him fine.

no, not really, I said, *but i'm just down in south bend, so it'll get to you quick in any case*

hehe

ok, where do you want to meet to give me the gold?

Luna, said Red, and it was the first thing he'd said all afternoon that made things easier for me. For Luna, of course, had been my home city, and Great Lakes my home shard, so that unlike non-Brit deliveries on other shards, this one would not require any horseback riding through mongbat-infested wildernesses. I could

< 233 >

just hit the runestone I'd marked HOME, pop up instantly in front of my old house, and run around the corner to the bank. It had been a while, and when I materialized at the old spot I saw, to my mild dismay, that the "artist" Bob had sold the plot to had already erased my airy, welcoming palace of light, replacing it with a locked and windowless cubic monstrosity of dark gray stone. There was no time to linger, though. I found Red waiting for me at the bank around the corner, where the gold transfer went off with surprising efficiency.

Then back to IM:

k the other thing about mailing your money, I said, *is it's gonna require someone to be there to sign for it--will there be?*

let me check brb

yah its coo

thanks man

try to send it out tonight if u can

i'll see if i can, I said, not remotely intending to schlep out to the FedEx store at this late hour.

i owe u my life, said Red.

lol--wait till the money gets to you before you start writing me any IOUs

heh

god im gonna get so fucked up this weekend

lol

me and my friend drivin down to fuckin summit and gettin some weed

its gonna be sweet

we got a 8th for 15 last time

lol

well hell man you are gonna get damaged this time then lol

I felt a mild self-disgust at my pandering thus to the young delinquent's fantasies of weekend oblivion—and saddened to

< 234 >

contrast it with the tender concern I'd once felt toward Radny's similar proclivities. But mostly I felt relieved that after a full fifty minutes of this second-rate Beavis and Butthead episode, the conversation appeared finally to be over. I closed the window on Red and alt-tabbed away to other onscreen business.

Only to see Red's name light up a moment later alerting me to another message, which was this:

shit them homless guys down there

I blinked and stared at the words, uncomprehending.

Was he talking to me?

they have shity pot but still fucks u up

Um . . .

fuck 400 buxs prolly get us a pound too

Ah, OK.

I reread the lines now, finally understanding:

shit them homless guys down there

they have shity pot but still fucks u up

fuck 400 buxs prolly get us a pound too

And then, I read the lines yet one more time. And would you believe me now if I told you that this little haiku, windblown across my screen like a snow drift of tawdriness and mystery, worked a sort of magic on my soul right then, opening some secret chamber of my heart to the humanity in Red and every other hapless, hungering player out there awaiting the provision of my humble services?

Yeah, no, I didn't think you would.

< 235 >

CHAPTER 36

⬇ **Monday, February 09, 2004**

My $85-an-Hour Job

A reader writes:

Hello, I enjoy your site, and use Ultima also to make "spare" cash on the side since I consider it a hobby. Yet I must ask you take something into effect and that is your time. Time is money and when you consider a sale and stuff you only have ebay and/or paypal considered as costs. Yet think about who/what you do and what you could make with the time you spent. (I know there are MANY other variables to consider.) But this would make your posts a bit more interesting at least I think so. Maybe dont throw in the cost of your time, but at least throw in the time (estimate) took for a certain item you sold.

Fair enough.

First, though, let me explain that I have so far refrained from breaking down my UO income on an

< 236 >

hourly basis for the same reason I try to avoid calculating my hourly wage as a writer: I don't like to depress myself. Two-dollars-a-word has a nice, round, George-Plimpton-at-the-top-of-his-game sort of ring to it. Ten-fifty-an-hour (no, believe me, I write very slowly) has more of a gym-teacher-moonlighting-at-the-Dairy-Mart thing going on.

Having dared to do the math, however, I am pleased to report that as a UO retailer my wages seem to be verging on Beverly-Hills-plumber-fixing-your-basement-leak-on-a-Sunday territory.

Consider the numbers on a recent wholesale currency purchase of mine. Yesterday I received 45 million Britannian gold pieces for $405, or $9 per million. The seller lives in Russia, a country that PayPal appears to have blacklisted, so paying for the gold involved a 20-minute trip to my local Vietnamese grocery store, which happens also to be the nearest MoneyGram agent. Arranging to pick up the gold and then actually picking it up in game probably involved another 20 minutes. The score so far: 40 minutes, $405 in the hole.

By the end of the day today I had already sold off 25 million of the gold, in two lots of 10 million and one of 5 million, for a total of $334.97. Subtract $28 for PayPal and eBay fees, figure about 15 minutes for each transaction (including listing the eBay auctions, corresponding with the buyers, making the deliveries), and the tally is now 85 minutes, $98.03 in the hole.

< 237 >

Now, assuming the sales continue at more or less
this rate, the remaining 20 million will net me $245
and cost me another 45 minutes in transaction time.
Sum total: 130 minutes, $175 profit. Or roughly $85
an hour.

OK, let's not kid ourselves. I'm leaving out all
kinds of overhead (UO subscription fees, unsold eBay
item fees, time spent reading UO information sites,
time wasted talking to "potential" customers) that
could easily bring that wage down to $50 an hour or
even halve it. What's more, that one deal may be my
sole source of UO income this week, and multiplied
by 52 weeks that's not a whole lot of per annum.

Still: $85 an hour. Can I break out the Cristal now?

Oh indeed, this was more like it. Had I calculated the hourly return on a deal as time-consuming and penny-ante as the one I
struck with Red, I would have wept to see the numbers. But this
Russian supplier, bless him, was the soul of efficiency: Regularly
stocked with large amounts of gold, he'd supplied me enough
times by now that our transactions were a practiced routine.
Even the awkwardness of trekking to the Vietnamese grocers to
make the payments had its upside: As the only major gold buyer
willing to put up with the hassle of sending dollars to Russia, I
had a keen advantage when it came to negotiating prices with
this particular supplier. Generally speaking, in any case, prices
were better on higher-volume deals than low, and as I was also
coming to realize, big volumes meant faster turn-arounds too:
Compared to five Red-type deals for 10 million gp each, for instance, a single Russian deal for 50 million gp not only cost me
ten percent less cash, but took me 80 percent less time.

< 238 >

If only all my suppliers could have been Russians. Or better yet: Rich Thurmans. Two weeks after the featured Russian deal, I would make a purchase from Rich that dwarfed it both in volume and in savings: 120 million gold pieces for $960, or $8 per million. Who knows what sort of hourly rate I could have totted up from those numbers and paraded on my blog? A corporate lawyer's?

Then again, the deal with Rich was not the sort of thing I felt like going into too much detail about with my readers. For that matter, even the Russian transaction had some aspects I'd thought better left unmentioned. For it's not as if the Russian supplier's product was an awful lot more wholesome than Rich's. The Russian extracted the gold he sold me from his control over a handful of shardwide markets in the Blade of the Righteous, a rare daemon-slaying sword that gave +10 to hit points and a 50 percent boost to damage and could mostly be acquired only from other players, for around 20 million gp down at West Brit Bank or as much as $275 on eBay. The only other way to get your hands on this "artifact" was to max out your stealing skill and then be lucky enough to happen upon the sword in the formidable depths of the new Doom dungeon—opened to the UO public the same day Age of Shadows launched—or cheesy enough to script a bot that lurked in those depths unattended, around the clock, waiting for the random monthly moment when the sword spawned and could be snatched up automatically. That the Russian's methods involved far more cheese than luck was obvious to me even before the day a GM busted him for macroing and he IM'd begging me to call customer service and plead his case:

I was there talking to gm when he found me. how he can suspend my account?

yeah ok friend, but just one question, I felt compelled to ask. *Um . . . how do i put it?*

< 239 >

have you *not* in fact been running unattended scripts in Doom?

:-)

Still, the Russian's dirty gold was chump change compared to the ill-gotten gains of Mr. Richard Thurman, whose role in the mysterious Publish 21 exploit was at long last coming into focus for me. In our conversations of the preceding weeks, Rich—being Rich—had not quite managed the air-tight secrecy he and Mithra had agreed on, dropping a hint here, blurting out a detail there, until eventually, and though I wouldn't hear the whole story for another several months, I got the picture: Rich and Mithra had scored big. They'd pulled off possibly the biggest duping scheme in UO history and gotten away clean, with style even, losing not so much as an account between them or a single solitary piece of the billions in gold they amassed.

From the moment Publish 21 went live, Rich and Mithra had run their programs top speed, nonstop, until the day Mithra happened to look in on one of his two-bot teams and found the pair of them neither hard at work nor frozen in the stillness of a bot gone off its rails but simply, and unsettlingly, dead—each one a gray ghost haunting its own corpse. Quickly, Mithra rezzed the bots and searched the crime scene, eager to find out what had become of the two characters' pack beetles, which by now should have been loaded with checks totaling as much as 50 million gold pieces between them. But the money was gone, and the beetles were dead, their corpses looted and the missing contents clue enough for any looter curious as to what had been going on here.

It didn't make sense. Player-versus-player violence wasn't permitted in this particular region of Britannia, and the high-level monsters that surrounded the desolate hamlet Mithra had chosen for his worksite never wandered into town by accident. Somebody must have led the monsters down from the hills, pulling

< 240 >

them intentionally into combat with Mithra's bots. But who would have done such a thing? Strictly speaking, it could have been anyone. Pulling trains of monsters onto innocent bystanders was a traditional form of dumb-ass fun in MMOs, and if the bystanders were perceived as not-so-innocent—the way Mithra's suspiciously bottish characters just might—the pleasure might be all the richer. But this was weird all the same. Why would someone come all the way out to this godforsaken desert whistle-stop just to play the jackass? It seemed so improbable.

No more so, however, than what soon proved to be the true identity of the bot killer. For as Mithra learned the very next day, it so happened that in his quest for the loneliest spot on the Britannian globe, he had selected the exact same location another bot farmer had already staked out. And as if that weren't already quite sufficiently absurd, the farmer Mithra had moved in on turned out to be none other than—well:

ok rich I know that's you so don't try to play any of your fucking little games, announced Lee Caldwell, bursting in on Mithra's operations that second afternoon.

now, Lee continued, *this is how it's gonna go*. He proceeded to outline the terms of a blackmail little different from the one he'd once excoriated Rich and the EUO cartel for giving into when the prize had been the precious exevents routine: Now, in return for Mithra/Rich's full disclosure to Lee alone of the technical secrets behind this obvious gusher of an exploit, Lee and his associates would agree not to make his farming life a living hell of round-the-clock GM harassment.

Mithra, who didn't know Lee personally but had heard a lot about him from Rich, gave the proposition a moment or two of thought and then replied, *i'd sooner cut off my own leg.*

He meant that almost literally, too. Immediately, Mithra flashed news of the encounter to Rich, who quickly got hold of Lee via

< 241 >

IM, sweet-talking him with promises of full cooperation just long enough for Mithra and Rich to set in motion their plan for the day when other farmers caught on to their method and inevitably began to dilute the value of its output: They were going to shut it down dead. Through the secure channel of a UO account untraceable to any of their others, Mithra contacted a GM in-game and proceeded to describe, in exquisite technical detail, the workings and implications of the Pub 21 bug. Within hours, and with only the most inscrutable wisps of public explanation, OSI shut down every shard in the game to patch in an emergency fix to the server code, and the bug was gone. Between the moment it had started working and the moment it stopped, no more than seven days had passed.

"Probably Rich and I should have talked about that decision a bit longer," Mithra would tell me a couple years later, in a phone call from Little Rock. "But we spoke on the phone and we'd agreed: once it looks like everybody is catching on, we need to shut it down ourselves." Mithra had little to complain about in any case. In its brief operation, the exploit had netted him 17.5 billion gold pieces. Rich ran into delays getting his Pub 21 bots up and running and ended up accumulating only about 4 billion gp, but unlike his partner in crime, Rich had a day job, and he was more than happy with his haul. Never once detected by OSI in any aspect of the scheme, the two of them spent eight months gradually selling off their hoard, careful not to swamp the market, and in the final tallying of profits, Mithra walked away with roughly $130,000 and Rich with about $30,000, for a total payout of well over $150,000.

Six thousand three hundred and sixty dollars of which—according to my PayPal records from the months subsequent to Publish 21—came straight from me. And like I said, although hard figures and precise details of how it all went down were not

< 242 >

available to me at the time, I already knew the score: My best suppliers were among the biggest exploiters in the game.

I suppose this should have caused me at least a moment or two of serious soul-searching, but at this stage, frankly, I was not in the mood. Maximum return for minimum outlay: That was the power player's approach to Ultima Online, and as a style of play it was decidedly not for everyone. But in the game I was playing now it happened to be the only style on offer: There was no other path to a win. I still didn't know how Bob and Markee Dragon did it, really—how exactly they achieved their awesome efficiencies remained something of a mystery to me—but for me the way forward was getting clearer all the time. I had a finish line just two months ahead of me, and if I was going to cross that line a winner, I could not depend on average players alone for my supply. I couldn't even depend on Chinese factory workers, it seemed, judging by the measly $305 my collaboration with Gordon had produced thus far. No, to win at my own game fair and square, I was going to have to rely at least in part on people who cheated at theirs.

< 243 >

CHAPTER 37

Market Watch

Astonishing growth in overall sales--the market total has risen steadily over the last month for a total gain of over 30 percent. This could be just a seasonal uptick after the Christmas slump, I guess. But the sales number is growing faster than volume, which means the average item price is getting higher, which in turn might mean lots of things but to me suggests mainly one: The artifacts market is heating up.

Ah, artifacts. Plucked from the monsters of the new dungeon Doom, these rare, powerful weapons and armor are the rarest of rares, sometimes only one to a shard. Indeed, when they first started popping up in the game, just a year ago, they were too rare to even register on the economic radar. Now, though, there seem to be just enough of them out there to fuel desire for more, yet not quite enough to sink

< 244 >

the prices much--which range from $100 for the humble Leggings of Bane to as much as $800 for the coveted Ornament of the Magician. After a long slide toward commodity pricing, in other words, the UO market seems to have rediscovered its first love: luxury.

I better get off my butt and get me a piece of this while it lasts.

Now here it is--your weekly UO eBay market snapshot, based on average sales figures for the preceding 14 days:

Market sales total: $171,224 (+11,338 from last week)
Market sales total, annualized: $4.5 million
Market volume total: 3,852 sales (-35)
Exchange rate: $14.48 (-0.10) per 1 million Britannian gold pieces
Price of an 18x18-tile mansion: $155.03 (-0.76)
My gold holdings: 58.65 million gp ($849.25)
My dollar holdings: $1,600.47
My profits, last 12 months: $3,588.92

Monday, February 16, 2004

The Home Stretch

Dear readers:

Time is running out for me and this nutty little project of mine, and I must thank you, from the bottom of my heart, for the kindness you have shown in keeping your traps shut about the fact. There is

< 245 >

no longer any ignoring it, however: the April 15 deadline I set myself is now less than two months away.

Will I make it? Can I? Take a moment to review the terms of the proposition set forth atop the left-hand column of this page:

> On April 15, 2004, I will truthfully report to the IRS that my primary source of income is the sale of imaginary goods—and that I earn more from it, on a monthly basis, than I have ever earned as a professional writer.

You will see that in their strictest sense, I have already failed. The income-tax return I file in April will of course pertain only to money made in 2003, and as I've already reported, my profits from the sale of imaginary items last year amounted to a measly $3,131.42, or a little more than 6 percent of my income.

Where there's a weasel, there's a way, however, and as a greater weasel than I might put it, this all depends on what the meaning of "truthfully report to the IRS" is. Consider, too, the stipulation that "I earn more from [this project], on a monthly basis, than I have ever earned as a professional writer," and note the ample wiggle room in the phrase "on a monthly basis." So: While the good folks in the U.S. government may not want to know on April 15 just how I earned my money in the preceding three and a half months, there's nothing to stop me from telling them, is there? And if during some one-month period

< 246 >

between now and April 15 I make more from selling
imaginary items than I ever made on a monthly basis
as a writer ($4,600, let's say, considering that my
writing income has approached but never attained the
magic figure of $55,000 a year), then I may
"truthfully report" that, may I not?

OK, so this is the moral equivalent of cheating at
solitaire. And yes, I do feel a bit dirty, thanks
for asking. But there's no time to dwell on that
now. I've got work to do:

Between this day and April 15, the Play Money
enterprise must earn me during some one-month period
a minimum of $4,600.

One month. Forty-six-hundred dollars.

Go.

⬇ **Friday, February 27, 2004**

Living the Dream

And so it begins, again.

Wife out of town, all other professional commitments
set aside, I end this project the way I started it,
and the way I meant to run it all along: working
around the clock. My daughter's still with me, and she
still owns the hours when she's not asleep or in day
care, but the rest of the time I'm right here at the
computer, buying and selling a whole lotta nothing.

These next two weeks are critical. I mean to focus
now on preparations that may not be real profitable

< 247 >

in the short term but could help put me over the top in the final month of the challenge: exploring the markets, setting up a Web storefront, placing advertisements. I'll keep you posted as the campaign unfolds.

Meanwhile, my first strategic decision is this: it's all about suits. Suits of armor, that is, which funnily enough is also how I got the ball rolling here, selling 100% lower-reagent suits to Mr. Big for gold. Their eBay price has dropped by almost half since then, and Mr. Big can't really be bothered with them anymore, but for me they've turned into a nice little business. Nothing major, but the margins are pretty sweet (I can buy a lower-reagents suit for about $5 worth of gold and sell it for $20, minus fees), and as a core competence, suits definitely give me room to grow. There are now a number of marketable suit configurations--high resistance for player-versus-player action, high luck for hunting monsters--and such is the genius of UO's current loot-production mechanics that as one configuration saturates the market and falls off the high end, others will start emerging to replace them.

All very sensible business considerations, yes. But there's one other thing that draws me to suits. Unlike the gold I've been almost exclusively dealing to keep my hand in the game these last few months, suits are not pure exchange value. People don't just turn around and spend them on something else--they use them, live with them. And because of the

< 248 >

complexity of UO's item-modification system, each
suit is entirely unique, composed of qualities and
quirks that sum up to a whole whose essence only a
connoisseur can judge. I'm not a true connoisseur
myself yet, but there are times now when I get my
first look at a lower-reagents suit someone's
offering me and know it, I swear, just as intimately
as any twenty-year veteran of the garment trade
knows a jacket from the feel of its lapel between
his fingers.

And the day I can do that with a nine-piece dyeable
all-seventies resists-mage suit--man, that's the day
I can retire with dignity. Here's hoping it happens
in the next ninety days.

< 249 >

CHAPTER 38

Is There an Accountant in the House?

The terms of the challenge seemed clear enough when I laid them down: Between now and April 15 I must post a profit of $4,600 within a one-month period.

Now that I've had some time to ponder the meaning of the word "profit," however, I'm beginning to understand why they pay those corporate CPAs the big bucks. Like any other high-profile business readying its quarterly earnings report, I hear the siren call of dubious accounting schemes and know enough to try to shut my ears against it--yet I'm not sure I know enough to tell the difference between the truly dubious and the merely creative. Even the most basic rules of accounting, after all, can be fairly counterintuitive, and I sure as hell don't want to let my ignorance of the art of bean-counting screw up my shot at winning this race.

< 250 >

Obviously, for example, it would be the height of cheesiness to invest all my dollar holdings in gold and other inventory, spend a month selling it off, then claim all that revenue as profit. But what about existing inventory? How do I value that, for the purposes of a final reckoning? Just counting the dollars I invested in it won't do, since that wouldn't account for inventory acquired merely from buying and selling within the game. How do I count it, then?

And what about expenses? Clearly, monthly outlays like subscription fees must be deducted in full from any monthly revenues. But what about one-time fees like hiring a designer to ready my Web storefront for business? Can I amortize that cost, and if so, over how many months?

Sigh. By the time I post this Wednesday's market figures, I will need to have come up with some rational--and ethical--scheme for calculating the benchmark numbers of my progress toward success or failure. Surely there is someone out there with the training, the spare time, and the esprit de corps to lend me a hand?

Tuesday, March 02, 2004

No, Seriously

OK, maybe I was a little too coy in my plea for help yesterday. Let me try again.

By tomorrow I need to figure out a credible scheme for calculating my profits and losses on a weekly

< 251 >

basis. By tomorrow, if past server statistics are anything to go by, some eight hundred people will have looked at this page. By tomorrow, therefore, the chances are good that these words will have been read by a professional accountant, or an amateur accountant, or a person whose father was an accountant, or someone who got halfway through writing a novel about an accountant--any one of whom knows at least three thousand times more about accounting than I do. And maybe that someone is you.

It is?

OK then: Help!

Send me an email, an instant message (the contact info is on the lefthand sidebar, can't miss it). Give me a clue! How do I do this?

And yes, I'm asking for free advice. It's called keeping costs down, for God's sake. Isn't that what you accountants are always telling us to do?

As for you 799 other slackers: You want to pitch in? Go buy some of my stuff. Damn.

⬇ **Wednesday, March 10, 2004**

Market Watch

This week's Market Watch features newly sensible figures on my progress, thanks to the patient assistance of Mr. Lance Leger (better known to denizens of the Pacific shard as Sarlock Longbow), Play Money's new in-house accountant. For the first

< 252 >

time you can see how much profit I actually racked up during the preceding week. Neat! Not so neat is the fact that I seem to have ended this week in the red. Nothing Sarlock can't fix with a few clever recalculations, I trust. We'll see how it goes next week.

And now, once again, here's your weekly UO eBay market snapshot, based on average sales figures for the preceding 14 days:

  Market sales total: $163,414 (-7,070 from last
    week)
  Market sales total, annualized: $4.2 million
  Market volume total: 3,589 sales (-129)
  Exchange rate: $13.58 (-0.22) per 1 million
    Britannian gold pieces
  Price of an 18x18-tile mansion: $182.27 (+31.78)
  My gold holdings: 177.2 million gp
  My dollar holdings: $1,670.14
  My inventory: $608.20
  My net worth: $3,397.84
  My profits this week: -96.56 (!)
  My profits, to date: $7061.76

*(Numbers crunched with help from HammerTap's
DeepAnalysis, an eBay market research tool, and
Lance Leger, professional accountant and
guildmaster, Ancient Order of Elves.)*

< 253 >

CHAPTER 39

The retention of Sarlock Longbow, elven CPA, was not the only announcement I posted that day. There was another development to discuss, not quite so significant for the outlook of the enterprise perhaps, but from a personal perspective somewhat more consequential. I had flown to New York City for a few days on various sorts of family business, and I'd come back with news I felt obliged to share with my readership:

⬇ **Wednesday, March 10, 2004**

The Art of Losing

I'm back. If we can call it that. Somehow every trip I take lately seems to entail losing a little piece of myself along the way.

You may remember the disastrous hard-drive crash of my last trip to San Francisco, which took with it years' worth of email and other memorabilia. Then there was the suitcase lost on my return from Brazil two months ago, gone with gifts for wife and child and twenty of my favorite CDs. And last night I came

< 254 >

home from New York to find that we'd been burglarized while I was away. The DVD player, the ReplayTV unit, and a telephone were taken--no great loss, all things considered, except that I truly had been looking forward to the *Sopranos* season debut recorded on the ReplayTV.

I should mention, too, that I spent the weekend letting go of things much dearer. My 97-year-old grandmother, a sweet, witty, legendary woman who will be mourned by half of Greenwich Village when she finally goes, is going. I was glad to get to see her again, and hold her bony hand.

And there are more unsettling losses afoot, about which I may or may not say more here later. I'm not sure why I'm going on about all this right now in any case; its connection to the business at hand is figurative at best. I could relate these lessons in loss to the nature of this enterprise, I guess--talk about how I deal in nothingness all day, how I trade in desire for things that aren't real, and how I should probably just sit back, enjoy the Buddhist wisdom of it all, and find solace in knowing that all desire, in the end, is for things unreal.

But honestly, there's only one real reason I should even be alluding to how tough things have gotten, and that is to advise you all that the drift of my life may soon entail a change of plans for the Play Money undertaking. Or anyway a change of venue. I'll need to be hitting the road for a while, is what I'm

< 255 >

saying. Destination: California. Means of transport: Honda Civic. Place of business, while en route: the Flying J chain of truckstops, which I'm told has wireless broadband service now, and where I plan to continue my trading activities during those hours when I am not putting pedal to metal.

After that, who knows? I have family in L.A., we'll figure something out.

And here, I guess, is the place to say a few words about a question that will soon be on your mind, in any case, unless I head it off now.

When Bob Kiblinger remarked to me in one of our first conversations that he'd made his first wife an "Ultima widow," I chuckled, unfamiliar with the term and with its many variations (World of Warcraft widow, Star Wars: Galaxies widow, etc.) and even less aware of the oceanic depths of domestic heartache that had rendered it cliché among MMO players. I was inclined, in any case, to treat with skepticism the notion that a video game could be, in any meaningful sense, addictive. But later, after UO got its hooks in me, my skepticism gave way to puzzlement, and in the midst of casting around for more informed accounts of compulsive MMO play, I came across a motherlode of first-person evidence: the legendary EverQuest Widows listserv, an online, ad-hoc support group for people whose spouses or lovers had left them, either in fact or in effect, for the attractions of a virtual world.

It was a never-ending catalogue of hurt: conjugal beds abandoned for nightly forty-player dungeon raids; wives stealing away in minivans to make new lives with alcoholic wood elves

< 256 >

from Tennessee; children left unfed and unretrieved from day care because their daddies were too busy stalking Zi-Thuuli of the Granite Claw through the Dreadspire Demi-plane of Blood. To be sure, there remained a lot to be skeptical of. Members of the group—among them Liz Woolley, the much-interviewed mother of a seriously depressed young man who shot himself to death at the computer in the midst of a week-long EverQuest binge—seemed a bit too quick to downplay the role of non-virtual issues in contributing to their woes. But the stories themselves rang true. And as I pursued the question into less anecdotal realms of discussion, I found among the best-informed observers—gamer-friendly psychologist Nicholas Yee, for example, whose in-depth player surveys are models of both rigor and nuance—no disagreement with their central truth: More frequently exaggerated than understood, the power of virtual worlds to play havoc with real lives is, nonetheless, nothing to scoff at.

All of which I tell you principally to make it clear that I've considered the problem at length, in depth, and from a multitude of perspectives, and that I speak with some authority, therefore, when I say that the sudden collapse of my marriage in the early months of 2004 had absolutely nothing to do with Ultima Online. Honest. Like the death of my grandmother, it's just something that occurred during a period of my life when I happened also to be spending my workdays selling enchanted leather armor and other fairy-tale commodities to invisible strangers. And I only mention it here, as I said, because in the end it reshaped those workdays in certain ways I think require an explanation.

To wit: after several weeks of increasingly dramatic unpleasantness between my wife and me, a cooling-off period was thought advisable, and I agreed to go spend some time with my

< 257 >

sister and her wife in Los Angeles. As discussed, the drive from Indiana to California would cut into my work schedule as minimally as truck-stop Internet connections permitted, and once I arrived I was welcome to clear a spot for myself at my sister's dining room table and set up shop there. The going would not really get any tougher, I assumed, but it was probably going to get a bit weirder. And I just thought my readers should know.

< 258 >

CHAPTER 40

My departure was set for the 24th, two weeks away, and a few things needed finalizing before I hit the road.

For one, it was clearly time for me to let go of Gordon L_____ and all the possibilities he represented. Having failed repeatedly to hit competitive production rates with his Final Fantasy gil-farming team, Gordon was now trying to retrain his Beijing "colleagues" (as he charmingly referred to the workers at his factory) as a power-leveling service—players-for-hire paid to take control of their customers' characters for a few days and speed them all the way to maximum skill level. Bob, who had some experience with the power-leveling business, was patiently walking Gordon through the protocols, even though he had long since declared Gordon, officially, a "disaster," and didn't seem to expect much of this new strategy either. Deep down, I knew our collaboration was going nowhere, and I had already given up hoping for any revenue from it whatsoever. But it was harder to accept that I had lost the chance, yet again, to set foot in an actual, functioning virtual loot factory.

It helped some that I now had an actual, almost-functioning virtual loot storefront to call my own. The design of the Play Money supply store was nearly complete, and it was lovely: elegant and

< 259 >

minimalist, and tricked out with a custom-coded back-end interface that inspired me to play around for hours adjusting item prices and stock quantities. The pretext was that I needed to iron out all the kinks and go live before I left town, but the truth was that my Web-designer friend had made me, basically, the coolest lemonade stand a kid could want, and I probably would have been delighted just to spend the remainder of my days in South Bend twiddling its buttons and pull-down menus.

But I didn't, of course. For there was money to be made.

⬇ **Wednesday, March 17, 2004**

Market Watch

The good news: I turned a remarkable $996.99 in profit this week. The bad news: I turned a remarkable $996.99 in profit this week, which means that in the three weeks ahead, I must average an even more remarkable $1,200 a week if I'm to make my goal.

Now here's your weekly UO eBay market snapshot, based on average sales figures for the preceding 14 days:

```
Market sales total: $158,380 (-5,034 from last week)
Market sales total, annualized: $4.1 million
Market volume total: 3,392 sales (-197)
Exchange rate: $13.56 (-0.02) per 1 million
   Britannian gold pieces
Price of an 18x18-tile mansion: $168.58 (-13.69)
My gold holdings: 182.45 million gp
My dollar holdings: $2,689.36
My inventory: $470.60
```

< 260 >

My net worth: $4,555.13
My profits this week: 996.99 (!)
My profits, to date: $7,887.75

Audited statements available upon request.

(Numbers crunched with help from HammerTap's DeepAnalysis, an eBay market research tool, and Lance Leger, professional accountant and guildmaster, Ancient Order of Elves.)

⬇ **Friday, March 19, 2004**

Oh, Crappy Day

What a crappy day. A lousy $225 in revenues, but that's the least of it. I have run up against the dreaded supply crunch. My accountant, Sarlock the Elf, advises me to keep my cash flowing, but it's pooling instead. My PayPal account fills up with dollars while I beat the bushes desperately for inventory at prices I can live with. It's an endless haggle, and I have discovered I don't especially like haggling.

Not when it doesn't go my way, in any case. Today I spent a good 45 minutes appraising a pair of accounts some random prospect was looking to sell, only to be met with what sounded like genuinely wounded indignation when I made an offer that stood a remote chance of securing me a living-wage return on the deal. I know, I know: the guy probably spent the best hours of his adolescence building up this asset, and it's my problem if I can't learn the art of lowballing with charm. But still, it's bad enough

< 261 >

to blow a deal without feeling like you've stepped on someone's pet puppy in the process.

To make matters worse, my beloved Tradespot, the bazaar of first resort for anyone looking to load up on UO stuff, has become uncomfortable territory for me. I was warned today by the people who run the place to stop spamming the boards with links to my eBay auctions, and to limit my total posts there to four or five a day. Guilty as charged, and the restrictions are fair enough. But soliciting the torrent of goods I need is not going to be easy now that my access to Tradespot has dwindled to a trickle.

And to think just days ago I was pleading with you all to buy from me.

For God's sake somebody please sell me something.

Well, somebody did. The next day I got a phone call from a gentleman with an improbably refined-sounding Southern accent offering me 250 million gold pieces at $8 per million. It was Mithra, hitherto just a name I'd heard Rich Thurman mention now and then, and though I had a pretty good idea how he had gotten this gold, I accepted his offer with gratitude and relief.

Three days after that, Gordon cc'd me on an email to Bob, yet another message brimming with unearned optimism about the prospects for our joint venture. Had I known that this would be the last I ever heard from him, I would have wanted to offer my solemn good wishes in reply, I think. In the end, I barely noticed the message when it arrived: I was already on my long way out West.

< 262 >

PART TEN

On the Road

CHAPTER 41

⬇ **Wednesday, March 24, 2004**

All Hail the Flying J!

I write to you from exit 292 of interstate highway 80, in Davenport, Iowa, USA. I'm in a back corner booth of the local Flying J truckstop, which along with diesel fuel, hot showers, laundromat, Louis L'amour audio books, and other necessities of the modern truck-driving life, now offers broadband Internet connections for the reasonable rate of $4.95 per day, $24.95 per week. The air conditioning is on too high, but my little office here is otherwise comfortable enough-- handsome faux-wood-laminated particle board table and banquette, warm fluorescent lighting. The connectivity options include modem, Ethernet, and Wi-Fi. I am going with Ethernet at the moment, the wireless currently being a little more Wi than Fi.

I've been sitting here conducting business for almost four hours, which is surely the longest stretch of time I have ever spent inside a truckstop. I have

< **264** >

always been fascinated by these places, though of course, as a pointy-headed college boy, I've never much felt at home in them. Culturally, this is alien territory for me: solidly working-class, Southern-inflected, lots of big bellies in T-shirts and mullets flying proud. The distance is underlined by the odd truckstop apartheid that lets the general public in to shop and eat but sets aside various areas and amenities for "Drivers Only."

Yet here I sit, surrounded by truckers gazing at their laptop screens, not really so different any-more. Truck drivers may be the last American cowboys, but like me, they're in a business that plays weird games with geography and uses the latest telecommunications technology to do so. Their trucks are tracked by GPS as they drive, their lives go on by email and EverQuest when they stop. Right now I'm meshed into the same network of highways and data vectors, only mirrored, talking to friends and family on the cell phone while I drive, getting back to work when I stop.

Two, maybe three more days of this, and I'll be at my sister's house in California.

Six hours later, a hundred and sixty miles on, I checked in with my readers once again:

Market Watch (Now With Fewer Data Than Ever!)

So, here I am at the Flying J in Des Moines, a little after midnight Central Time, waiting for DeepAnalysis

< 265 >

to stop being broken. I think I've waited long enough. We'll just have to skip the eBay market numbers this week and get straight to my financials. This is unfortunate for two reasons. One: I am very curious to see how the price of gold is doing two days after OSI's announcement that characters can now move between shards with all their possessions. Rumor has it that there are vast hoards of gold on the Asian shards (where gold trades at a much lower rate than elsewhere) just waiting to flood into the North American shards. Should be fun to watch.

And two: My financials this week are nothing I'm in any hurry to look at. Profits are down, alas--$933 against last week's $997--pushing the average weekly number I have to post in the time remaining up to a staggering $1,335. The only bright spot is that the vast majority of my assets are now in inventory and gold (yes, the supply crunch is over), so I am poised for some serious profit-taking in the week ahead.

My gold holdings: 332.28 million gp
My dollar holdings: $1,441.82
My inventory: $1,030.60
My net worth: $5,488.83
My profits this week: 933.70
My profits, to date: $8,821.45

Audited statements available upon request.

(Numbers crunched with help from Lance Leger, professional accountant and guildmaster, Ancient Order of Elves.)

< 266 >

On the Road

⬇ **Thursday, March 25, 2004**

Clocking Out

It's after midnight, Central Time, and I have just
finished a seven-hour shift here at the Flying J in
North Platte, Nebraska. The bandwidth remains solid,
but the circumstances tonight are somewhat less
accommodating than yesterday's. The communications
nook here at the North Platte stop shares space with
the TV area, and I have struggled to stay focused on
my work while a rotation of uniformly burly truck
drivers watched and commented on *Charmed* ("Oh you've
never seen it? Cute show. These gals are witches,
and that guy there is supposed to be some kind of
mentor to them. The outfits can get kind of skimpy
too, so that's nice"), *Law and Order* ("Oh man, that
kid killed the guy just for some Chinese food? Boy,
if I'd have done something like that when I was that
age, my daddy would have-- I wouldn't have been able
to run away from him fast enough!"), and the 1998
Julia Roberts/Susan Sarandon weeper *The Stepmother*
(this one left them speechless, actually). I did
about $320 in sales and posted something like
seventy eBay auctions. I'm exhausted.

Home now, to my bedroll at the Rockin' DH campground
and trailer park, just across the interstate.

The Rockin' DH was an unkempt swatch of former rangeland,
and it had utterly charmed me when I checked in earlier that day.
The manager, a leathery old cowboy type, had taken my $8 cash
payment with a nod and then apologized for having to write

< 267 >

down my license number in a battered ledger book. "Government makes us do it now," he said. "I guess they're afraid some child molester will come hole up here or something."

"It's really not a problem," I'd replied, laughing. But now, as I pitched my tent by the glare of my headlights, I could sort of see where the government was coming from: The place was creeping me out. Ledger book or no ledger book, I got the feeling this campground even now harbored more than its share of potentially homicidal castoffs from the bottom rungs of the socioeconomic ladder, and the contrast between this rough unwanted patch of dirt and the fantasy land I'd been working in all evening somehow didn't much amuse me anymore. I crawled into the tent and pulled the sleeping bag tight around me, and had I not been preoccupied with thoughts of my imminent disemboweling by a Kmart bowie knife, I might have spared a thought for Hiro Protagonist, the central figure in Neal Stephenson's *Snow Crash*, who in the Metaverse owns vast tracts of valuable real estate, but in the real world lives in a shed. How many of my customers and suppliers, I might have wondered, lived in similar suspension between virtual wealth and actual squalor? How many felt its queer aesthetic appeal even to the limited extent I'd managed today?

I fell asleep in spite of myself and woke up washed in morning sunlight and calm. It was time to move on.

↓ **Saturday, March 27, 2004**

Having Fun Yet?

Greetings from the Richfield, Utah, Flying J. I
started in Denver this morning, having stopped over
to visit a dear old friend there. I caught snow

< 268 >

flurries coming over the Rockies, descended into the sun-baked, John Ford glory of the Utah canyonlands, watched far-off rain storms drift for hours on the horizon.

And then I sat here for five hours, watching the computer screen. I toted up about $1,100 in sales, did a half dozen deliveries, haggled with gold sellers, fretted about cash flow.

Was it fun? I've been wondering. Yesterday, over at Terra Nova, the Wired News story about me got written up, and TN regular Staarkhand commented as follows:

> I've been keeping up with Play Money for some time now. Quite interesting, although it has been depressing to observe the transition from witty and insightful commentary on [virtual worlds] and general human nature to PLZ BUY FROM ME WTFOMG. I think we can probably cut him some slack though based on the merits of earlier work and his pretty harsh deadline coming up.
>
> After all, it's just business. Wait, that's what's depressing. The archives reveal that Julian rather enjoyed the game at one point.

I can't disagree. Not with the last sentence, anyway. UO was once a much simpler diversion for me, it's true. Yet I'm not sure that I'm really enjoying it any less now. Or even that it's "just business." Yes, I am buying and selling Ultima items, trying to get more of them all the time, but so are thousands of other players. And the emotions I'm experiencing

< 269 >

as I enter this final phase of my "game" are complex--
not pleasant, exactly, full of deep anxieties about
outcome and social standing, yet not unlike emotions
I've felt in other games.

In particular I remember an almost gruesomely
involving six-month game of e-mail Diplomacy I
organized three years ago. I think I meant it as a
kind of farewell to the carefree days of
childlessness in the months before Lola was born.
And yet in practice it turned out to be anything but
carefree. Diplomacy is a fiendishly complex game of
negotiation, bluffing, confidences honored and
betrayed, and for the months I played that last game
I went to bed with knots in my stomach and woke up
in cold sweats, sick with worry over what the next
round held in store for me.

I loved it.

And I'm loving this, too, though I'm not sure why.
Let's just say that among the many strangenesses of
life in late modernity, not the least is that we have
come to play games that defy any simple understanding
of what the word "fun" could possibly mean.

That night, short of gold on several shards, I sent a desperate
IM to Rich Thurman, who phoned back to offer another quarter
billion pieces of the Pub 21 hoard. He seemed almost excited to
be contributing to my efforts.

"We're all watching you, you know, wondering how it will
turn out," he said, and I refrained from asking who exactly he
meant by "we." As much gold as he and all the other farmers

< 270 >

moved, it just about made sense to think of them as the UO economy itself, cheering me on, and I preferred to. It was a nutty notion, of course, but somehow buoying, and it lightened my mood all the way into the next morning and the Nevada desert.

Monday, March 29, 2004

Farewell to the Road

I came to the Southern California finish line of my journey last night, but not before one final Flying J--the impressive Barstow, California, outpost of the truckstop chain. Such is the degree of professionalism at the Barstow Flying J that as a nontrucker I was explicitly banned from using the facilities in the "Drivers' Lounge" and was obliged, therefore, to set up shop in the amply wired coffee shop. I leave you with this image of me in my "office," kindly taken by the waitress with a crappy little $35 digital camera I'd bought a few truckstops back:

And here, for good measure, is a picture of me completing a delivery of 5 million gold pieces at the bank in Skara Brae, a city in the far west of

< 271 >

UO's mythic land of Britannia. I'm the gray-haired guy in reddish robes, on the lighter horse, thanking and being thanked:

Flying J. Skara Brae. Which is my true place of work?

The question is left as an exercise for the reader.

< 272 >

CHAPTER 42

Thursday, April 01, 2004

Market Watch

This week I did nearly $3,000 in sales and rose to the number-two spot in the top UO eBayers list, beating out such legendary sellers as uotreasures, rdial1, and markeedragon. Save the applause, though, ladies and gentlemen, for my profits were dismal: a mere $780.

My weekly target for the remainder of the challenge now rises to $1,450. Can I possibly make it? In some kind of Horatio Alger universe where dreams conquer every obstacle, maybe. But here's a reality check: If I sell everything I have in stock between now and next Wednesday, at the roughly 25 percent margins I've been getting, my profits will just barely top $1,300.

Time to get selling, I guess.

< 273 >

Meanwhile, here's your weekly UO eBay market snapshot, based on average sales figures for the preceding 14 days:

  Market sales total: $163,648 (+5,268 from two
    weeks ago)
  Market sales total, annualized: $4.3 million
  Market volume total: 3,392 sales (+160)
  Exchange rate: $13.06 (-0.50) per 1 million
    Britannian gold pieces
  Price of an 18x18-tile mansion: $128.01 (-40.57)
  My gold holdings: 415.09 million gp
  My dollar holdings: $1,013.37
  My inventory: $1,525.03
  My net worth: $6,269.21
  My profits this week: 780.38
  My profits, to date: $9,601.83

Audited statements available upon request.

*(Numbers crunched with help from HammerTap's
DeepAnalysis, an eBay market research tool, and
Lance Leger, professional accountant and
guildmaster, Ancient Order of Elves.)*

⬇ **Saturday, April 03, 2004**

Wonder of Wonders

Well I'll be damned. In the two days since my last, gloomy post, I've done more than $2,000 in sales. If this rate holds, I will make my numbers for this week and then some.

< 274 >

Onward and Upward

Another red-letter day for revenues: $1,150 in receipts, for a total of about $4,150 so far this week. If I do the same tomorrow, my profits are sure to hit their target for the fiscal week. If I don't, I'm still in the game for April 15. Not bad.

And yet I'm cringing now thinking of all the ways I betrayed the enterprise in the last few days. Going to see a movie with my mom and my sister and her wife, weeping through the surprisingly moving *Eternal Sunshine of the Spotless Mind* while inventory went untracked and unreplenished. Spending a day with my mother at her monthly oncology treatments while the desperate pleas of customers went unanswered. Talking to my wife and daughter and far-flung friends and family on the phone when my focus should have been nowhere but on this laptop stationed on the diningroom table in the middle of my sister's house.

What would Donald Trump say?

Market Watch

And now, as they say, the numbers.

As if to swat my optimism of last night on its wet little nose with a rolled-up newspaper, today was my worst sales day in weeks. I started the day in the

< 275 >

red, with chargebacks from two fraudulent PayPal payments knocking me down about $44, and I only just clawed my way out of the hole by the end of the day. Result: $1,086.69 in profit for the week, my best weekly posting so far, and still much too low for comfort.

Let's break the situation down once more. I need to post a one-month profit of $4,600 before April 15 to top my best month as a writer. My profits for the last four, record-breaking weeks total about $3,780, so it's no use looking backwards. All hope lies in the week to come. With a running start of $3,248 for the last twenty-four days, I'll need to make $1,352 in the next seven days to hit $4,600.

I intend to.

Now here's your weekly UO eBay market snapshot, based on average sales figures for the preceding 14 days:

  Market sales total: $167,099 (+3,451 from last week)
  Market sales total, annualized: $4.3 million
  Market volume total: 3,525 sales (−27)
  Exchange rate: $13.06 (+0.01) per 1 million Britannian gold pieces
  Price of an 18x18-tile mansion: $167.94 (+39.93)
  My gold holdings: 275.02 million gp
  My dollar holdings: $3,097.32
  My inventory: $1,856.80
  My net worth: $7,355.90

< 276 >

My profits this week: 1,086.69
My profits, to date: $10,687.99

Audited statements available upon request.

*(Numbers crunched with help from HammerTap's
DeepAnalysis, an eBay market research tool, and
Lance Leger, professional accountant and
guildmaster, Ancient Order of Elves.)*

< 277 >

PART ELEVEN

Judgment Day

CHAPTER 43

Homeward Bound

I'm writing this on a 737 headed east from
California, though of course I won't be able to
post it until I get home to Indiana tonight.
Strange to think that the truckstops of America have
better networking tech built into them than the
passenger jets.

Strange, too, to be heading home so soon. I had
meant to stay in L.A. until after the fifteenth,
the better to finish out the project undistracted
by travel and, I guess, domesticity. But the
reasons I left home in the first place were never
so practical . . .

So I'm flying home early now, for various reasons,
none so clear to me as my desire to be there
tomorrow when my daughter goes on her first real
Easter egg hunt. And in all probability this means I
have chosen that opportunity over the chance to meet

< 280 >

my financial goal. The day of travel and the hours of
child care now coming out of my schedule almost
guarantee a reduction in sales this week. But it
wasn't a very hard choice, to be honest.

Still, I have to wonder why that choice, broadly
speaking, seems to be a recurring theme in this
chronicle. Remember that the project began in
earnest with a similar separation, and a similar
push to reach a near-term business goal, ten months
ago. That separation wasn't so obviously related to
marriage problems, but the tension between work and
family was much the same. Not that it has to be that
way, of course. Indeed, many of the people I've
talked to who trade in virtual items for a living
say they do it largely because it lets them work
from home, near spouses and children.

Nonetheless, there's something about the nature of
this work that forces the question. And it really
boils down to the much simpler, yet more baffling
question that I have asked myself every day of this
job: What is it that drives people to spend
hundreds and thousands of dollars (or what amounts
to the same thing, hundreds and thousands of hours)
to get their hands on playthings they can never
really hold?

I still don't know. But more than ever I suspect
it's the same thing that drives people to value the
playthings of material life in general, the
trappings of success, the visible tokens of
accomplishment that keep us on the treadmill of

< 281 >

production and make the economy go around. I don't
say this in judgment of my customers (may they ever
prosper). If anything, they're closer than the rest
of us to the sort of enlightenment that frees you
from the treadmill, if only because they know that
their striving is just a game.

May we all know it sooner or later. Soon enough,
anyway, to see and hold the things that matter.

As for the things that pay the mortgage, my sales
yesterday included 40 million gold pieces, a couple
of high-end suits of armor, an extremely rare weapon
known as the Staff of the Magi, and a somewhat less
rare warfork known as the Taskmaster. Taken
together, these items had a value to their buyers of
just more than $900.

Monday, April 12, 2004

Tax Day Minus Three and Counting

And you'd think I'd be checking my profit numbers on
an hourly basis at this point.

But I don't dare. Or don't care. Not sure which.
Sales have been slow the last two days, and Lola came
home from day care today with a fever and
instructions to stay out for twenty-four hours, so
tomorrow's sales are bound to be even slower. My
elusive financial target looks more elusive than ever.

No regrets here, though. The Easter egg hunt alone
was worth every lost sale. I hard-boiled half a
dozen eggs, colored them with Hi-Liter, "hid" them

< 282 >

around Lola's room, and held her basket for her as she went around finding them.

"Hide them again," she said.

And we did. Six times.

Market Watch (Moment of Truth Edition)

Let me begin by saying what an honor it is to receive this handsome cherrywood-veneer plaque commemorating my third week in a row as Number Two Seller in the eBay Ultima Online market. I know that when my great-great-grandchildren seek someday to understand what the life of their illustrious ancestor was about, they will find in this single accomplishment the Rosetta Stone of my existence. I'd like to thank God and Meg Whitman for making it possible.

As for that other accomplishment I've been pursuing here, well, today's the day, isn't it? I suppose I could wait to see how sales go tomorrow and mail in my tax payment at midnight, but let's face it: the numbers are in. And as predicted, they are short of the mark.

Six hundred and eighty-three dollars short, to be precise. Even taking into account my shortened hours manning the store this week, sales were catastrophically slow, and my profits withered accordingly to $668.71. In the last month (31 days), I turned a profit of $3,917. Annualized, that's a

< 283 >

$47,000-a-year gig--nothing to sneeze at, of course, but nothing I haven't achieved as a professional writer, either. Game over: I lose.

But where there is a loser, I am told, there must also be a winner. And I don't see anyone else here but me. Do you?

Now here's your weekly UO eBay market snapshot, based on average sales figures for the preceding 14 days:

  Market sales total: $156,857 (-10,242 from last
    week)
  Market sales total, annualized: $4.1 million
  Market volume total: 3,403 sales (-122)
  Exchange rate: $13.08 (+0.01) per 1 million
    Britannian gold pieces
  Price of an 18x18-tile mansion: $167.97 (+0.03)
  My gold holdings: 262.57 million gp
  My dollar holdings: $4,770.33
  My inventory: $1,134.20
  My net worth: $8,024.61
  My profits this week: 668.71
  My profits, to date: $11,356.70

Audited statements available upon request.

(Numbers crunched with help from HammerTap's DeepAnalysis, an eBay market research tool, and Lance Leger, professional accountant and guildmaster, Ancient Order of Elves.)

< 284 >

Taxed and Burned

As of a few hours earlier this evening, it's official: I have paid taxes on my income as a trader of virtual items. I listed $3,131 in profits from Play Money on my 2003 federal return. And in my Q1 2004 estimated tax payment, I included $2,056 to cover my $8,225 in Play Money profits for the year so far.

That should leave me with a nice little sum to blow now on the indulgence of my choice--a $4,000 ticket to the TED conference, say, or (as a gold-farming acquaintance of mine recently did with his revenues from retailers like me) a down payment on a Prius. It should, that is, and yet it does not. For it turns out, as the tax preparer informed me to my profound dismay late yesterday afternoon, that my wife and I still owe a whopping $6,650 on our 2003 income taxes. And thus, in the final, crowning irony of a project that has never lacked for ironies, the entirety of my assets in this improbable business must now be handed over to the government, there being no other liquid funds available to pay the tab.

On the plus side, when I dropped by South Bend's main post office at 5:30 to mail the payments, they were giving out free Krispy Kreme doughnuts.

And then?

< 285 >

I went home, ate the donuts, and more or less immediately fell into the deep, black hole of depression I'd been circling since autumn. And I didn't really stop falling, I would say, until about the first week of June, when the Zoloft started kicking in.

Nobody had to ask me what had finally pushed me over the edge—they could take their pick of proximate causes. Friends and family mostly blamed the shattering of my marriage, but others recognized that my career was in a crisis, too, neither clearly reinvigorated by the year at Stanford nor presently sustained by much more than the hanging thread of a magazine contract I had now blown off for too long, it appeared, to earn renewal when it ran out in a month or two. Personally, my darkest thoughts focused on the career, which in my gut I knew to be over, while my marriage, something told me, would in time recover.

That I proved dead wrong about both, however, doesn't embarrass me quite as much as my failure even to consider, until now, the possibility that neither crisis so convincingly explained my sudden emotional collapse as the one that immediately preceded it: The end of the Play Money project. Loss. Defeat.

I don't mean simply the fact that it ended—which considering how long and well the project's sheer momentum kept my mental health on track, deserves some credit—but the way that it ended. Which is to say: in failure.

Sure, I tried to shrug it off. I told myself, as I told my readers, that it had only been a game, and not a very consequential one at that. But I of all people should have known better, having just emerged from thirteen months inside a living deconstruction of every precept separating the playful from the serious. That games are merely simulation—only shadows of real life—may have been an easy thing to believe back when the complexities of life more generally and resoundingly overshadowed those of games,

< 286 >

but no longer. And if it now grows harder to resist the thought that games are not so much an imitation of life as one of life's more tricksterly incarnations, then what's the ending of a game than a different sort of death?

Death calls for mourning, and mourning at its best entails a reckoning: a summing up of what has ended and a final settling of accounts. I'm guessing now I should have mourned Play Money better than I did. I should have recognized its failure for what it was and acknowledged what it meant to me, which basically was a kick in the existential nuts. I'm thinking maybe then it wouldn't have come to haunt me quite the way it did.

< 287 >

CHAPTER 44

Monday, April 19, 2004

Post-Game

And so it ends. April 15 has come and gone, my winnings have been tabbed and taxed, the tribe has spoken.

Not that the world took notice or anything. But there was commentary here and there. Wired News checked back in for a wry post-mortem. The gang over at Terra Nova opened a congratulatory thread. And e-mails trickled in from wide-eyed strangers the world over, wanting variously to know (a) how they too can quit their day jobs and make $3,917 a month selling imaginary suits of armor and (b) what lies next for me and for Play Money.

In answer to (a), all I can say, my friends, is RTFB: read the blog, from start to finish. There's not much I could tell you that isn't there already.

As for (b), I wonder myself. In the near term, I do have a writing career to catch up on--a contract

< 288 >

with *Wired* magazine that I will have to hustle to comply with, a book proposal that needs some revising (can you guess the topic?). I have therefore decided to limit my trading, for the time being, to the buying and selling of Britannian gold pieces, the least time-consuming activity in the business.

I will also be updating this blog much less frequently, if at all--except to continue posting my weekly market report until I have compiled a full year of numbers, sometime in June. Watch for pretty graphs upon completion.

You may consider this entry, then, my farewell. And as such, it comes I guess with an obligation to share with you some thoughts on what this has all meant to me and, if it's not too presumptuous to consider, the culture at large.

For me, I think, what this project has been about is the relationship between play and work. I began my involvement with Ultima Online as a player, and I took up this enterprise wondering if it might not lead me to an El Dorado I have looked for all my adult life: a place where work is play.

It didn't, of course. Not exactly. It took work to make Play Money, and the work was hard, and more to the point, the work did not fit any definition of play handed down to us by tradition. It was not simply a diversion from the path of life; it was the path itself, for a time, and just as fraught with existential care as that path ever is.

< 289 >

The funny thing is, though, that more and more nowadays this curious confusion of entertainment and existence is the definition of play. The games we choose for our amusement are becoming so complex, so involving, that the line between gameplay and career, between gameworld and society, begins to blur. In the course of this project, I met many players of UO who were just as much laborers in the UO economy, even if they wouldn't have said so themselves. I also encountered ethical dilemmas, questions of economic justice even, that would never have troubled me as they did if the economy in question were merely a game.

What this says about the culture we are building, and about the strange promise of the technologies that increasingly shape that culture, I'm not quite certain. But you can rest assured that if the book *Play Money* ever gets written, these will be its central questions.

So now the book is written, and I've tried to keep my promise. Insofar as it's been possible, I've made my story speak to what I see as a peculiar moment—possibly the most peculiar ever—in the twisted history of work and play. Yet as I look back again on the unfolding of events that ends here, with the words I wrote above, the only question that, for me, persists as central is the same one I have asked myself almost every time I re-read that farewell post: Why *does* it end here?

Why did I quit?

Bob Kiblinger read that final post the day I made it and emailed a message of what amounted to condolences. "What a

< 290 >

sad day :(," he wrote, the frowny face a touchingly effortful departure from his customary genial optimism, which quickly reasserted itself: "If you change your mind I seriously think we could do something together with up and coming MMORPGs. My long term plans are to compete/beat IGE in every single game I can get involved with. If you want to give it a try—just let me know and I am sure we can work something out. If I don't see you on IM—good luck and I hope everything is working out well with your family!!"

"Hey, Bob . . . don't write me out of your plans just yet," I answered, still wanting to believe it wasn't over. Just a few days earlier, Rich Thurman had shared with me the list of his top-ten customers for fiscal year 2003, and I had just made the cut with my $3,690 in purchase of fresh-farmed gold. At the very top of my list? None other than Bob Kiblinger, the source of $35,000 in revenues that year. The rest of the line-up was nicely rounded out by Markee Dragon himself and several members of the illustrious Markee Dragon team. Though I should have been shocked, I guess, to find out Bob and the others had been buying from Rich all along, I was mostly gratified, because it meant that in the end, whatever other business goals I'd failed to achieve, I hadn't failed to learn the secret to being a successful, rule-abiding trader. There simply wasn't any secret. As long as there were large-scale farmers in the game, the only way to make a living was to buy from them. And so my purchases from Rich and Mithra, I realized, had not so much excluded me from the inner circle of top traders as ushered me into it: We were all gold farmers, more or less, and Play Money, it turned out, was as legitimate an operation as any of them.

But it was over, all the same. In the months after April 15 I made a couple more low-end gold purchases from the Russian, but

< 291 >

otherwise Play Money was a permanent fire sale, the inventory auctioned off piece by piece until at last the only bits left were crap not even worth the trouble of logging in to delete, and I was obliged to recognize that I had quit the game.

But why?

It's not like the pay or the conditions were so bad. As discussed, a $47,000 income wouldn't have topped my best year writing, no—but on the other hand, to be honest, it would have topped all the other years. And it wasn't exactly hardship pay either: Even in that last crazy month, I wasn't putting more than fifty hours a week into the job, all of them in the comfort of whatever I chose to call home.

Other people have put the question to me as well, and I have tended to shrug and say, "I guess I figured out I'm just not a businessman." And this is true, as far as it goes. But at the time the project ended, and in the months that followed, I was also more uncertain than I'd ever been that I was a writer. How then could I have been so sure, under those circumstances, that the less agonizing, more reliable line of work wouldn't have suited me better in the end?

I wasn't sure at all, is the truth. But here I am, a writer again, and not a merchant of make-believe, and if there's any explanation for this state of affairs, I'm still not very well equipped to say what it is. So let me hazard, in lieu of an explanation, a guess.

On December 9, 2005, the *New York Times* published on its front page an account, datelined Fuzhou, China, of what the story called a "gaming factory": forty computers packed into the basement of an ancient, shabby building, each one running the same online game, each manned by a worker diligently "playing" the game while upstairs, in cramped dorm rooms cluttered with hot pots, off-duty workers slept in bunk beds. The workers were called "gold

< 292 >

farmers," the article explained, and it was their job to play online all day, every day, gathering artificial gold coins and other virtual loot that "as it turns out, can be transformed into real cash." The workers were among as many as 100,000 Chinese earning a living in gold farms, the factory itself just one of hundreds like it throughout China, maybe thousands even, all "tapping into the fast-growing world of 'massively multiplayer online games.'"

"For 12 hours a day, 7 days a week, my colleagues and I are killing monsters," one 23-year-old gold farmer told the *Times*. "I make about $250 a month, which is pretty good compared with the other jobs I've had." Pretty good compared with most other gold farmers, too, who generally make less than 25 cents an hour, not counting room, board, and of course, all the free gaming they can fit into their hard-working days.

I learned two things from this article. One, that Gordon L____, who'd claimed to be paying his workers $1.50 an hour, evidently *six times* the going rate, was either not quite as savvy as I'd imagined or not quite as honest. And two—

Well, how to put it? That it hadn't all been a dream, I guess. That the clue I'd chased all the way to Tijuana, and from there, in a sense, all through the thirteen months of my own attempt to spin a living wage from virtual loot, hadn't simply been a con man's story. The curious rebirth of play as production—of which I'd caught glimpses in Edward Castronova's econometrics, Bob Kiblinger's sales figures, Rich Thurman's gold-per-minute rates, and all the other numeric abstractions that structured the virtual economy—was finally every bit as concrete, robust, and luminously strange a social fact as the rumor of the virtual sweatshop had implied.

All the same, I wasn't sure just why I cared so much. "You realize of course that the whole virtual-sweatshop thing is essentially a myth," Brock Pierce had told me two months earlier—

< 293 >

still looking not a day over ten and still presiding, as CEO of IGE, over the world's largest reseller of virtual currencies—and I hadn't even bothered to argue. By then I was wholly willing to admit he might be right. With the explosive success of World of Warcraft in both the U.S. and China, millions now spoke knowledgeably of the plague of "Chinese gold farmers" and the factory-size operations that employed them. But no eyewitness news account had ever turned up such a factory, in China or anywhere else, and I had begun to make my peace with the possibility that it was all an urban legend, and maybe even all my fault—a myth sparked by my brief report on the Blacksnow sweatshop in *Wired* three years before and thenceforth nurtured by the anxieties of the average North American MMO player, haunted as they no doubt were by the specter of an alien doppelganger whose playing was as literally laborious as his own so often felt.

But the *New York Times* had brought the myth out into the light and shown it to be fact. It was official: work is play and play is work. The only question now was what that could possibly mean.

Not that I hadn't already given that one some thought. By now I had finally read my Huizinga and my Caillois and the Situationists on play—and found them bracing in their variously elegiac, analytic, and inflamed attempts to salvage play from the margins that modernity had cast it into. They were everything I could have hoped for, in fact, in that long-ago moment when I'd watched my daughter rapt in play and wondered how it was that daily life, and work especially, could have fallen so far from that state of grace without provoking, somewhere, a critique as eloquent as the howls Lola would have loosed if I had snatched her up just then from the wonder of her toys.

Except that this was not that moment any longer, and what I wondered now was what exactly those impassioned twentieth-

< 294 >

century ludologists—no friends of the modern productive regime, insistent that "play, radically broken from a confined ludic time and space, must invade the whole of life"—would make of the invasion that was finally coming to pass. Could the daily grind of a Chinese gold farmer possibly be the ludic utopia they'd had in mind? Could they find a way to celebrate the nightly drudgery that had built Troy Stolle's tower, or make out anything like liberation in the strange reshaping of production it seemed to herald?

Consider this: In an essay on work and play in MMOs, the psychologist Nicholas Yee proposes a thought experiment. "Given that MMORPGs are creating environments where complex work is becoming seductively fun," Yee asks, "how difficult would it be for MMORPG developers to embed real work into these environments?" As one possibility, he suggests that the screening of diagnostic scans for cancer be outsourced not to low-wage technicians in India—as is routinely done now—but to players who would actually pay to do the job, so long as it contributed to the advancement of their characters. The proposition is at least as plausible as the Chinese gold farms, and implemented in a science-fiction world like Star Wars Galaxies, it wouldn't even disrupt the players' immersion in that world.

Nor is Yee's thought experiment entirely hypothetical. The multiuser online world There, as Yee points out, started out as a sort of semi-covert test-marketing environment, in which companies like Levi's and Nike paid There to let its paying customers wear virtual versions of the companies' products. When this attempt at extracting value from player activity didn't pan out, There, Inc., renamed itself Forterra and shifted its focus to a similar exercise in interweaving the playful and the productive: supplying the U.S. armed forces with vast, multisoldier

< 295 >

training grounds in cyberspace, virtual Kuwaits, Afghanistans, and Baghdads.

The military, of course—with its rich history of war games dating back through the eighteenth-century Prussian *Kriegsspiel* to the Persian origins of chess—has long been ground zero for the confusion of play and productivity, but lately it seems to be outdoing itself. Never mind the military's collaborations with game producers to create marketably playable simulations like Pandemic Studios' Full Spectrum Warrior. The rumor these days is that planners at the Pentagon have adopted as a kind of bible Orson Scott Card's science-fiction novel *Ender's Game*—in which a small army of children believe themselves to be playing a sophisticated video game when in fact they are telematically leading a campaign to annihilate a race of ruthless space invaders. (How many of these planners, I wonder, have read the sequel, in which the leader of these children spends the rest of his life atoning for the richly complicated sin of unknowing genocide?)

And if all this strikes you still as rather more speculative than momentous, consider, then, the increasingly ludic production of that most transformative of contemporary commodities: computer software. There's a Web site called TopCoder.com, where programmers compete in juried contests to win prizes for the best computer programs for a given task, while the site itself sells off the winning programs at a profit. It's a quirky little business model, not much imitated and not especially well known, yet it illuminates a similar but much more talked-about phenomenon: the production of open-source software, in which dozens or hundreds or thousands of unpaid programmers join in loose collaboration to create a computer program none of them will own and anyone can modify. With open-source software running most of the Internet's infrastructure and the open-source Linux operating

< 296 >

system making serious inroads against Microsoft Windows on business and government desktops, tremendous effort now goes into figuring out what sustains so much and such high-quality "amateur" product. But what hundreds of analyses of the open-source software movement have failed to get a handle on is precisely what TopCoder builds its business on: the essentially playful urges behind open-source production.

Why do they do it, the TopCoders and the open-source programmers and the free-software hackers? Not for salaries, obviously, or for the cash prizes, really, or even for the high-minded philosophical reasons most often and most closely examined—the commitments to open-source methodology as a more socially responsible or technically powerful way of writing software. No, above all they do it for the agonistic glory of having their contributions singled out for inclusion in the final product and the ineffably geeky joys of writing the slickest code you can. "Jouissance" is the broad term anthropologist of technology Gabriella Coleman applies to this ludic impulse at the heart of open-source creation. But Linus Torvalds, creator of Linux, has put it more plainly: "The computer itself is entertainment," he declared in his foreword to Pekka Himanen's *The Hacker Ethic*, an elucidation of the ideas behind open-source creation.

Consider it all, then. Look at Troy Stolle's late-night pointing and clicking, at Blacksnow's sweatshop, at Nick Yee's cancer-screening parable, at the military's dreams of death-dealing games and the hackers' play at writing code that works. Each on its own might not amount to a historic moment, but looking at them all together I can't help sensing the emergence of a curious new industrial revolution, driven by play as the first was driven by steam. As steam did then, so now play lives among us as a phenomenon long ignored by the machinery of production—evanescent, vaporous, unexploited—and inasmuch as production

< 297 >

abhors a vacuum, it was perhaps just a matter of time before it moved to colonize the vacant, vacuous space of play.

Such were my thoughts, at any rate, in the weeks after the *Times* confirmed the existence of the Chinese gold farms. And like I said, I was at a loss to fit them into the frame of reference I had found in (and once shared with) Huizinga, Caillois, the Situationists, and other high-modern champions of play. For all of them, to one degree or another, the modern system of production was so radically unplayful that even imagining that system capable of incorporating the energy of play would have been a challenge: Any such incorporation, in their view, could only subvert the system or destroy the play.

And yet, if you think about it, the logic of the system isn't really so antithetical to play as that. In fact, if you think about it hard enough, you might conclude that play is where that logic has been headed all along. Max Weber, for instance, who thought about it very hard indeed, seems to say exactly that in those final pages of *The Protestant Ethic and the Spirit of Capitalism* where he denounces the "iron cage" of meaningless hyperefficiency the Puritan economic reformation has left us in, in which "the idea of duty in one's calling prowls about in our lives like the ghost of dead religious beliefs." Those are the oft-quoted words anyway. Just below them in the same passage, however, Weber curiously, yet much less famously, suggests that dead religious beliefs don't only survive as ghosts: "In the field of its highest development, in the United States, the pursuit of wealth, stripped of its religious and ethical meaning, tends to become associated with purely mundane passions, *which often actually give it the character of sport* [emphasis added]."

Weber doesn't elaborate the point, but it makes sense: Drained of the religious significance that gave it meaning, the economic system we inhabit must either bind us to its pointlessness against

< 298 >

our wills—a costly proposition, like any prison system—or contrive new meanings for our daily grind. And what easier way is there of contriving meaningful activity than through the mechanisms of play? Add computers to the historical picture, effectively building those mechanisms into the technological foundation of the world economy, and the contriving gets so easy that it starts to look inevitable. The grind must sooner or later become a game.

Call it a theory of ludocapitalism, and don't feel too obliged to take it seriously. Just keep in mind that this is where my thoughts wound up after chewing on the Chinese gold farm for a while, and please accept it as the closest I can come to saying why it was I left the business when I did. I had gone into it thinking I might find a way *out* of the grind, an escape from modernity's productive regime, but, by the end, I think I'd begun to understand what I'm here to tell you now: I'd been attempting the unnecessary. The grind was already escaping from itself.

< 299 >

PART TWELVE

Unsettling Accounts: An Epilogue

CHAPTER 45

It isn't over till it's over, though, and it wasn't until April 15, 2005, that I filed my last tax return on income from Play Money, reporting the money I made in the final months of the project. Even then I felt I still had unfinished business, a single loose thread still in need of tying up. Technically speaking, I had, as promised, informed the IRS of my earnings from the virtual trade: I had reported the monetary amounts of those earnings and paid the requisite taxes. But I still felt as though I'd cheated somehow. I hadn't given the IRS the chance to engage with the challenge I'd presented them, hadn't fully informed them of the game at hand or, more important, of its stakes.

What's more, I wasn't sure what the stakes were myself. I was done with the real-money trade, to be sure, but if I kept on playing UO or other games, and if I kept on acquiring virtual items, could I really claim that in those moments of play I had left the real economy behind? Once upon a time I might have thought so. But whatever sense I'd ever had of the distinction between the real and virtual economies had long since blurred, and I wasn't sure I could trust the IRS to draw the line for me. I needed answers to the tax questions that had both amused and troubled me from the outset of my enterprise: Were virtual trades taxable as

< 302 >

barter? Was loot wrested from the corpse of a fallen orc as taxable as cars won on game shows? Did the IRS really mean what it said about "fair market value," even if it meant robbing millions of MMO players of their escapist illusions?

So two months later I walked into my local IRS office in downtown South Bend, Indiana, and sat down at a help desk, face to face with agent John Knight, to get some answers.

"Hi, there, I have a business that's kind of unusual," I began, "and I want to sort of go over some weirdnesses about it and try to make sure—"

"What sort of weirdnesses?" asked Knight, so casually I almost didn't hear him. He spoke with a downstate twang, had a weatherworn, pickup-driving look to him, the graying hair of an aging rocker and the skeletal gaze of a downscale Willem Dafoe. He didn't appear to think much of my chances of posing any kind of tax conundrum he hadn't already roped and tied many times over.

"Well," I said, "are you familiar with the phenomenon of massively multiplayer online role playing games?"

"No."

"Dungeons and Dragons? That kind of game?"

"No."

"OK. It's like on the Internet—"

"Yeah, I know about games on the Internet," said Knight.

"Right, so it's a game on the Internet, and people go in and they—how do I explain it? There are thousands of them playing at once, and they have characters that go around in this world—"

"And that's your job?"

Knight didn't seem to be joking, but I gave a brief chuckle just in case he was. "Sort of," I answered, and as I went on to explain the business as clearly as I could, Knight furrowed his brow, warming to the challenge of figuring out what the hell I was talking about.

< 303 >

"OK," he said, "so I got a fake jewel that's worth 80 million points, gives me all kinds of invincibility, but I got two of 'em, or I don't want to play anymore, and so I can go on eBay and sell my jewel to some other character?"

"Yeah."

"And you sell these . . . things?"

"Yeah."

"You have a lot of these things. The sword, the dragon, the houses, you got a lot of stuff—and you go on eBay and you're selling all this neat stuff and you're makin' a profit?"

"Yeah."

Another pause. It seemed to be sinking in. And at last John Knight was able to offer me what I had come here for today—his informed, considered opinion:

"That's so weird."

A nonbinding opinion, presumably. Followed by an elaboration that did little to dispel the impression Knight had nipped into the supply room shortly before my arrival and smoked a righteous bowl:

"So now we're selling intangibles in an intangible world. *For* an intangible world."

He let that hang in the air between us for a moment.

"But we're using real money, and you're gonna have a tax liability," he continued, quickly recovering his sense of professional mission. "If you paid eight thousand dollars for a flaming sword and you got nine thousand dollars, obviously you had an eight-thousand-dollar basis, so you only made one thousand dollars." And obviously, as a business profit, that income would be reported on the Schedule C, Knight told me. But for some reason, the notion that I and others might also acquire valuable items not only by buying them but also by playing the game seemed to flummox him. "If you're playing the game and you got a shining

< 304 >

jewel for nothing, and sold it for three thousand, looks to me like . . . It's kinda like me going out and maybe, I don't know, finding something in the ground and it's eight thousand years old and it's an artifact and me selling this thing and getting ten grand from the museum . . . It's like selling a collectible. It's not really inventory, but it could . . ."

Knight groped for words, struggling to locate in the vast cosmic order of the tax code a place for loot. "It's so bizarre," he said at last. "Because you're getting stuff for free, and that doesn't happen in the real world."

For *free*? I believe at that moment actual tears of dismay came to my eyes. Yes, even the deepest theorists of play had defined it as a waste of time, but was it really still so hard to accept that play can also be productive? Even when its productivity stood visible, for all the world to see, in the closing prices on eBay? I thought of the hundreds of sellers who had come to me bearing the fruits of their hunting, their crafting, their conniving, their cheating. I thought of the hundreds of thousands of effortful hours those items represented. And I wondered how anyone could possibly think those items had been gotten for free. Knight had misunderstood, I supposed, and I suggested as gently as I could that perhaps a better way to think of the MMO player's hard-won items was by analogy with the farmer's crop, which, for instance—

"But you're not gonna go out and *find* a truckload of watermelons out there, are you?" Knight said, cutting me off. And there was no stopping him now: "A truckload of watermelons would go on a Schedule F, which is a lot like a C. It costs you money to make the watermelons, and that's a business expense, and you realize gains when you sell them. But when you just sell tokens and talismans, certain symbols, certain powers, that you acquire for free... that might be almost like a collectible, which

< 305 >

would be on a D, and it might be a higher rate of tax . . . See, it's really a highly technical question. I might have to refer you to a specialty line."

I suggested we set aside, for a moment, the highly technical questions and focus on a more pressing one: What was I supposed to tell the IRS about my virtual wealth now that I'd left the business for good? Say I kept on playing UO, or switched over to one of the newer and hotter MMOs like World of Warcraft or Lineage 2, but never made another dollar from my efforts? Wasn't it clear by now that I would still be acquiring genuine assets, income like any other, whether or not I ultimately chose to turn it into dollars?

Knight gave me a quizzical look and addressed me now in the slow and careful tones of a high-school guidance counselor working with a confused but promising student:

"These things you deal in? They aren't worth anything. I mean, I've got a bunch of stuff, my guns, my cars, my motorcycles. But if I don't sell some of them, I've just got *stuff*, see what I mean? A person can have all the virtual talismans in the world, and it might end up selling for a million dollars... but until then it's just like any kind of thing. Stuff can sit forever, and if it doesn't generate any coins or currency or gain, they can't tax you on that."

For a brief moment it all made sense. What had I been thinking? Of course: Stuff was stuff, and money was money. The realm of material value looked crisp and clean again, the way it had before I'd tumbled down the rabbit hole of virtual economies.

Then the moment passed, and I wasn't sure I had the slightest idea what Knight was getting at. Yes, the tax code does at times quite tidily distinguish between stuff and money—between income in kind and income in cash—taxing certain forms of in-kind income only at the moment it gets sold (a moment aptly referred to as a "realization event").

< 306 >

"But what about barter?" I asked. "And prizes? If I win a truck on a game show I don't have to sell the truck to be taxed on it—"

"Yes, that's because . . . it's a real thing. But if you have this thing that's in a cyberworld, it's not *in* the real world."

"But it's *valuable*," I insisted, somewhat wearily, my run-in with PayPal customer support having long before tapped most of my patience for Socratic dialogues with help-desk guys about the nature of reality.

"Well, I'll tell you what," said Knight. "You're right, it is valuable. But at this point the Internet's still new, and the whole concept of the cyberworld is new, and the government, we're still dealing in the third dimension. So if you win a truck, we know we can get into this truck and we can go somewhere with that, and we know it holds value. Whereas if you look at me and say, well, I've got fifteen of these things and seventeen of these powers, I'm gonna say, well, so big deal. See if it'll buy you a beer. Well, it can. But to me it can't. And to the government it can't— yet. It doesn't look like it's holding value at this point.

"And as soon as it starts holding value, you're gonna wish it didn't, you know what I mean? Because how are they going to keep track of it? The game company'll have to start sending out 1099s for every time somebody gets a bag of grapes or a gold coin or a shiny emerald—the game companies are going to say we don't want to do this anymore, because we're not making that kind of money. And your online subscription's going to triple. Just to keep the paperwork. You'll see the game collapse the moment they start putting value on that."

I could see his point there. But I couldn't help feeling, I don't know, the slightest bit hurt by the U.S. government's failure to recognize the value of the Britannian economy.

< 307 >

"But what *about* barter?" I persisted. "When I sell my house for a million gold pieces in the game—"

"It's not a million of *our* stuff. It's not a million *dollars*."

"It's a currency," I said, a little more testily than I meant to. "I can tell you the exchange rate."

I could have, too. I could have told John Knight, right then and there, exactly how many gold pieces his salary was equal to, or how many millions I had earned from trafficking in all this worthless stuff: 868.25 million, to be precise, at the April 15, 2004 exchange rate.

"Yeah, but I don't think the government would recognize it," Knight calmly replied. "I might not be the final word on this, but I don't think we're recognizing Dungeon and Dragon currency as legal tender. You can't spend it outside your game, really; you can't change it at a currency exchange. You go into the exchange rate sites, you don't find Dungeon and Dragon—or what do they call their thing?"

"The Britannian gold piece?"

"You're not going to find the Britannian gold piece in the currency exchange sites. It's all, like, the Iranian this and the Iraqi that. Though come to think of it the Iraqi *that*'s probably worth less than the Britannian gold piece, by about 1,400 to 1."

John Knight thought that was pretty funny. He let out a big laugh about it anyway, and I, at last, laughed, too. I liked him well enough by now.

But as I left the office I clutched tight the phone number he'd written down for me, the IRS's Business and Specialty Line. I was definitely going to get a second opinion.

"Thank you for calling Internal Revenue Service, this is Mrs. Clardy, badge number 7500416, how may I help you?"

< 308 >

Truth be told, Mrs. Clardy didn't sound very interested in helping me at all. It was minutes before five o'clock in the greater D.C. area, and she was probably not thrilled to catch a final call involving "unusual issues," having no doubt heard her share of them already. She worked in the Barter Income section, to which my call had been transferred after my questions had stumped the Small Business specialist I'd spoken to first. Waiting on hold, I'd had a good feeling about finally reaching Barter, a sense that here at last the complexities of my case would be recognized and thoughtfully addressed. Now, though, I wasn't so sure. In fact, I was pretty sure now that Mrs. Clardy would in a few moments be dismissing those complexities as confidently as John Knight had, only less jovially and more authoritatively.

"Well, are you familiar with online role-playing games?" I asked.

She wasn't. So I launched into my second mini-seminar on virtual economics that afternoon, explaining the games and the business as quickly as I could without short-shrifting the complexities, which was about two minutes, speaking at a brisk but personable pace.

"Right," said Mrs. Clardy, audibly glancing at her watch.

So then there was nothing to do but offer up my long-cherished theory of virtual trades as taxable barter income—and await her judgment.

"Sounds like barter to me," she said.

"So . . . both parties to a virtual trade would have to report the value of the items traded?" I asked, not altogether certain I had heard correctly.

"Right."

"Even if they don't turn around and sell them on eBay?"

"Right."

< 309 >

I wasn't sure what else to say or whether the conversation was over at this point. And that was when, for some reason, Mrs. Clardy asked if she could put me on hold for a moment while she consulted some reference materials.

Sixteen minutes later, she returned, a bureaucrat transformed:

"OK," she said, breathless, almost giggling. "We just had this little *discussion*, several of us all work here in the same area. And it sounds to us like what you described would be— yes—Internet barter." Here she paused, whether to catch her breath or to let the epic surreality of the conclusion sink in, I couldn't tell. "However," she went on, "there are no regs, there is no code, there are no rulings to rely upon. This is our *opinion*. What I would do if I were you is request what's called a letter ruling that says this is the way it should be treated. Because you can take that to the bank, if you get a letter ruling, whereas my opinion is just my opinion. And the opinion of a couple others here."

She then explained where to get the forms for filing for the ruling and how to fill them out. "You're gonna need to give all the information about how you can take the items and actually sell them on eBay, so they actually do have a value. And explain the entire thing like you explained it to me, and say, 'When we trade them inside the virtual reality is that bartering that would be taxable under tax law?'

"Because at some point in time," she continued, "they're going to have to go toward the Internet. They haven't been touching the Internet or are afraid to go there or whatever, but we have to get some of this on record, because there's so much going toward the Internet that there's just not a choice."

Trying to keep up, I asked her about the other question on my mind, the notion that simple loot drops could be taxed as well, like game-show prizes.

< 310 >

"I would include that question also—because you're still in the virtual field, and we don't have things addressing the virtual field yet. I mean, you may be groundbreaking, because you may be the only one who ever asked this."

Miss Clardy laughed; she seemed delighted at the prospect.

"Well, yeah," I said, "I'll be very interested to see because, of course, if this type of thing is ruled bartering, there's hundreds of thousands of people in these games who—"

"Oh I know! The ramifications are *enormous*. Obviously the ones you do on eBay, that's not a question—you get in some profit, so that has to be considered income. But inside the virtual world, you know, we don't have rules. Our *opinion* here is that yeah, if that's something of value, which it is because you're able to sell it on eBay, then that would be a type of barter. But we don't have a rule that says virtual is the same as real. So it's the virtual aspect that nobody has addressed yet. And you're probably one of the first ones to request an answer to a virtual question."

"OK, well, here we go," I said, otherwise at a loss for words.

"Break new ground!" said Mrs. Clardy, by way of farewell.

And reader, I truly meant to. But it turned out Mrs. Clardy had neglected to mention the $500 fee stipulated in the letter-ruling request instructions, or the tax lawyer I would have to hire to write the request with any effectiveness, or the six months or more I would have to wait for a final response, in any case. And even if none of these obstacles had stood in the way, there was still John Knight's laconic, drawling voice in my head, reminding me to think twice about seeking official recognition for play money: "As soon as it starts holding value, you're going to wish it didn't, you know what I mean?"

I did. I knew what he meant. Of course, I knew better than to think play money hadn't started holding value long before I sat

< 311 >

down at John Knight's desk, but it occurred to me that right now maybe it was holding just about all the value it could handle.

That same week in China—land of a hundred thousand gold farmers—a judge had issued a suspended death sentence in the case of 41-year-old Qiu Chengwei, who had murdered a younger man in a dispute over a prized virtual sword. Qiu had acquired the rare Dragon Sabre the year before, questing in a popular Asian MMO called Legends of Mir III, and subsequently loaned it to 26-year-old Zhu Caoyuan, who sold it out from under him for 7,200 yuan ($871) and pocketed the cash. Told by police that nothing real had been stolen and therefore no theft charges could be filed, Qiu had gone to Zhu's house with a very real knife, burst in on him as he lay sleeping, and killed him. "He was barely able to put on his pants before Qiu stabbed him," said Zhu's grieving father. And yes, perhaps the tragedy might have been averted if the local police had had a better understanding of what was at stake, but the fact that the tragedy occurred at all suggested it might well be a while before anybody really understood.

Meanwhile, back on Bob Kiblinger's side of the globe, business was booming. Anchored as always in the dwindling but still robust economy of Ultima Online, Bob had branched out into more than a dozen new games, establishing a market presence not quite big enough to rival IGE's, but profitable enough to attract a buy-out bid from Brock Pierce and company (briefly entertained and ultimately spurned). He'd left the Ford Explorer behind for a zero-year Cadillac Escalade, lived in a much larger and much nicer house than the one I'd met him in, and was negotiating now to build himself a fantasy home along the lines of Ultima creator Richard Garriott's famous Austin, Texas, castle. I wished him well, still do, and haven't come much closer to deciding whether the effects of businesses like ours on games like EverQuest, UO, and

< 312 >

WoW are in the final balance good, bad, or indifferent—or even whether it matters that the question be decided.

It's not like there's any shortage of people thinking about these issues, in any case. The curious new field of virtual-world studies, which I had once suspected wouldn't survive its infancy, now toddles confidently, with a professional association in the works and conferences like State of Play becoming annual events. And on the message boards, mailing lists, and chat channels of MMO players and developers, all the same questions are being posed and sorted with, if anything, even greater rigor and insight.

I suppose that's why, in the end, I chose to keep my $500 and forgo the ruling Mrs. Clardy had so winningly exhorted me to seek. I didn't really want to know whether play money should be taxed or not, I realized; I wanted to know whether this society, or any, was finally capable of making sense of it. And all things considered, I trusted the people I'd been playing and trading and arguing with all along to make sense of it a lot more than I trusted the Internal Revenue Service to.

And no offense. I'm sure someday the IRS will catch up with reality, and when they do I'll trust them to have the first idea what it really means to say a Britannian gold piece holds value.

In the meantime, though, it'll be our little secret, OK?

< 313 >

INDEX

< 315 >

< 316 >

< 317 >

< 318 >

< 319 >

< 320 >

< 321 >